About the author

Ailsa Piper is a writer, director, teacher and actor. She has been nominated for Green Room Awards as both an actor and director. Her play, *Small Mercies*, was joint winner of the Patrick White Playwrights Award in 2001. She is director of LuminoUS, which investigates and illuminates classic texts through detailed work with actors and light. She is yet to win an award for walking.

SINNING
ACROSS
SPAIN

A WALKER'S JOURNEY FROM
GRANADA TO GALICIA

AILSA PIPER

VICTORY
BOOKS

VICTORY BOOKS
An imprint of Melbourne University Publishing Limited
187 Grattan Street, Carlton, Victoria 3053, Australia
mup-info@unimelb.edu.au
www.mup.com.au

First published 2012
Text and internal photographs © Ailsa Piper 2012
Design and typography © Melbourne University Publishing Limited, 2012

Characters in this journey have had names and some other identifying features changed to protect their identities, and some characters have been melded together for the same reason.

Permission to reproduce the line from Dorothea Mackellar's 'My Country' by arrangement with The Mackellar Estate, c/– Curtis Brown (Aust.) Pty Ltd.

Cover design by Trisha Garner
Typeset by Sonya Murphy, TypeSkill
Printed by Griffin Press, South Australia

National Library of Australia Cataloguing-in-Publication entry

Piper, Ailsa.
Sinning across Spain: a walker's journey from Granada to Galicia/Ailsa Piper.

9780522861396 (pbk.)
9780522861402 (ebook)

Piper, Ailsa—Journey—Spain.
  Pilgrims and pilgrimages—Spain.
  Hiking—Spain.
  Walking—Spain.
  Spain—Description and travel.

796.5109461

For Peter

My true north

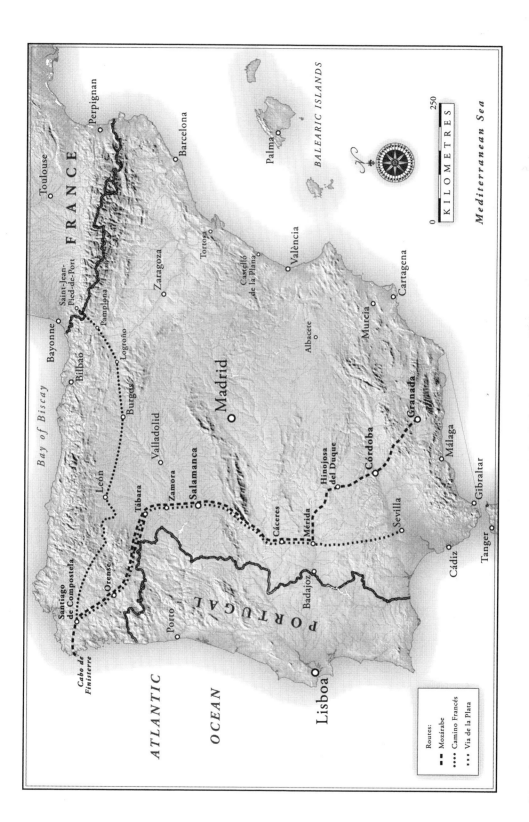

BALEARIC ISLANDS

Mediterranean Sea

250

KILOMETRES

0

FRANCE

Perpignan

Barcelona

Palma

Toulouse

Saint-Jean-
Pied-de-Port

Pamplona

Bayonne

Bilbao

Logroño

Zaragoza

Tortosa

Castelló
de la Plana

València

Cartagena

Bay of Biscay

Burgos

Valladolid

Madrid

Albacete

Murcia

León

Zamora

Salamanca

Tábara

Granada

Hinojosa
del Duque

Córdoba

Málaga

Orense

Santiago
de Compostela

Cáceres

Mérida

Sevilla

Gibraltar

Cabo de
Finisterre

Porto

PORTUGAL

Badajoz

Tanger

Cádiz

Lisboa

ATLANTIC

OCEAN

Routes:
— Mozárabe
•••• Camino Francés
··· Via de la Plata

CONTENTS

PROLOGUE   1
  1   Indulgences   3
  2   Doing the Crying   12
  3   Flying *Sola*   20
  4   Sin City   26
  5   Coincidences   34
  6   Granada   43

ACT ONE
  7   Moor, Moor, Moorish   53
  8   *Sin* Sin   63
  9   Rehab   72
 10   Road Testing   80
 11   Córdoba   89
 12   Weathering Storms   102
 13   *Peregrina Sola*   113

INTERVAL
 14   Mérida   127

ACT TWO

15	Pilgrims	139
16	*Tentación*	148
17	Keeping Company	160
18	Making Sense	167
19	A Swag of Sins	174
20	*Gracias a la Vida*	182

INTERVAL

21	Salamanca	193

ACT THREE

22	Into the Wind	205
23	The Walking Village	214
24	By Heart	225
25	Return to Galicia	236
26	*Regalos*	244
27	Rising	255
28	Three's Company	265
29	Sunny Santiago Sunday	277

CURTAIN CALLS

After Words	287
The Stuff in the Swag	289
Sinners, Saints, Guardian Angels …	291

PROLOGUE

I WILL WALK OFF YOUR SINS
Pilgrim seeks sinners for mutually beneficial arrangement.
Proven track record.
Tireless. Result-oriented. Reliable.
Seven Deadlies a specialty.

THAT'S WHAT STARTED IT.

Words on a page.

Less than a month later I found myself hiking through olive groves and under translucent pink blossom on a road called the Mozárabe, making my way north from the legendary Spanish city of Granada, towards the cliffs at Finisterre in the far north-west.

Springtime in Spain.

It wasn't all *flores* and *fiestas*.

One afternoon, after eight hours of incessant rain, I was trudging along a flooded dirt road in waterlogged boots and drenched khakis, feeling far from home and even farther from reason. What on earth had made me imagine I could skip across a country carrying other people's sins on my back, let alone abstain from committing any of them myself?

Only that morning I'd given in to the sin of anger when I tripped into a ditch. I stood ankle deep in tadpoles and shouted profanities at the drizzling sky.

Pride fled as I knelt beside a freeway scrabbling to find my map, which had blown into a pile of mouldering rubbish.

Lust was yet to claim me, but it was waiting, choosing its moment to transform me into a stew of heat and confusion. Thankfully, that afternoon, I was unaware it was planning an assault.

'Just get on with it,' I instructed myself, hoicking my pack higher. 'The road won't walk itself.'

I kicked sloth into the Spanish sludge and sped up. One foot then the other. Eventually I had to get somewhere.

The icy wind persisted, but the rain gradually eased to silvery mist. Sun peered through bullet-grey clouds. The path was still a quagmire, but to my right, a rainbow's arc began to form and young corn swayed like seaweed in a warm current.

'*Hola, peregrina!*' I heard a voice shout. Hello, pilgrim!

To my left was a shepherd with his flock. He waved his wooden staff to beckon me over, then watched as I navigated my way through the mud to his side. He asked how my walk had been.

'*Duro,*' I said. '*Pero hermoso.*' Hard. But beautiful.

The shepherd grinned to reveal toothless gums.

'*Como la vida,*' he said. Like life.

This is the story of that hard but beautiful walk.

1

INDULGENCES

WALKING TWELVE HUNDRED KILOMETRES from Granada to Galicia with a swag full of sins was never going to be easy, but I didn't embark on the quest lightly. Over the years, I'd hiked a variety of Australian miles, whether along bayside tracks in Melbourne, Swan River paths in Perth, harbour circuits in Sydney, inland trails through central Victoria, the Overland Track's wilderness in Tasmania, or the desert sand of Uluru and the Larapinta.

I'd also walked in Spain.

Only seven months before, I had undertaken the 780-kilometre Camino Francés, a pilgrim trail that crosses Spain from east to west, finishing at the cathedral in the mediaeval city of Santiago de Compostela. It was late September. Northern autumn. The days were breezy and the skies clear. Villages were spaced along the track as evenly as beads on a Spanish matron's rosary, and each offered the possibility of a hot *café con leche*, a stone seat under a shady tree, or an encounter with a local, smiling and wishing me '*Buen camino*'.

Buen camino. Good road. Good path. Good walking.

The Camino Francés is best known because the Catholic Church grants indulgences—forgiveness—to those who walk it for religious reasons. When I considered setting out on it, friends quizzed me about my reasons.

'Is this some spiritual endurance test, with a few bedbugs for good measure?'

'What is it you're looking for? *El Dorado?*'

'You're not going off to find God, are you?'

Undoubtedly, I liked the idea of time and space for reflection, coupled with physical challenge and immersion in a different culture, but the indulgence I was seeking was definitely not religious. I wanted more. More of what I access in my walking. When I hear long-time meditators talk of their experiences, they might be describing the way I feel when I walk, particularly if I'm alone and in nature.

Empty. Peaceful.

Finally, though, what made me embark on the Camino Francés was a poem called 'The Summer Day', by the American poet Mary Oliver. In it she muses on creation, prayer, death and a grasshopper, but it was the last two lines that changed my life. Mary demanded to know what I was going to do with my time on the planet. Her poem called me to walk out into the world's wonders.

After completing the Camino Francés, I came home to Australia knowing I was changed, but uncertain of what that meant. I longed for the fractured Esperanto that is the language of that road. I craved figs, sunflowers and dusty tracks leading ever west, but most of all I yearned for the journeys I had taken outside my body.

I'm a fairly earthed creature, raised in rural Western Australia and shaped by loss as much as by luck. I'm sometimes sentimental, but I'm not prone to flights of fancy or hallucination. Nevertheless, something strange happened on the Francés. Daily, along the *camino*, a part of me hovered above myself, observing the steps, sweat and smiles, but not feeling them. Out of body, but wholly embodied. I was entirely functional, crossing busy roads, monitoring water intake, observing muscular twinges and ensuring I had plenty of nutrients by way of peaches and blackberries, but I was flying, without wings and wide awake, tracking the pilgrim-snail below.

I told myself it was endorphins or an overdose of *vino tinto*, until I returned to my normal life and found myself aching to lift off to the end of that kite string, to fly away.

I live in Melbourne, in the bottom right-hand corner of Australia. It's a city of boulevards and alleys, contemporary chic and conservative ritual. It's a UNESCO City of Literature, and the home of Aussie Rules football. It has the third-largest Greek-speaking population of any city in the world, a Chinatown that bustles day and night, and a coffee culture that was imported by our Italians. There's even a small Spanish quarter.

Melbourne is also where I locate my personal village.

I have a tribe made up of all ages and creeds, a multitude of friends with mighty hearts and minds. My two sisters relocated to Melbourne from the west, and are my touchstones and cheer squad.

Melbourne gave me my husband. I was a touring actor and he came backstage to compliment the cast. I long ago lost my urge to perform, but thankfully I have never lost him. We've crafted a marriage that's a haven, encompassing our mutual need to follow distinct and sometimes separate paths. Base camp, as he calls it.

So it wasn't a desire to be somewhere else that unsettled me, driving me to research the history of pilgrimage. I wanted to understand what had happened as I flew above myself and perhaps, more importantly, to rationalise the connection I'd made with one particular *compañero* on the road.

Compañero. One with whom you break bread.

He had been my on-and-off companion on the Francés. We walked together effortlessly, which was odd because we were both seeking solitude. We established immediately that even if the road brought us together, we would separate if either needed space. Ironically, the freedom to part made it easier to keep company. Like my experience of marriage, time together has more value when it's a conscious choice.

My *compañero* practises Chinese medicine, working in places where other angels fear to tread. It was he who treated my body when it threatened to give out on me, and it was he who reminded me, in English and in Spanish, that there is beauty in the sedate progress of a snail. Geographical distance and cultural differences don't lessen my conviction that he is mine. Clan and kin. When I met him on the Francés I felt we'd been reunited after a long separation. It was a home-coming. It felt fated.

I can say that now. I wouldn't have dared to back then, because I was still seeking logical answers to the questions posed by my flights and by our time walking together.

In my search for answers, I trawled through accounts by long-distance walkers and mystics. I quizzed Buddhists, priests and yogis about other lives, past or parallel. I interviewed shamans and shysters. Among a pile of historical material, I found information about pilgrim traditions through the ages. None of them could explain my flying, or my conviction that my *compañero* was clan, but one bizarre notion struck me: the belief, in mediaeval times, that a person could be paid to carry the sins of another to Santiago, and by doing so, could absolve the 'sinner' from punishment. It sounded like a scam, cooked up by the church and some rich, lazy philanderers as an occupation for unemployed serfs. Nonetheless, I was intrigued.

I found myself wondering about indulgences, hellfire and damnation. They had never featured in my thinking, though I am drawn to the idea of communal responsibility. I've always believed we can help each other to heal; that, when necessary, we can walk in the shoes of another. Here was a way to do it literally.

Sin is a kick-to-the-stomach word. Hard. Two consonants separated by a thin, hungry vowel. Even though there are less challenging terms, like crime, transgression or offence, 'sin' persists, and not just inside churches. It's a favourite of advertisers and comedy writers as well as preachers, because it packs a punch. Everyone reacts to it. I certainly did.

But I was not sure I believed in it as a concept, let alone in carrying it. I was not even sure if I believed in a god. Faith eluded me.

Research told me that the coming year was a Holy Year, meaning pilgrims arriving in Santiago de Compostela would receive what the Catholic Church called a 'plenary indulgence'—the removal of all punishment for sins committed up to that point. A quarter of a million were expected to walk the Camino Francés, more than double the norm. Presumably only faith and the idea of absolution would make anyone choose to be part of such a pilgrim traffic jam.

Trying to understand, I probed the differences between societal codes of behaviour and the 'flaunting of divine authority' that categorised a sin. Often they overlapped, but sometimes a sin was not even an action. It could be a thought or an emotion. And there was punishment for these sins, tough punishment, to be meted out in a life beyond this one. An afterlife.

I wasn't sure where I stood on afterlives. In spite of my Catholic education, I was more inclined to read poems than gospels, but there were many people, from different religions and cultures, who had no doubt there were second and even multiple lives, or another world beyond this.

'What's it like to believe in a hereafter with a resident rule-making parent?' I asked anyone who would listen. 'What's it like to be sure?'

I drew plenty of blanks and headshakes but the questions persisted, and I couldn't let go of the possibility that walking, the thing I love to do, could be of service.

I tried to be realistic. Even if it was possible to believe in walking as communal caring or of my footsteps having heavenly consequences, I'd barely returned from one gruelling walk. As much as it had been transformative, it had also involved blood, sweat, knee pain and tears, and I was in no rush to take that on again. Plus, my coffers weren't exactly overflowing, nor was my husband doing cartwheels at the prospect of another separation hard on the heels of the Francés.

But the fascination held. The compulsion grew.

I woke at night, stumbling to the dictionary to clarify the difference between gluttony and greed. I sweated the subtleties of sins, misdemeanours, misdeeds and crime. I wrecked a couple of dinners by asking people to cough up sins, and I couldn't tear myself from the theology aisles of the local library.

As Catholic schoolgirls, we were instructed to pray for God to send us a vocation. I waited, but it never came. No insistent banging on the door of my soul.

Until this.

Despite that Catholic education, I hadn't been able to hold onto faith as an adult. I recollect a sensation from childhood, when God felt like a hug from my favourite nun; like being enveloped in layers of ironed cotton that smelled of Palmolive soap. As I grew that was replaced by the prickles of rational thought and the itches of lived experience.

'So what am I meant to do with this call now that it has come?' I asked my sister. 'Should I stand on a corner and hold up a placard? Set up a makeshift confessional?'

She laughed, told me not to whine, and reminded me of a story my mother used to tell about me as a four-year-old.

My little brother was inconsolable, sobbing over some calamity. I rushed to comfort him, repeating over and over, 'Don't cry, don't cry. Let me do the crying.' It became a family joke.

Now the surrogate-weeper was morphing into the sin-carrier, and eventually, after my husband urged me to 'do what you have to do', I gave in. I would take to another pilgrim road, one with almost no foot traffic, and approach the journey as a writing project, to give me a framework. I sold two paintings, bought in memory of my mother when she died, to pay for the air ticket, and I blanked out six weeks in my calendar. Decision made.

But I still had no sins to carry.

Nineteen days before leaving I sent a letter to colleagues, sponsors and friends.

Words on a page. A bit like a poem that changes your life.

This is what I wrote.

I WILL WALK OFF YOUR SINS
Pilgrim seeks sinners for mutually beneficial arrangement.
Proven track record.
Tireless. Result-oriented. Reliable.
Seven Deadlies a specialty.

I WILL WALK OFF YOUR SINS will be a monologue for performance, the first draft of which will be written along a 1200-kilometre pilgrim trail called the Camino Mozárabe that stretches from Granada via Córdoba and Salamanca, to Santiago de Compostela, in the north-west corner of Spain.

The Mozárabe is a solitary road, steeped in the history of the period of co-existence and collaboration between Jews, Muslims and Christians in mediaeval Spain, and the wars that ripped the peace apart.

My project springs from research I've been doing into mediaeval pilgrimage, including the curious notion that a person could be paid to carry another's sins. Some mediaeval Christians believed that by paying someone to walk to a designated sacred place on their behalf, they could gain absolution from sin.

I will examine the consequences of just such an undertaking as I walk the Mozárabe with the 'sins' of my contemporary community for company. I will explore personal and global responsibility, faith, walking and weather—but hopefully not the Spanish medical system.

And how can you help?
Well, I'm hoping you might consider paying for me to carry a sin. It can be on your behalf, or for the wider world. These sins will form the focus for my walk and my work. In effect, you'll be a co-writer.

What are the details of the undertaking?

I'll spend Easter in Rome for the rituals, then two days in Granada at the Alhambra, before beginning to walk north to Santiago on the Camino Mozárabe. I've allowed a Biblical forty days to walk in the wilderness, with a day of research in Córdoba. That requires me to average thirty kilometres per day, something I know, after walking the 780-kilometre Camino Francés in northern Spain last year, is achievable if somewhat daunting—but walking off sins is not meant to be a picnic!

What can you contribute?

I draw the line at mortal sins. My shoulders and psyche can't carry violence or brutality. I'm interested in behavioural sins, sins of omission or violations of a moral code. And of course, consider the Seven Deadlies: anger, greed, sloth, pride, lust, envy and gluttony.

In terms of payment, please evaluate what you think your sin is worth: its weight to the pilgrim; the benefit in having it erased; the benefit of focusing on it for forty days. Think of it as buying indulgences.

The Australia Business Arts Foundation (ABAF) have approved the project and confirmed that my supporters can make a donation to ABAF's Australia Cultural Fund. ABAF will provide you with a fully tax-deductible receipt, and send me your 'sin info'.

So what about that pilgrim list?

Here are a few of the outgoings to which the pilgrim will apply her walking wage. All amounts are rounded from euros to Australian dollars …

Feed a pilgrim for a day on the road: $35 (forty days needed)

A week in pilgrim refuges: $120 (six weeks needed)

Journals for the journey's words: $25 (six required)

Maps and guidebook for lone pilgrim: $70

Airfare Rome to Granada (I can't walk it!): $210

Muchas gracias!

Thanks so much for considering the request. If you are still with me here, you will hopefully be with me for twelve hundred kilometres of dusty Mozárabe road.

    Now I just need to get to Santiago.

    With your indulgence …

2

DOING THE CRYING

THE FIRST FINANCIAL DONATION was generous, from a friend with no spare cash to throw at pilgrims. I'd hoped she would contribute reflections, maybe even a sin with a small pricetag. I called to say she had given too much and I couldn't allow it.

'It's not your business to allow or disallow. You're not the boss of me, my friend.'

'No, I know that. Of course. And I'm really grateful, but I don't think it's—'

'That's right. Don't think. Just say thank you. Go and walk, and don't assume you know what's best for me.'

I'd been brought up sharp by a sin of my own.

Pride.

I'd always valued an idea of myself as someone strong—the one who 'can do' when a need arises. Had that led to an unwillingness to accept help from others? Or an idea that help had to be given on my terms? Could it be that I was intractable? Only content when I had the upper hand? Pride-full?

I wrote to my friend to address my sin, but it was the beginning of a lengthy dialogue with pride. It's one of the Seven Deadly Sins, and topped the list when I transcribed them into my journal:

Pride
Anger
Greed
Sloth
Lust
Envy
Gluttony

I wrote my name beside Pride. A confession, though I had no idea to whom I was making it. A hotline to heaven, to the great forgiver and wish-fulfiller, remained elusive. I hoped the sin-walk might help me embrace humility, the Contrary Virtue to pride.

I was becoming quite the expert on sin.

The Contrary Virtues come from the *Psychomachia* ('Battle for the Soul'), an epic written by a Christian poet called Prudentius, around 410AD. Practising them is supposed to protect you against the Seven Deadly Sins: *humility* against pride, *patience* against anger, *liberality* versus greed, *diligence* versus sloth, *chastity* to counter lust, *kindness* for envy, and *abstinence* against gluttony. They're a spiritual insurance policy and useful if you know your sinning tendencies.

It turned out I was pretty conventional in mine.

A Vatican report from 2009, carried out by the Jesuit scholar Father Roberto Busa, stated that pride was the sin most commonly confessed by women. It was followed by envy, anger, lust then sloth. Men had most difficulty with lust (or at least, they confessed to it most frequently) followed by gluttony, sloth and anger. The Vatican also admitted that almost a third of Catholics no longer went to Confession, and ten per cent actually believed it to be an obstacle to a relationship with God.

Most surprising was the Vatican's list of modern sins. Among them were genetic modification, causing poverty, environmental pollution, experiments 'on the person' and the taking or selling of illegal drugs. They gave me an insight into the thinking of the contemporary Church.

Current thinking about sin from outside church walls was reflected in responses to my letter:

> *Being a total atheist, I have a little intellectual problem with the concept of 'sin', but being an atheist is not anti-theist, so I can handle the idea of sin as either part of a person's belief system or as something ethically or morally wrong. Always though, sin is in the eye of a sinner, it has to be self-recognised to become a sin that can be expressed to the pilgrim.*

That implied an inbuilt moral compass, something 'natural' to tell us when we veer off course. I wondered about that. I had managed to go a long time without staring down my pride.

> *I have great trouble with the word 'sin' and the whole frame-work that goes with it. I wish it would disappear from the language. I think there's clarity and knowledge beyond that word. It holds us back, I think, from seeing ethics and morality as rules that allow this group of animals to prosper.*

Words. They persist for a reason, usually because they are nec-essary. Sin wasn't going anywhere. When I googled it, there were 1,250,000,000 results! Difficult to argue that sin was irrelevant in the digital age, even if definitions and interpretations varied.

> *I love it. And I want to help. But I'm uncomfortable about the idea that it might be 'worming my way out' of my own respon-sibility. Would it make me somehow a bigger sinner to attempt to offload it onto you? I am already judging myself for even contemplating allowing you to shoulder a burden like that on my behalf. In fact, I am already imagining others judging me for it, too … What kind of friend could I be to let you take it on? And how could it possibly make me less guilty in my*

own eyes? In fact, the thought of attempting to on-sell a sin is making me writhe in shame ...

People gave me plenty to digest.

And yes, people gave me sins. From the first day, there were confessions, even some from strangers who'd heard of the quest. I began to get an inkling of what I was going to shoulder. Also, I knew something of the weight I'd carry, because I had committed most of them. In fact, I'd say I was as experienced a sinner as I was a walker.

These were among the first sins to arrive:

> *My sin is a desire for vengeance to be visited upon the woman who had the affair and caused the break-up of my marriage a few years ago. I'm carrying it around and I don't even care anymore but I still can't stop secretly wishing it.*

I've wished for vengeance. It was because of emotional cruelty inflicted on someone I loved—or at least, my perception of cruelty. I dreamed of the perpetrator in agony. I would wake shaking, still able to see the car that had ploughed into a tree as a result of my wishing, and the rivulets of blood running down a familiar forehead, as help failed to appear. It appalled me that I could imagine such scenarios.

But I could.

> *White lies to spare the feelings of others—or perhaps more honestly, to protect how others may feel about me. Is this wholly wrong? Could I/do I want to stop? Is it kindness or weak selfish self-preservation?*

White lies can protect both liar and recipient. I don't ever want to hear the words 'Your bum looks massive in that', even if they are the gospel truth. I wondered if I could travel a day without a white lie, let alone a week ... or six weeks? Because it did seem to me that carrying the sins for others implied that I would try not to commit them myself.

The sin I wish you to walk off for me is sleeping with my best friend's husband. Not once, but four times. Over a three-month period.

This act, this period of my life, has cost me dearly. I carried it alone for fifteen years. I finally confessed to my friend last year.

I did a three-month retreat, thirteen or fourteen years ago, specifically to expunge the stain from my consciousness, clearing my karmic debt.

But it still remains in my heart.

I believe that this act has prevented me from connecting/finding/meeting the partner I so wish to love and who will love me for who I am. A life shared. A love shared.

I don't wish to carry the remnants of guilt and shame anymore.

I would be so grateful if you would walk off what remains. I have done the best I can with owning it, dealing with it, seeing it. And tried very hard to forgive myself.

I have understood so much about human nature from this mistake I made.

But I don't truly know if I have forgiven myself. I think I have. But it was so big for me. Maybe I should go to Confession?

Whatever it takes. Maybe you'll find the answer. Who knows?

I knew that sin, too.

Many years ago I had an affair with someone who was in a long-term committed relationship. There had been no ceremony and no rings, but they were married. Let's not quibble on technicalities.

Pain was caused, and I had my face resoundingly and publicly smacked. Sense was slapped into me but I regret the hurt I caused to this day.

So, I knew the territory.

Sin.

It's such a little word.

The translation for it in Spanish is *pecado*. It sounds like a confection or a foible. Delicious but harmless.

Pecado.

That first sample convinced me that *pecados* were anything but harmless. I was shaken by the forthrightness of the admissions and by the reactions they evoked in me. I became protective of my 'sinners'.

'Have you had actual sins told to you?' I was asked.

'Yes, I have.'

'Big ones?'

'Well, they're painful for people, so that makes them big ...'

'BAD ones?'

'What's bad? Tell me what you think is bad?'

I saw what it had cost to disclose. I wanted to ease my sinners' struggles, and to forgive them. To make it all better.

I wanted to do their crying.

My brother and I are two years apart in age and live on opposite sides of the continent. Brett spent most of his life in the bush where we grew up, while I've lived a city existence in the performing arts. He has two children. I have none. While our love for each other is fierce, it's rarely verbalised. The upcoming sin-walk made it possible for us to discuss the respective choices we had made—and to speak that unspoken affection.

One morning, we were laughing on the phone, joking about the seductions of a 'devil-may-care' life. Brett was telling me that he and his wife Sue were making changes that excited them. True childhood sweethearts, they'd been together since their teens. Now that their children were adults, they were dreaming of new horizons and adventures. The day was sunny and warm on both sides of the continent. Full of promise.

Six hours later, Sue was dead.

She had gone to work healthy and full of vigour, at a job she enjoyed. At morning coffee, she said to one of her co-workers that she didn't feel well. With that she fell to the ground, unconscious. She never woke up.

The world was altered in a heartbeat.

Brett's eulogy to Sue was a tribute to her endless capacity for giving practical, tangible love. These are a few of his words:

> *Sometimes it seemed that she loved everybody, and she wanted everyone to love her. It was difficult to explain to her that the world doesn't work that way. She would be dismayed, when I would try to say that respect is not bought with love alone, that sometimes you had to be strong, or even tough, to gain respect and not be taken for granted.*
>
> *Sue didn't get it, because all she had was love.*

I wrestled with the old chestnuts.

How can there be a god when things like this happen? How can a good person be taken too soon, when others live on, not wanting to be here or causing pain? Surely that's a sin committed by God, if a god exists?

It's pointless. There's no logic or justice in death, only sudden then lasting sorrow. Our mother died at the age of fifty-seven, a full-force gale to the end. Years later, it still cuts deep.

I watched Brett being a father; being a grieving husband; being stoic, funny, wise, afraid and courageous. Mostly I just saw my little brother suffering.

And I couldn't do his crying.

Brett was adamant that I 'get on with living', so I went home from the funeral to prepare to depart for Spain forty-eight hours later. Flying east to Melbourne through the night, I looked out at endless black. There may have been stars but they're not what I remember. I saw nothing but a void.

3

FLYING *SOLA*

ON MY RETURN, A FRIEND said she was worried I was tempting evil by embarking on the sin-walk. She wrote that she knew *the potency of guilt and sin and willingness*, and urged me not to *sacrifice yourself for something unworthy. I know there are forces that we don't understand*, she wrote, *and that they might hijack your beautiful intentions.*

I was already nervous after Sue's death, having been reminded once again that we're all merely a breath away from the end. I considered pulling out of the Mozárabe, or even delaying, but I'd been employed to carry a swag of sins and I heard my brother's voice urging me to live, not simply take up space, so I farewelled my husband and boarded the plane for Rome. Then, in my window seat, I admitted to myself that I was terrified and I cried, much to the embarrassment of the honeymooners beside me.

The journey from Australia to Europe by air takes roughly twenty-four hours. For me, it was a chance to regroup.

I figured practicalities would help me to ignore grief and fear. As sunset turned the centre of Australia dusty pink below me, I opened the guidebook to the Camino Mozárabe. It was five years old—the most recent available in English, because the road was so little travelled—but it was all I had. Sue's sudden death meant I was leaving without completing my research and planning.

My prep is normally exhaustive. For the previous year's Camino Francés I'd read two guidebooks cover to cover, scoured websites, grilled *camino* veterans, downloaded Spanish podcasts, replaced my heavy boots with lightweight Merrells, and sourced a smaller backpack. I rehearsed saying *por favor* and *buenos días* as I hiked favourite sections of Victoria's Great Dividing Trail. It runs through gold country and still bears century-old scars of the hopes that brought people from all around the world to scrape and dig. It's hard ground, pockmarked and pillaged, yet when you investigate, it hums with life.

Yellow everlastings, pale spider orchids, and egg-and-bacon plant carpet the feet of gnarled gums. Red, blue and green parrots swoop, like visitants from a tropical jungle. At the base of eucalypts, echidnas snuffle. Kangaroos and wallabies bound between shadows, lizards and snakes slither, and galahs scream at intruders to get out of their patch.

People say the Australian bush is monochrome grey, not vivid in the way of European woods. And that's true. But to me it's more wonderful for the diversity it nurtures. And always, if I take myself too seriously out there, a kookaburra's chuckle will set me straight.

So I walked my Australian trails, with visions of Don Quixote's windmills in my eyes. I practised calling 'Hola!' to magpies and crows. I savoured the name of my destination, Santiago de Compostela, rolling it around my mouth like a boiled lolly. *Santiago* is Spanish for 'Saint James', who is Patron Saint of Spain and was one of Jesus' apostles. *Compostela* translates as 'field of stars'.

Saint James of the Field of Stars.

Stories about him abound.

One account says that his remains were brought to Spain from the Holy Land in a stone boat in about 44AD. Centuries later, they were supposedly found in a secluded forest near the coast at Finisterre, the westernmost point in Europe, believed to be the edge of the known world. The name means 'land's end' in Latin.

Another story says that in the year 814AD, there was a man called Pelayo. He was a shepherd or a monk, depending on the account you read. One night he was guided to some very old bones by a star, or stars. The local bishop sniffed an opportunity and immediately claimed the bones in the sarcophagus as those of Santiago.

This was massive news. King Alfonso II came to see for himself and so became the first Christian pilgrim, or *peregrino*. The story of the *camino* had begun, and it provided backing for the assertion that that region of Spain was Christian territory and Moors must not be allowed to claim it.

Santiago was made protector of the Christians, and in 844 he was said to have appeared on a white horse to lead them in battle. He became known as *Santiago Matamoros*—St James the Moor-slayer— an incarnation that seems at odds with his other persona, *Santiago Peregrino*—St James the Pilgrim. In this, he is usually depicted wearing a hat, robes and sandals, carrying a staff, and with a scallop shell around his neck.

Peregrinos took scallop shells home from Finisterre as a memento of the arduous conditions of pilgrimage and as proof of success. In words that all *peregrinos* come to know by heart, Sir Walter Raleigh wrote:

> *Give me my scallop shell of quiet;*
> *My staff of faith to walk upon …*

The shell relates to the pagan history of the *camino*, and may well be a leftover from the Romans' worship of Venus, because some claim the shell is a fertility symbol. It was appropriated by Christians when Santiago was supposed to have intervened to help a knight who had been swept under the waves. In that tale, the knight called to Santiago, and when he and his horse resurfaced both were covered in shells.

Seduced by these stories, I'd walked my Spanish talk back when I was preparing for the Francés. Myths and legends had tumbled in my head as I learned to say *pueblo* (village), *mochila* (backpack), and *albergue* and *refugio* (the hostel-style pilgrim accommodation in most *pueblos* along the way).

I'd doused my belongings in a vile-smelling concoction, developed for the US Army, which promised to repel bedbugs for six weeks. I'd fretted over pack loads, compiling lists of every item I was to carry with its individual weight, right down to the twenty grams for spare shoelaces. I'd obsessed over a schedule, finally deciding thirty days was reasonable, and booked return travel based on that, congratulating myself on a job well done.

I had been *so* ready when I set off for the Francés.

But I was headed for a very different road on the Mozárabe, and remembering that did nothing to reassure me *en route* to Rome, as the honeymooners snuggled beside me and Indonesia passed below.

After Sue's funeral, I'd pulled my trusty *mochila* from its hanging place and stuffed it full of the same old gear. I did buy a replacement pair of my beloved Merrell boots, and I visited my osteopath, who assured me the knee twinges I'd been experiencing were not a problem.

'Probably caused by fear,' he said.

Fear was keeping very close company as the plane droned north. Unable to walk, which is what I usually do when I'm afraid or on edge, I looked for another salve.

Poems are my internal guides. My maps and markers. My signposts.

They came alive for me when I chanced on Dorothea McKellar's 'My Country' in a school anthology. *Core of my heart, my country!* she wrote. I was a bush-raised girl in a city school, and as I read her description of a *pitiless blue sky*, I went home. She woke me to the possibility that words could conjure places, sensations and memories. Thanks to her, I think of Australia as both *wilful* and *lavish*, and I know that Dorothea was right about my homeland:

All you who have not loved her, you will not understand.

Only once have I ever deliberately memorised a poem. As a little girl, I had to compete in an Eisteddfod, and I can still recall those lines of Mr Robert Louis Stevenson's, learned by rote and not by love:

I saw you toss the kites on high
And blow the birds about the sky;
And all around I heard you pass,
Like ladies' skirts across the grass—
    O wind, a-blowing all day long,
    O wind, that sings so loud a song!

I wore a starched white frock with pink embroidered dots on it, white ankle socks and patent shoes, and I don't remember any connection to the words except for the quality of being held in check, stifled by the idea that there was a 'right' way to approach poetry. In my child's head, meeting that Scotsman's poem was like meeting the Queen. It required best behaviour, a straight back, rounded vowel sounds and polished shoes.

Not so the poetry I love. It transforms the mundane to the magical, and even at thirty thousand feet it can turn fear to calm. As the newlyweds snoozed, I whispered 'The Owl and the Pussycat' to the black ocean below. From my birth, my mother recited it to me every night until I went to sleep. She did it for years, until I could recite it back to her.

It's still vivid for me: a pea-green boat bobbing in a wide star-lit sea; a runcible spoon scooping slices of quince; bong-trees shading a be-ringed piggy-wig; and that impossible couple, owl and cat, dancing on the sand under the light of the moon. I know it by heart. By my heart and her heart. It lives right at my centre, one of my mother's most precious gifts to me, and a way for me to keep her alive.

Just after I decided to walk the Mozárabe, I heard a psychologist talking about the importance of the stories we're given as children, and the damage we can do with promises of handsome princes rescuing impossibly beautiful but helpless princesses who complain about peas under mattresses. Wicked witches and demure damsels.

He believed the best model anyone could offer a child was Edward Lear's 'The Owl and the Pussycat'. Words like 'runcible' can be explained, he said. Don't let them put you off. His theory was that, as a model for relationships, it had it all. They love and celebrate their differences, and set out on a great quest together. They have plenty of all they need—honey and money. The decision to marry is instigated by the cat, and the owl loves her strength.

My mother had fitted me well for the road, but the thing Mum didn't know was that Mr Lear left unfinished a poem about the children of the Owl and the Pussycat. I wish she had seen it.

> Our mother was the Pussy-cat, our father was the Owl,
> And so we're partly little beasts and partly little fowl,
> The brothers of our family have feathers and they hoot,
> While all the sisters dress in fur and have long tails to boot.
> We all believe that little mice,
> For food are singularly nice.
> Our mother died long years ago. She was a lovely cat.
> Her tail was five feet long, and grey with stripes, but what of
>   that?
> In Sila forest on the East of fair Calabria's shore
> She tumbled from a lofty tree—none ever saw her more.
> Our owly father long was ill from sorrow and surprise,
> But with the feathers of his tail he wiped his weeping eyes.
> And in the hollow of a tree in Sila's inmost maze
> We made a happy home and there we pass our obvious days.

A motherless family, at home in fair Calabria.

Italy.

My first stop in Europe.

I gave myself over to sleep as we flew farther from the Southern Cross towards the field of stars.

4

SIN CITY

It begins.

That's what I wrote in my journal at Bar Roxy, where cellophane-wrapped, bow-tied Easter eggs overflowed the counter, 'Sweet Home Alabama' played on the radio, and a coiffed matron sipped her aperitif as she fretted over a crossword. We were in the Roman suburb of Parioli, where embassies rub shoulders with research academies, and the *signore* at the next table spoke to me of *sesso*. Jet-lagged and still tuning in to Italian, I had to ask him to repeat himself. It took three attempts before I realised he was saying that men need daily sex, and that was why he took lovers outside of marriage.

It is only *sesso*, he said. '*Fa niente.*' It's nothing. And no, his wife would not want to know about his lovers.

When I asked if his tolerant, disinterested *sposa* could take a lover, he snorted. Women are different, he said. They are all *sentimenti* and *pensieri*. Feeling and thinking. They don't live here, he said, grabbing at his crotch.

Roman men often did that—a quick check that all the bits were in place.

'Relax,' I wanted to say. 'No one has taken the old feller away in the night.'

How did he think God felt about these other women, I asked.

He laughed.

God? At present, He must be very busy, he said. All those priests who have made the *pedofilia*. It is not good. Not good. No, God had bigger work than to worry about something *naturale* like a man's needs. God understood they were *normale*.

I didn't have the energy—or the vocabulary—to quiz him further. I must have been tired, because languages are one of my chief pleasures.

I've worked with language all my life, as a writer, theatre director and teacher. I relish English and its vagaries. I speak enough Spanish to chat about the times if not the tides; have passable schoolgirl French; and enough Italian to know when I'm in a discussion that is going down a one-way street. Having also been an actor, I'm not bad at the language of the body either, which is, in many ways, the most eloquent idiom of all.

At Bar Roxy, I crossed my legs and hunched over my journal, inclining my body towards the coffee machine. No interpreter was needed for the *signore* to understand that the conversation was *finita*.

Bar Roxy's coffee was working wonders on my jetlag.

Caffeine. A small sin. An addiction that took hold when I first came to live in Melbourne, sharing a house and a coffee plunger with my friend Susan, now a Roman resident up the road from Bar Roxy at the British School. Over cups of tea from a familiar pot, we'd caught up on news before I headed to the Parioli shops to provision my corner of the fridge and to locate that caffeine fix.

Walking back past ivy-covered, terracotta-coloured mansions, I considered writing the sins into my journal. Committing them to paper would begin the project in earnest, but I wasn't ready. Fear still niggled.

Roman spring was in full showy flight. Shop windows brimmed with purple and green artichokes. Asparagus and fennel tumbled from market stalls. Wisteria scented the air and pink cherry blossoms wafted on the warm breeze. The grass was strewn with white button-flowers, and an impeccably turned-out *bambina* offered a posy of wild daises to her elegant *nonna*. A gardener slipped me a red rose through the wrought-iron grille of an embassy gateway. Surely there was a film crew?

But no, it was just Rome. As bountiful as ever. And as complex.

Rome was my first landfall outside of Australia, thirty years earlier, with my then-love, my first-love. Wisteria draped itself over the Forum's Virgins, and we wandered between them, marvelling. My most recent visit had been three years earlier in high summer with my husband, to celebrate Susan's birthday in August heat. Seeking relief from scorching cobblestones, we had stood under a shaded sign that read *Carpe Diem* before toasting Susan with *prosecco* on the terrace of the British School. It had been a celebration of seizing the days.

Now, on my way to walk the Mozárabe, those snapshots of previous visits flicked across my internal screen. I climbed to the Piazza di Spagna and sat in the sun, watching the parade of tourists, lovers and hawkers. I tried to imagine the real *España*, waiting across the sea, but it was impossible with the language of Verdi and Rossini babbling about. All around me, couples twined limbs around each other and kissed. Italians always appear to be in flirtation overdrive. If they are having as much sex as it seems, then they are also champions at contraception, because for decades they've had one of the lowest birth rates in the world.

There were rumblings from the Vatican. People waited to hear whether the Pope would comment on the paedophilia scandal that threatened the church's credibility and appalled the world. The sins of the Fathers had not been addressed, and Easter was an opportunity for acknowledgement. Confession.

I wondered why it is so hard for those in power to admit culpability, or even to admit to reality. The dome of the Vatican contemplated me across the jigsaw puzzle of rooftops, palms and pines, giving away nothing.

As a Cardinal, Pope Benedict had been in charge of the office that dealt with sexual abuse cases. Did the men inside those Vatican walls never wonder if their failure to confess might be part of the reason why the faithful were turning their backs on the confessional? Were they so out of touch they thought it could be ignored? And did they think it would be possible to regain trust without an apology?

Like sin, sorry is a little word, but it seems difficult for the powerful to utter it.

When Australia's then-new prime minister made an apology to the Aborigines of the Stolen Generations, we stopped and cheered in our homes, in public squares, in offices. That act of contrition, to coin the Catholic phrase, meant something. It still does to me.

The next day was Thursday. April Fool's Day. I woke pre-dawn on Susan's sofa, looked out at the clear sky then rolled over. Tomorrow, I thought. Tomorrow I'll get up and watch sunrise over the eternal city. And then I snuggled in, assuming I would have a tomorrow.

That's the necessary arrogance of living. There'll be a tomorrow. But it's not a given, as I'd recently been reminded, and if we want to leave behind a clean slate, knowing we have not given pain, then probably we have to stare down our sins at some point.

Sin. The word has history and bite and danger.

Like the paintings of Caravaggio.

I went to a retrospective of his work with Susan. We stepped out of twenty-first-century spring, and into Caravaggio's world of grinning cupids with dirty toenails, rotting fruit, weary Madonnas and oriental-eyed youths, crowns of thorns and blood, two feasts at Cana and three John the Baptists. The paintings were fleshy and immediate, and a group of children howled with delighted horror at the sight of Judith hacking Holofernes' head.

We emerged into bright sunshine to sip blood-orange juice. Rome may be a diva with grubby bra straps, but she still knows how to have a good time. Fountains sprinkled drops of light. Sinners, saints and pilgrims converged in the Piazza del Popolo, slurping *gelato*, chocolate and coffee. The city glowed apricot and pink as we climbed home to Susan's, arriving to emails from my husband on her computer.

In the coming weeks, communication would be limited. The cost of international calls, the time difference and my desire to fulfil my pilgrim responsibilities meant that chats would be rare. Emails would only be possible from larger towns where I had access to, and time for, internet connection. Because I needed to average thirty kilometres per day on the road, there would be very few hours for seeking out net cafés, so the correspondence in Rome was doubly welcome.

My husband wrote that there'd been a 3.6 earth tremor across Melbourne the previous night, just after 263 masseurs had set a new world record for delivering simultaneous rubs in the Victorian goldfields. There was no indication if these facts were connected. He was off to eat Lebanese food with friends and hoped I could find a hot cross bun in Rome. I couldn't!

On Good Friday I had the seven hills to myself as I watched the sun chase the moon from the sky before visiting the Church of Trinità dei Monti, at the top of the Spanish Steps, where a congregation of twenty joined with eight white-clad nuns and four priests, who sang a liturgy in French, their voices like glass bells.

In Australia, cities are quiet and trading slows for Good Friday. In Rome, I emerged from Mass to see a homeless man being shunted aside as a shopkeeper lifted his shutters and straightened the doormat. The ladies at Luisa Spagnoli on the Via Veneto filled their windows with new season's clothes, breakfast coffees lined up on bars, and two American kids sipped morning cocktails at Harry's Bar. Sunshine, romance, cuisine and commerce. *La Dolce Vita* was in full swing.

Susan and I went in search of a vigil. Around Piazza Navona, all the churches were closed or in tourist mode. We wandered by the Pantheon, that great pagan–Christian temple, where they were ushering out sightseers because—lo!—they were holding a Mass. Easter Vigil in the Pantheon for a congregation of twenty.

A Christian church since the seventh century, the Pantheon is thought to have been built to honour the Roman gods. Clouds floated across the eye to the sky in the dome's centre as Mass began. I listened to the story of the death of Christ and hymns from the six-person choir as I tried to imagine the layers of story and devotion in that place.

Afterwards we had coffee and cake, browsed antiquarian book-stalls, selected postcards and tested expensive perfumes. There was no evidence of pilgrim faithful on the streets.

By contrast, in the rain of Easter Sunday, St Peter's was packed with microphones, super-size screens, broadcast vans, digital scanners, police, private security, hamburgers, hot dogs, flag-waving, elbow-shoving, position-jostling and voice-raising. It was the kind of gathering that might have been evicted from a temple for bad behaviour. Faithful and sightseers crammed together, thousands of us under our umbrellas, looking towards the Pope as he said Mass on the steps. Were we all hoping for the same thing? Apologies? Compassion? Miracles, perhaps?

IN HONOREM PRINCIPIS APOST …

The inscription on the façade of St Peter's.
'In honour of the Prince of the Apostles.'
The man beside me fingered a strand of over-sized rosary beads and prayed in Latin. A couple nearby explained the proceedings to their curly-haired children. Mr Rosary Beads turned, hissed and gave them the finger, before returning to his prayers.

I left. I hoped my sinners would understand my early departure from that day's research. I'm not sure how the Prince of the Apostles might have felt.

Crossing the eternal city in damp hiking clothes and sodden spirits, fear kicked back in. I was reminded of what lay ahead: weather; the challenge of staying focused when the way was dispiriting; the possibility that sins might overwhelm me. I still didn't know why I wanted to do this thing, and Rome kept her answers close to her ample chest.

I ducked into a warm *enoteca*, and sat with a bowl of lentil soup, remembering lines I had read in a *pueblo* called Ventosa, out on the Camino Francés:

Per aspera
Ad astra
A través de caminos difíciles
Llegaréis a las estrellas

Through hope,
through difficult ways,
you'll arrive at the stars …

It was hot then. Baking. Another lunchtime stop, but in very different circumstances. I'd already travelled a few difficult ways. I'd nursed pain in my right knee for three days—a new experience. Sharp twinges stabbed at me, mostly on downhills, and I had to sit more often, and for longer. To learn to be a snail.

I'd watched pilgrims toiling through Ventosa in the heat haze and considered those who had walked the way before me. Millions of footsore seekers. Did they all believe in the act of pilgrimage? In sin and redemption? In God?

Did I?

The morning at the Vatican, among the zealous and devout, had provoked the same questions, and again I had found no answers. In the dim light of the *enoteca*, I shivered as I journalled:

Belief.
Devotion.
Dogma.
Credo. (In Italian it also means 'I believe' …)
Faith.

Warming my hands on my soup bowl, I stared at the list.

Faith was where it finished.

Next morning, Susan watched me pack my *mochila*. Sleeping bag, rain pants and jacket, thermal leggings and top, sarong and pashmina. Mini-towel, mini-torch and mini-Swiss Army knife. The precious journals, my sister's camera and a friend's mobile phone with charger. My scallop shell. Seven hundred grams of toiletries and medicals. Tampons and toilet paper. A hat, sunglasses and one extra set of what I was wearing: hiking pants, T-shirt, socks, undies, bra.

As I stuffed red Crocs into the pack, Susan, an ex-theatre designer, winced.

'World's ugliest shoes,' she laughed.

'Ugly but good,' I said. Like all the contents of the pack. Serviceable and plain.

I hunched it onto my shoulders and stood in front of her, holding my walking poles. We both collapsed into laughter. What was I thinking?

Her computer tinged and she checked it. Sure enough there was mail for me. Three more 'sinners'. One nominated sloth, saying she didn't walk enough. Two others, both of them walkers whose energy I was grateful to have winging my way, separately nominated selfishness.

I stared at the word.

Selfishness. Selfish. Self-ish.

How exactly was it a sin? Did it give hurt? Was it a species of Deadly, or more common-or-garden? I knew I'd committed it frequently, but had no idea how to categorise it.

The word swirled. I could make no sense of it.

'You're just nervous,' Susan said.

'I'm not ready,' I heard myself say. 'I feel like I'm in that actor's nightmare where I'm being forced to go onstage with no script and no rehearsal.'

'You'll be fine,' she said. 'You've got your costume. Just improvise.'

5

COINCIDENCES

I FIRST SAW LEONARDO and Ricardo when I stood behind them at the check-in counter in Rome, eavesdropping and trying to decide if they were Italian or Spanish. They were tall, lean and dark of eye and hair; model-beautiful; and both wore sweaters in shades of grey. Their bodies inclined towards each other like compass needles seeking true north. They had a pile of shrink-wrapped luggage that dwarfed my backpack as we inched forward in the queue. Leonardo wore a cream cap, and smiled when our eyes met. Ricardo, in designer stubble and gold hoop earrings, didn't turn around.

I was seated beside them on Flight VY6103 to Barcelona.

At take-off, Leonardo's breathing was shallow and rapid, and he gripped Ricardo's arm. I found my eucalyptus oil, opened it, and the scent of Australia wafted about the cabin. I held the bottle out to him.

'*Respira,*' I said. Breathe.

I was back in the goldfields, kookaburras laughing at me. Leonardo calmed.

'*Usted es un koala,*' I said. You are a koala.

He wore a bracelet engraved with the name 'Ricardo'.

'Is that you?' I asked.

'No,' he said. 'It's him.'

Ricardo turned from the window and looked into my eyes, his features unmoving for what seemed the longest time. Then he smiled. Another world. I had passed the test.

Leonardo and I chatted in a mix of Italian and Spanish. When I told him I was planning to walk alone across Spain, his dark eyes widened. He took my hand, leaned in to me, and whispered, 'No sei nervosa?'

When I admitted that yes, I was nervous, he reassured me, speaking of the heart—corazón—and of the spirit, of the miracle of nature. Your walk will be beautiful, hermoso, bello, he kept repeating, over and over like a mantra. He was as changeable as the Melbourne sky on a spring day, joking one moment and concerned the next. No te preocupes. Don't worry. Don't worry.

Ricardo reached across and touched my forearm.

'Mira,' he said. Look.

He took a plasticised holy picture from his wallet, and gave it to me. I had not held anything like it since primary school, when I'd collected such cards, each shielding me from some evil or giving me a particular strength.

'He is a patron of pilgrims,' Ricardo said in slow, deliberate Spanish.

It was an image of a long-haired child wearing a pilgrim hat and holding the pilgrim's gourd and staff. A scallop shell was pinned to his cloak. At his feet were pink roses, and in one hand he held a Red Riding Hood-style basket.

Santo Niño de Atocha. The holy child of Atocha.

'He is my patron,' Ricardo said. 'For you.'

The Santo Niño is an incarnation of the Christ child. Legend has it that he smuggled food to Spanish prisoners of the Moors in the town of Atocha in the thirteenth century. It was a precursor to the stories that lay ahead of me in Andalucía, where Christian armies conquered the Moors after eight hundred years of co-existence.

It was a coincidence that Ricardo should have an image of a pilgrim saint. But then 'coincidence' is the way of the camino.

After less than ninety minutes, we were landing in Barcelona. Leonardo insisted I take their phone numbers.

'If you need anything, *cara*; if anything goes wrong—nothing will go wrong, nothing—but if anything does—it is very important—*muy muy importante*—that someone in Spain knows where you are.'

They waited with me for my backpack, and made me promise to text when I had a phone in Granada.

'*Una promesa, sí?*'

Yes. I promised.

They kissed me farewell, hugging me like I was their own, before walking away, hand in hand. Lovers. Of each other, and of nervous pilgrims.

My chest hurt. I'm not sure if it was envy—they were going home together to a familiar domestic life—or if it was a memory of some much earlier farewell. Because it felt like I had found them after a very long separation.

'Spiritual gobbledygook,' I murmured, as I rode the escalator to find my connecting flight for Granada. 'They're just two kind strangers.'

And yet I knew such things were possible.

My thoughts shifted to a man in South America, healing with acupuncture and reflexology. My *compañero*, taking his skills to the dispossessed. He makes me glad to know there are such people, and simultaneously aware of my own timidity.

I had met him at the opening of the second act of my Camino Francés.

Pilgrim lore says the Francés is like a traditional play, dividing into three acts.

Act One is Basque country, from the mountains of the Pyrenees to the elegant city of Burgos. It's said to relate to the physical: feet, terrain, weather, equipment. During this stage the pilgrim is taught lessons by the body.

Act Two, the *meseta* from Burgos to León, is an open tableland that many pilgrims describe as relentless. That is the province of the mind. Some avoid it altogether, taking a train between the cities that bookend it. Others go *loco* on its scorching plains, with nothing but thoughts to distract them.

The final act, up through the mountains and mists of Galicia, is said to be the realm of the spirit, where pilgrims reap the rewards of their struggles with body and mind, and may get to understand something of the thinker behind the thoughts.

As it transpired, that was almost exactly how my Francés panned out.

Act One was behind me when I met my *compañero*. It was my first day on the *meseta* and I was nursing my knee, fearful of the shooting pain that had forced me to stop for two days in Burgos, pain that kept reminding me to slow down. Learning to walk at snail's pace was the lesson of my first act, but it was never going to be easy for me.

I crested a hill and there it was—the *meseta*—stretching away from me, bleached and endless; dove-grey sky, sand-coloured wheat stubble, and the faint whisper of the north wind. A lone shepherd with his puffball sheep inched across the foreground, his whistles merging with the tinkle of their bells.

I grew up in equally panoramic vistas, but was accustomed to flocks spread over miles and mustering on horseback or motorbikes. That image of the shepherd and his charges drifting across baked fields was a perfect blend of landscape and activity. Their world appeared unified and peaceful.

The *meseta* holds all the beauty of solitude. One mound of earth can dance before the eyes for miles. A wild rose will thrust out of the soil and produce a bloom in defiance of all the forces of nature. Trees are twisted into mangled, sculptural shapes by the scented wind from Africa.

Sirocco.

What a word. I rolled it around as I walked, reminding myself that the hot winds in Spain come from the south, whereas in Australia we speak with dread of the northerlies that bring scorching heat and firestorms.

There was no Sirocco that day. It was cool. Light rain fell. I was simultaneously in Spain and in the west of Australia, remembering the water-starved regions where I grew up, and remembering my mother. Thinking how she would have loved the *meseta*. Talking to her. Wondering if there was something left of her to hear me. Before I knew it, I was out of my body, flying through the shimmer.

My knee jabbed, reminding me I had to stay grounded and walk like a snail if I wanted to reach Santiago. A yellow arrow pointed to a building with a domed roof and a scallop shell painted on its wall. This was San Bol, a ramshackle construction with no water, electricity or toilet. I'd been told by other pilgrims there was nothing there but 'dirt'. Why turn in? The body would cope. Go another five kilometres at snail-rate to the next village with its multiple *refugios*.

But something about the place called, so I hobbled down the road, castigating the *camino* gods for landing me in a place with no Chinese medicine. One acupuncture treatment, I thought, and I'd be free.

On arrival, the room was dark, but there were candles lit and flowers on the table. A brown-eyed man leaned into the light and said he was an acupuncturist and could treat my knee if I felt comfortable with the idea.

Comfortable? Only the coincidence was unnerving.

He took needles from his backpack and inserted them into my head, legs and wrists. My breathing slowed as I relived the *meseta* walk. I sat a long time.

My next clear memory is of the eyes of the acupuncturist as he kneeled in front of me and asked if I was 'doing okay?' I nodded. He stayed a while, watching me, and I remember saying I thought we'd met before. From his first appearance he'd felt familiar. I said I must have seen him on the road earlier.

'No,' he said, 'I'd remember.'

That night I lay in my bunk with acupuncture seeds in my ears, listening to the breathing of other pilgrims and watching stars through a window above my healer, who spoke a full sentence aloud from his dreams. I wanted to answer, but wasn't sure about the etiquette of holding a conversation with a sleeper.

Next morning, though, we talked. In the half-light, we walked out to look at a sliver of moon still visible through the trees. *Camino* legend says the spring at San Bol has healing properties, but I'd found my own miracle-worker. My *compañero*. We passed his coffee mug back and forth to warm our hands, and spoke of dreams and possibilities and snails. He left before me and I remember thinking that if our paths didn't cross down the road, it was okay, because at least I had found him again.

Back in the Barcelona airport, I waited for my flight to Granada. Meeting Ricardo and Leonardo had braced me, and I decided it was time to commit to the sins. Make them ordinary, I told myself. Normalise them.

So I opened my journal to the first blank page and wrote, in the terminal, on my knees and with no ceremony:

THE SINS I CARRY
Sloth

Sloth is the sin of *not* doing. I carried several versions of it for different people, one of whom categorised his as accidie: 'a state of restlessness and inability either to work or to pray'. My sinner wrote of his expectations of himself, and of his inadequacies; of expecting too much and falling short; and of the arrogance and stupidity in trusting that things will go well.

Another described his sloth in terms of shallowness. He felt deep regret for action, or actions, not taken, before a friend committed suicide. Had he intervened, he wrote, might he have made a difference?

The question haunted him decades later, and he included *neglect, insensitivity, undue regard to what other people would think, and distraction* in his confession.

Another wrote of procrastination, a sin that is not so much about doing or not doing, but about putting off what must inevitably get done. Rather like me and the writing up of the sins!

Another wrote a meditation on sloth as apathy:

> *So many things in our lives are automatic, instant, pre-programmed, plug and play. It's easy for us not to think; to press a button for heating or cooling, turn on the TV and turn off our brains, to buy convenience foods because it's too effortful to cook properly.*
>
> *In food terms, people today talk about food miles— the distance between the produce and the plate. It's generally a reference to the amount of fossil fuels used in food production and transportation, but it also has a moral dimension. It is so easy for us not to face the consequences of our purchases. You buy a hamburger—you're not the one who has to raise or kill the animal. There is a vast distance between the eater and the producer, between the eater and the animal, and this is a fertile breeding ground for apathy, for not caring …*
>
> *It's not all that long ago that many people raised and killed their own chickens. It was hard, bloody work, often done by women. It's likely no one enjoyed it. But they had to do it. I think there is something of salvation in 'having' to do things. As someone who tends to laziness, I have often felt the pull of apathy, the seduction of easefulness.*

I pushed on, not wanting to fall victim to another sin I was carrying.

Anger

I had been given a lot of anger to carry, in different forms. One perplexed me:

> *I still carry anger towards John Howard and Philip Ruddock for the damage they did to refugees and to Australia's soul. I would like to know that I am funding part of your pilgrimage as an attempt to walk off some of this damage ...*

Is there such a thing as justifiable anger?

Australia's previous prime minister and immigration minister had implemented refugee policies that I too found abhorrent. I transcribed the 'sin', but felt it was really a badge of honour.

I empathised with another sinner's wish to dip into *an endless stream of comforting understanding*. She had flashes of shocking anger at her aged and infirm parents, and was battling guilt about feeling resentment toward those she loved.

There were the confessions to *adultery, vengeance* and *white lies* from my first days, and the admissions of *selfishness* from Rome. There was a lengthy acknowledgement of the sin of *envy*, mostly directed at me. The sinner had a perception that my life was lived free of fear, sadness or doubt. That 'good things' came to me unbidden. To me, awash in fear, it seemed the words were written about another person. It had been risky for my sinner to admit to envy, knowing it could perhaps compromise our friendship. I did notice the confession irritated me. I felt misunderstood, that assumptions had been made about me that were far from the truth as I experienced it.

There was also a *mea culpa* about the sin of *gossip*, which amused me when I looked up to see people flicking through glossy mags, lapping up the dirt on airbrushed celebrities. No doubt many of the famous felt misunderstood, too! The sinner gave no indication of whether they enjoyed gossip, or had damaged anyone with it.

Gluttony was the final sin, along with the admission that the sinner felt little remorse for committing it, so expected little to change. Was it sinful not to feel remorse for a sin? There was very little guilt in evidence in the airport as travellers carb-loaded or sugar-burst on pastries and chocolates before one-hour flights!

Sinners. All around. Looking just like me.

And in my journal, more sinners. My benefactors and co-creators.

I studied what they'd given me, their insights into what it is to be human, and I thanked them, as they slept on the dark side of the earth. Out on the tarmac, planes taxied through a heat haze that obscured the mountains beyond. Somewhere there was the home of my knights in grey sweaters. I turned over the holy picture. *Santo Niño de Atocha* regarded me with steady eyes from under the plastic protective cover. A red-haired woman beside me leaned closer to inspect the card.

'*Es bueno,*' she said. It's good.

'*Sí. Muy bueno.*' I wished I could tell her just how good.

She patted my arm and I lost all vocabulary. She wore a chunky silver bracelet and the one charm hanging from it was a silver snail.

Signs and portents.

Coincidences.

I must be in Spain.

6

GRANADA

GRANADA GLITTERED. FRUITING ORANGE trees lined the streets. Gargoyles squinted at my blonde hair. Sun sparkled on the ring of mountains surrounding the city.

The Sierra Nevada.

They looked impossibly high and were blanketed with snow.

Granada. The word means both 'pomegranate' and 'grenade'.

I had jobs to do. I bought a Spanish SIM card, and it didn't work, then it did, so I panicked then relaxed. Ironically, the network I chose was called Happy.

I texted my Barcelona angels and Leonardo phoned immediately, insisting that if I needed anything, I must call. No! Text, don't call! Calling is *caro*—expensive. Just text, and Ricardo or I will call you.

Next I needed the precious *credencial*, which identifies the holder as a genuine pilgrim, a *peregrino*. As such, we are offered assistance from police, town halls and *camino* associations along the path, and entry to *refugios* and *albergues* where they exist.

At the cathedral office, where *credenciales* were issued, the clerk had trouble locating them. It was clearly not an everyday occurrence.

She asked where I was starting my walk.

'Here,' I said, 'in Granada.'

'Granada?' she said, black eyes widening.

'*Sí*,' I said. '*Aquí.*' Yes. Here. No doubt about it. Here.

She shook her head, rolled her eyes, and said, '*Madre de Dios!*'

Handing over my passport, she wished me '*Buen camino*'.

I was a pilgrim. Hearing those two words, it felt real.

Outside, in the orange-scented air, I inspected my treasure.

On the cover was a woodcut of a pilgrim staff leaning against an antique wood door. A scallop shell and a gourd dangled from the staff. Inside was the crest of the Archbishop of Granada, with my details underneath it in the woman's curlicue print. She had stamped and dated it with the Archbishop's seal, and confirmed I was going to Santiago '*a pie*'—on foot.

To the right of the seal was a photo of a white road cutting through green fields, overlaid by the pilgrim's prayer to the *Apóstol Santiago*, with a colour photo of the apostle himself to inspire me. Or at least, a photo of a statue!

When unfolded, a map of Spain showed various pilgrim routes. The Via de la Plata was the longest, but the map didn't even show the Mozárabe, my longer road, which joined the Via at Mérida, four hundred kilometres to my north. I really was walking the less travelled road.

'*Comienza, peregrina*,' I whispered. It begins, pilgrim.

Pocketing my treasure, I climbed to the Alhambra.

The site is marvel enough, high on its hill overlooking the city, ringed by the Sierra Nevada. Then there are the palaces and fortress …

The Nasrid Palace is a feast of detail in tiles, carvings, arches, mosaics, wood and terracotta. And water: trickling, running, tinkling, pooled; the sound of it; the reflection of light on it; the relief of its cool dampness.

Al-hamra. In Arabic, it means 'the red one'.

The Alhambra was built from the red clay on which it stands. It literally rises from its own earth. Visitors massed over every inch of it. After two hours of splendours, I perched on a stone seat at the fortress, the Alcazaba, to thaw in full sun. Birdsong cut through the crowd chatter from the courtyard below. Trees were thick with crimson-pink blossom, against a cornflower sky. The mountains stood sentinel in the distance.

I wondered if other species strive to build for an aesthetic or to stare down mortality, to express a love of the divine or of another person.

The bowerbird came to mind.

The Alhambra had bowers: corridors and anterooms; spaces that fluctuated between intimate and generous; places for trysts and stories, intrigues and parties, pomp and romance. It exuded a powerful aura of peace, despite having been taken from its Muslim creators by Christian kings. Simultaneously a temple, citadel and domestic sanctuary, it invited awe yet gave me welcome.

In the Palace of Charles V, a great colonnaded amphitheatre, a grizzled German tourist launched into song. He flung wide his arms and let rip. The stones soaked it up.

Later, in the gardens of the Generalife, I roamed in the heat among Dutch iris, wisteria, magnolia, lavender, roses, peonies, marigolds, cockscombs, rosemary for remembrance, pansies for thoughts, and red poppies for the fallen. The waft of purple stocks reminded me of my mother, of childhood, my brother and his Sue.

For hours I wandered the Alhambra, losing myself in memories, then finding myself in centuries-old courtyards and archways. Hungry to walk, I followed a path along the Río Darro, which was all bubbling water, stone and blossoms, up to the lookout of San Nicolás, where I gazed beyond Granada to the north. My way ...

Down in the centre with its Moorish souk and Catholic cathedral among the orange trees, there were practicalities of a twenty-first-century nature: a battery charger for my borrowed camera; postcards and phone cards; and thirty euros of stamps—my village was waiting for news.

Strolling back to the hotel, the night air was chilly. Myriad flowers pumped scent into a starry sky. Shadows trailed me on the stones. Families were visible against the gold glow of candles and the blue sheen of television. Narrow streets wound me about, much as they would have if I'd walked them centuries earlier.

In 1492, Spain's Catholic monarchs, Ferdinand and Isabella, wrenched the Kingdom of Granada away from its Moorish ruler, Boabdil, after more than a decade of battles. It's said there is a spot where Boabdil, his heart broken at the loss of the city and the Alhambra, looked back over Granada. This place is known as *el último suspiro del Moro*. The Moor's last sigh.

The Catholic monarchs gave Jews and Muslims living in Granada four months to convert to Christianity or leave the country. In so doing, they created the *conversos*—converts. Those who abided by the law and converted were subjected to harassment and suspicion from both the community they left and the ones they attempted to join.

I recalled another stroll one morning through familiar antipodean streets. A man had stood on a corner near my home. He'd removed his hat, and held out a scrap of paper with an address on it: the local school.

'Please,' he said, his lips struggling to form the single-syllable word. 'Please,' nodding and looking into my eyes.

I indicated to him to follow and asked his nationality.

'Home,' I said. 'Where is home?'

'No home,' he said. 'Iran. Kurd.' He paused, repeated it, touching his chest. 'No home. Refugee.'

He held out both hands and looked at the ground, as though this was a personal failing, some mistake he had made, to be born Kurdish.

We were met at the gate by another Kurdish man who spoke some English. He explained it was a trial day; there might be permanent work as cleaners.

'Good luck,' I said, shaking their hands. 'I'm so sorry.'

Walking the Francés, I felt I gained some understanding of the plight of the dispossessed. There's no status to flaunt when you're trudging along a road, grubby and footsore, looking for a place to sleep. Walk the breadth of a country with reasonably settled politics, and you'll want that stability for all the world. The words 'peace' and 'freedom' felt personal and tangible out there.

But of course that's rubbish. I always knew I could go home.

'No home,' he'd said to me.

In the Arabian Nights air of Granada, a flamenco guitar played. Gypsy music. Different. Other. I hoped the Kurdish man had a job and was making a home.

At a *ciber*, a net café, there was mint tea and lines from a friend: *Whenever we are truly present, wherever we are, we bring peace.*

She'd put her finger on my problem of the preceding days. I'd been projecting into the future—the distance, the difficulties—and reflecting on the past—the grief, the warnings. You can't walk when your thoughts are ten miles ahead or ten years behind. Now. Here and now. All there is, is now.

Why had I forgotten that?

Next day I walked to the Convent of the Comendadoras de Santiago and knocked on the grille of their wooden door. It slid open, and a face appeared. '*Sí?*'

I held out the *credencial*.

'*Por favor, puedo tener un sello?*' Please can I have a stamp?

Each church, town hall, *refugio, albergue*, bar or restaurant along the way has its own *sello*, or stamp, which is pressed onto the pilgrim's *credencial* when they make a stop. The images vary enormously: civic, commercial, traditional, religious. *Santiago Peregrino* occasionally features. The stamps become badges of achievement for pilgrims, but they also serve a practical purpose. The *credencial* is examined to ascertain that you're a genuine pilgrim. Basically, that's to do with distances between stops. They're a way of checking that pilgrims are not being ferried along the road. Some pilgrims collect *sellos* from as many places as possible, even if they haven't stayed in a town, making a mosaic of multi-coloured inky memories. I always had my journal stamped too, so my scrawl was divided by *sellos*, like primary school notebooks with their stars and elephant stamps.

The nun took my passport and slid the grille shut. I waited. The grille opened, the passport appeared, and I heard 'Buen camino' as the grille slid closed.

I assume they are a silent order.

That first *sello* was red ink and oval shaped, with the cross of Santiago at the centre. I studied it as the ink dried, then photographed the convent's tiled pilgrim benediction, before turning to look for the first yellow arrow.

There it was.

On the grey wall of the building opposite, to the left of a broken downpipe, under a scrawl of graffiti, pointing the way for pilgrims to progress.

I walked.

I followed arrows on hydrants, fences and pavement. I hadn't planned it, but my feet led me out through the town. The streets were no longer beautiful, but no matter. I was walking and something was being restored.

After three hours, I realised I had better get back to my quarters. Wandering without sins was all very well, but there was a pack to load for the real business ahead.

On the bus back, I opened my journal and read the words of Rainer Maria Rilke that I had been sent to help me begin. Words on a page. Sustenance for the soul.

> A WALK
> My eyes already touch the sunny hill,
> Going far ahead of the road I have begun.
> So we are grasped by what we cannot grasp;
> It has its inner light, even from a distance—
> and changes us, even if we do not reach it,
> into something else, which, hardly sensing it, we already are,
> a gesture waves us on, answering our own wave ...
> but what we feel is the wind in our face.

I wanted to share it with the silver-haired woman leaning on her stick, trying to catch the chatter of the teenagers in front of us; to tell her that her city had helped me believe I could begin; to say I could feel the whisper of wind in my face.

I didn't have the words.

Instead I listened to the sounds of Andalucía. They don't always pronounce the 's' and so *Andalucía* becomes *Andalouia*. *Beso* becomes *beo*. I wondered how that had evolved, feeling my lack of knowledge of the Spanish people's different languages and cultures, and their complicated relationship to history, faith and tribalism. I only knew wildly impractical things. Poems, poets and pathways.

But I know how to walk, I told myself.

One foot down. Then the other.

And tomorrow I begin.

ACT ONE

7

MOOR, MOOR, MOORISH

I WOKE IN DARKNESS, allowed myself the luxury of a morning shower, and then read the list of sins. My new ritual. I tucked my journal into my *mochila*, filled my water bottles and crept downstairs, feeling the same nerves as in my acting days when the Stage Manager would call us from our dressing rooms.

'Act One beginners onstage please. Act One beginners to the stage.'

That was me. A beginner. The fluttering in my stomach confirmed it.

Chill air greeted me in Granada's lamp-lit streets as I left the Alhambra behind, hurrying through the suburbs of the previous day's mini-*camino*. With the sun rising over my shoulder, my ten kilos of pack inched left, then right, before eventually settling into its place. My hiking poles click-clacked along silent pavement and my legs found their rhythm. Walking. At last.

After about fifteen urban kilometres I reached Pinos Puente, a *pueblo* on the outskirts where I stopped for the vital first coffee. When I said I was from Australia, the truck driver beside me said it was *la otra parte del mundo*—the other part of the world. At school, he said, he had been taught that if you drilled a hole through the core of the planet from Madrid, you'd emerge in red desert surrounded by kangaroos.

I said that we refer to Australia as 'down under'—*abajo debajo*—but he shook his head and laughed. Perhaps I had missed a double entendre!

I pushed on into irrigation channels, birch trees and just-opening poppies. The sky was clear and the sun warm. I was focused and foot-sure. Until I got lost.

The yellow arrows had petered out, or been bulldozed by farmers, and my guidebook didn't mention any of the visible landmarks. The raging river in front of me was definitely not the trickle I was hunt-ing and the only bridge was made from sheets of plywood, which hung low, almost touching the torrent. I didn't fancy plunging in, so I forged on through mud and clay.

Eventually I came to a fence made of frayed lengths of rope strung between trees. It held dozens of suckling lambs, their tails wriggling as their mothers chomped on iridescent grass. A shepherd limped towards me. His breath was a blast of lethal spirits as he laughed at my quest for a bridge.

'No, no,' he said, pointing me back to the plywood construction. 'That way.'

He said it would be an extra twenty kilometres if I didn't cross there.

That sealed it. The temperature had already reached the predicted mid-twenties maximum, and the stage was over thirty kilometres—a mix of pavement, asphalt, sand and mud. I was not lengthening it. Back I went.

When I got close to the bridge I could see that it was flimsy, held together by rope and hope. Soil crumbled on the bank where the sup-port beams were inserted, and the river roared, confirming reports I'd heard of recent flooding. A willow hung low, making me think of Ophelia's death in *Hamlet*.

I looked around for a miracle, for a knight or a saint.

They weren't coming.

Dappled light danced on raging water, and the bridge was a dun-coloured ribbon across it. There was nothing for it. I stepped out.

The bridge swayed. I stepped back.

I shortened my hiking poles and hooked them through my belt loops, then placed my boot back on the wobbling surface. Despite the willow's shade, sweat dripped from my temples and nose.

Step. Toes gripping insoles. Step. Don't look at the water. Don't even glance at it. Step. Nearly there. Step. Keep breathing. Step. Step again. And …

Land! Solid ground!

I punched the air, twirled my poles like a cheerleader, high-fived myself, and shouted Hallelujah. My heart was pounding and my body was drenched. My boots were caked with mud, red dye seeping into their camel leather. They looked like they'd been walking for weeks.

'Get used to it,' I told them.

I loaded up, buoyed by my triumphant crossing, and hit a dusty white road that led into groves of olives. Miles of them.

Oliven. Aceitunas. Olive. Olivjen.

I was surrounded. On and on they went, their leaves catching the sun, making them glitter like chainmail. The trunks were effigies, and their features, formed from a constant tussle with the wind, gave nothing away as I passed between them, heading for the horizon outlined against cloudless sky.

My eyes already touch the sunny hill …

And I got lost again.

Another branch of the river cut me off. All I could see were gnarled trunks and grass in need of mowing. I wondered about snakes. I wondered about spiders. I wondered about wild dogs and boars. I wondered if I was going *loca*. As I attempted to orient myself by the sun, by buildings on hilltops and by my guidebook, the phone rang. Leonardo, the screen said.

'*Hola, amore. Cómo va?*'

There was no way I was admitting I was lost on day one, so I said everything was *bien. Muy bien.* Going very well.

Ah, pride. There it was. And a white lie, for good measure!

He stressed that if I was in trouble, or lost, just to call. 'Ricardo and I will come. *De nada.* No problem.'

Well, I was lost but I wasn't in trouble. His voice bucked me up and within minutes I found the farm building mentioned in the guidebook and was singing out loud in time with the tap of my walking poles, my body beginning to understand what was being asked of it. It wasn't necessarily happy about it, as my knees reminded me once or twice, but it was getting the idea.

The *camino* gods colluded to give me a taste of everything that first day—cold, mud, stones, pink apple blossoms, yellow mustard flowers, ploughed earth, flooded creeks, heat, mown grass, steep inclines and flat panoramas. And olives. No forgetting the olives.

In the town of Los Olivares, my river roared a greeting as it raced under an arched stone bridge. Elderly locals gathered on benches at the main crossroad and young mothers played with their children in patches of shade. In the bar, I demolished a *bocadillo*—a sandwich made from dense, white, baguette-style bread, filled with cheese, omelette, *chorizo* or ham. Sometimes a little tomato if you are lucky. No butter. No relish. No embellishment. Always good, but lip-smackingly delicious after a long walk.

The village's workingmen were in the bar. They smoked, watched TV and talked in gravel voices, all without uttering an 's'.

Bueno día they said, instead of *Buenos días*, for hello.

Ma o meno for *más o menos*—more or less.

Ma depacio for *mas despacio*—more slowly.

I had to say that a lot.

They were tough and furrowed like their earth, and they watched my every movement as I hoisted my *mochila* onto my back and walked out into the sun to make for the road to Moclín, the next village.

Depending on which guide you believe, it's only two or three kilometres.

I don't believe any of them.

It was a marathon. Straight up. And I do mean vertical.

Los Olivares dropped away, reducing to a toy town. In still afternoon heat, the olive-decked hills were a shimmering patchwork quilt and the ground blinding white as I slogged around a quarry. A pine grove gave temporary relief, and then up, up, up again in full sun on a narrow, rocky path.

Mercifully, the unfolding panorama distracted me from my screaming calf muscles. The track wasn't an incline, as my guide suggested; it was sheer perpendicular excruciation. For the final rock-strewn, rutted five hundred metres of slippery bleached shale, it did seem my nose was going to scrape the ground in front of me; but the path was lined with grape hyacinths and daisies, and at the summit, above the town, a fortress beckoned. I gasped my way up, inhaling blossom and cow manure, the fragrance of rural Spain.

At the last turn, with the beat of my heart a kettledrum in my ears and my *mochila* weighing on me like a crate of mortal sins, a farmer stood up on the other side of a wall. I thought my knees would give out. We stared at each other in silence and then doubled over with laughter. He gabbled at warp speed, pointing and grinning. I nodded, though he might as well have been speaking Hindi. I think he was saying I'd frightened him as much as he had terrified me.

When equilibrium was restored, he asked where I was going. The mirth stopped. He put a calloused hand on my shoulder and looked into my eyes.

'*Vaya con Dios*,' he said. Go with God.

I couldn't tell him I didn't know where or who God was; not after his blessing, out there in the heat and dung. I didn't want him to know I was uncertain, possibly unreliable as a pray-er of prayers. I thanked him and began the last few purgatorial metres, following his directions to the main square.

Moclín is a village of about four hundred people. Mid-afternoon on a sweltering April day, there was not a soul to be seen. The square was empty, save for a lone dog stretched on a shaded flagstone by the closed shop. Heavy shutters on all the houses kept the sun out and any signs of life locked in.

It was a big town in the fourteenth century, before the Catholics conquered it in 1486. At least that's what the lady in the *ayuntamiento* (town hall) said as she stamped my *credencial* and congratulated me on my achievement. On day one, I had walked more than thirty kilometres. I had climbed over two hundred metres in the last two kilometres from Los Olivares. Moclín lay at over a thousand metres altitude, she told me as she laughed and touched my cheeks. No wonder they were tomato red. She also said the *albergue* was closed—not enough pilgrims.

No pasa nada. No worries. There is a *hostal.*

As I shouldered my *mochila* for the last time that day, her parting words were '*Usted es un caracol!*' You are a snail!

I squinted my way through the glare of whitewashed houses, checked in and began my wind down. Day's end on the *camino* is a ritual. Everyone does it differently but most do something like this.

On arrival, present your *credencial.* Once confirmed as the real deal, the *credencial* is stamped with a *sello,* and you are given access to the *refugio* kingdom. My *sello* from Moclín showed a detailed woodcut-like image of the castle in crimson ink. Its delicacy contrasted with the stark red outline of Santiago's cross from the nuns in Granada, already a lifetime away.

Next, remove your pack.

Shedding ten kilos in an instant is orgasmic. Stand tall, feeling the spine realign, the head float free and the sweat-soaked back cool. Bend forward—ouch!—and remove boots. Leave them by the door, for obvious reasons. You can return later to douse the insoles with peppermint and ti-tree oils.

Most importantly, find a bed.

Top bunk is my preference, so I can lie with my feet up a wall, stretching, if the snoring from other pilgrims gets too loud. Near a window is a coup. Not too close to toilets, but with an eye to possible navigation difficulties in the dark.

Unpack soap and miniature towel, and head for the showers. A eureka moment ensues if water is hot and plentiful. If not, no matter. Washing hair and body is the ultimate reward for walking.

Apply moisturiser, liniment or olive oil as necessary. Step into clean clothes and sandals or the ubiquitous Crocs. Enjoy a moment of feeling human before heading for the troughs to wash the day's clothes. Attempt to feel fond connection with female ancestors who beat laundry on rocks. I think of my grandmother at her copper, steam billowing around her as a fire underneath kept the water close to boiling. Relish the sweet smells, and if you're an Aussie, revel in the absence of water restrictions. Hang clothes in sunshine on the nearest available space, using safety pins or pegs.

Every day. Wash and wear takes on a whole new meaning.

Then comes a moment of choice. What to do? Forage for food in a café or *supermercado*; have a coffee or beer; write in a journal; engage with others; seek a quiet corner; stretch; massage aches; treat blisters; lie prone; explore the town; find a church or an internet café; write postcards; pore over the guidebook for the road ahead; cook your dinner in the *albergue* kitchen, if there is one; do nothing …

Whatever combination of these activities is undertaken, most *albergues* insist on lights out by ten. The Spanish keep late hours but *camino* towns often provide an early pilgrim menu—salad, main and dessert, with bread, water and wine—for about seven to twelve euros, all delivered without ceremony so the *peregrinos* can get into their sleeping bags on time.

In the Moclín *hostal* I had sheets, blankets and privacy. Back into the pilgrim routine as though I'd never left it, I sluiced the day's dust, hung my washing to dry in the blistering late-afternoon heat and exhaled. The moment of choice.

My calves were throbbing and there was a journal to be filled, but a fortress waited above and the *señora* at the *ayuntamiento* had said it dated from the twelfth century when the Nasrid kings of the

Alhambra built their strongholds. For those masters of light, water and mystery, I could manage another climb.

I hauled myself up a stone path, singing fragments of Bob Dylan's 'Forever Young'. Watching where my throbbing feet fell. *Forever young …*

Gripping a handrail as my thighs screamed for mercy. *Forever young …*

Protecting the jelly that was left of my knees. *Forever young …*

It's a favourite walking song, but I'd last heard it less than a fortnight before at Sue's funeral, my brother's shoulders shaking as it closed the service. With my breath rasping and eyes blurring, it hit me afresh that Sue of the honey-hair and perennial suntan would never age. She had loved that song, even though she didn't believe in the god Bob prayed to in its first line. The irony of it as her farewell hit me hard as I climbed. I arrived at a church door, only to find it closed, and irony hit me harder.

I climbed on.

Gusts of cold air swirled as I reached the top. In spite of chirruping birds and commanding views in all directions, the place was a graveyard. Sections of wall, like skeletons, crumbled across the hillside. Dust to dust.

Nature had taken over, grass vanquishing stone. Thistles grew in what was once a courtyard. Pink flowers sprang from the remnants of a lookout tower.

It was like wandering through a painting by a European master, one of those symbol-laden meditations on lost realms. Or a *palimpsesto*—a favourite word, learned in my second Spanish class when I inherited a textbook from another student and was writing responses over the indents of his previously completed homework. The definition of palimpsest, the equivalent word in English, is:

> *A manuscript or piece of writing material on which the original writing has been effaced to make room for later writing but of which traces remain.*

Much of Spain is a *palimpsesto*, layers of story and life crowding on top of each other in a country that has been imagined and re-imagined, conquered and re-conquered.

The Moors of Moclín managed to hold off the Christians when the Catholic kings ordered an assault in 1485. My brochure told me one thousand infantry and horsemen stood their ground that day, but the following year, the Moors surrendered after another attack.

I looked back, trying to locate my road, but it was only one of many ant-trails. Mountains, villages, watchtowers, hermitages, fields, forests, nearby rooftops and far-off freeways laid themselves out before me. The panorama was endless in the clear light of day's end.

And those olives. They were like precision battalions, stretching to the horizon. Millions of them, waiting to march.

All was still and silent. It must have been terrifying for the Moclín locals as they watched the armies of Castilian Christians advancing for hours.

Los Reyes Católicos. The Catholic kings.

I was to become familiar with the phrase in the coming weeks. Ferdinand and Isabella were aggressive warlords or unifying innovators, depending on the tale being told. In truth, they were probably like all of us: both saint and sinner. Rather like Santiago himself with his dual incarnations of pilgrim and Moor-slayer. *Santiago Matamoros*, St James the Moor-slayer, is a knight in armour, actively engaged in lancing and beheading Moors. Was it not a sin if a saint killed in God's name?

An eagle's shadow passed over me and the wind whistled a dirge.

Maybe there was blood under the dollhouse roofs of Los Olivares. Dig into those oft-ploughed olive groves and there may be layers of bones of the past fertilising the present. The Romans, the Crusades, the Inquisition, Franco …

Walking the land revealed layers of self, too. Already, at the end of day one, my own history was uncovering. Past selves were emerging through the surface of the present self. The hiker from Australian trails. The sister wanting to do the crying. The actor wanting to inhabit the skin of others.

Palimpsesto.

Peeling back, trying to uncover the original without destroying the upper layers, those written with the skill and pain of experience.

As the sun set behind the olive-quilted hilltops, I opened my crimson journal in search of the list of sins, wanting to recite them to the air since I couldn't light a candle in the church. Instead, the book fell open at a poem.

Another layer.

Sent to me by a playwright I met on the Camino Francés, it's by Robert Louis Stevenson, author of my first rote-learned poem where the wind blew *all day long*. This time he was writing about France, but it might have been penned for that ruin at Moclín:

> *We travelled in the print of olden wars;*
> *Yet all the land was green;*
> *And love we found, and peace,*
> *Where fire and war had been.*
>
> *They pass and smile, the children of the sword—*
> *No more the sword they wield;*
> *And O, how deep the corn*
> *Along the battlefield!*

8

SIN SIN

THAT NIGHT, TO OUR mutual amazement, I met another walker at the Moclín café. Children of the *pueblo* played chasey around our table, while their parents traded stories at the bar and we tucked into roast chicken, potatoes and salad. I wondered about gluttony as I dipped bread into olive oil and sipped *vino blanco*, but after the day's mileage I decided it was fuel and not felony.

My fellow pilgrim was German, with a shiny bald head, grey eyes and a clipped white beard. He was certainly over sixty, but I thought it unlikely he had reached seventy. His English, his Spanish and his manners were formal, products of his time and his education. He was a veteran of several *caminos* and a theologian.

Herr Theologie.

As a young man, he studied under Joseph Ratzinger, the man we know as Pope Benedict XVI. What luck for a pilgrim walking with sin! Spain. Miracles and portents.

Our conversation was all walking: the condition of our feet, the quality of our guidebooks, and our anticipated arrival in Santiago. He said, in his courtly phrasing, that he hoped we might 'make some agreeable days'. I said I preferred to walk alone and have conversation at day's end, but we agreed to begin day two together. I tucked into bed at 9.30, the sky just darkening outside. Sleep came instantly.

Next morning, Moclín was hushed and shrouded in fog as we tip-toed up the main street, our calf muscles reminding us of the previous day's climb. As we descended from the town, gold light bathed the valley and picked out Moorish watchtowers on nearby hilltops.

Due to the floods of the preceding weeks, much of the track had been washed away, but where it was intact, it exploded with new life. Grass grew high and lush on the narrow shoulder of busy roadways, so even asphalt walking was made tolerable. *Herr Theologie* covered kilometres with a long springy step. Like many Europeans, he'd spent his life hiking and skiing in serious mountains. Warmed by sun and pace, we were removing outer layers and congratulating each other by nine—just before getting hopelessly lost in a rutted olive plantation on a vicious slope.

Up, down and around we went. Guidebooks proved useless, and eventually, after half an hour of panting and retracing steps, it was the frenzied pointing of a man on a tractor that directed us back to the *camino*.

'This was not the path,' *Herr T* gasped. 'Of course, we should have rested on the road.'

I seethed. I wanted to snap at *Herr T* to use the verb 'stay' instead of 'rest'. I wanted to blame someone, anyone, for the disaster, and he was near to hand.

Disaster?

Well, the 'one who can' had failed. Company distracted me, making me lose the way, so company created failure.

Crazy thinking. Irrational and emotional. We both had maps. We were both grown-ups. Never mind that I'd been lost twice the previous day when alone. This time my failure was public, thus intolerable.

Hello again, pride. How thoughtful that you've brought anger along with you.

I trudged under a black cloud of resentment as we passed green swathes of farmland and communal *lavadoras*, the traditional village washing troughs where women still gather to scrub and chat. They weren't out that morning. The wind was too chill.

Eventually we stopped in the *pueblo* of Ermita Nueva to rest. We'd walked sixteen kilometres in just over three hours. More like eighteen, if we counted the half-hour of scrambling through olives. A good pace. Cracking, for many.

So why was I agitated? It was a manageable 26-kilometre day.

We located a stone bench out of the wind, removed our boots, nibbled on my apples and *Herr T*'s cheese and watched locals emerging to greet the proprietor of a travelling shop. The *pueblo* was too small to have a supermarket, so the inhabitants supplemented their home-grown produce from a van that did a circuit of the countryside.

A group gathered. Heads nodded, hands waved, jaws dropped. Women jockeyed for position, turning from one friend to another to comment, and then back to the vendor for confirmation.

Spanish *pueblos* are rarely more than fifty kilometres from each other, which is nothing by Australian rural standards, but in Spain, such distances can seem sizeable. Whenever I arrived in a *pueblo*, I was aware of bringing news from the previous place or the wider world. Television and internet were never going to replace the pleasure of stories from the horse's mouth.

The van's owner winked, placing his finger to his lips as he handed over a parcel. He gave stories with small change, connecting the village dots. Women who had strained to walk up the hill, bent double or limping, straightened as they closed in on the action, weaving and dodging to get close to the source. Energy crackled.

Gossip.

The trade of soap powder and scandal made me reflect on how closely I'd guarded the sins I was carrying. I wished I'd always treated information that way. It's so easy to enjoy the moment of telling, whether good or bad news. When we are given information about someone, we have the goods. By passing on that information, we demonstrate our power and confer a little of it on the recipient. We're trading kudos, buying cachet by reducing a person to a commodity. We spend a little of one life to purchase a piece of another.

Often it's impossible to differentiate between news and gossip. 'Current affairs' has taken on a whole new meaning. I recalled the people reading magazines in the Barcelona airport, sampling the travails of the famous folk we know by their first names, whose perfect lives are often revealed to be less than the perfection they seem in pictures.

Is that part of it, too? A need to reassure ourselves that our ordinary lives are not so different from the larger-than-life charmed existences we read about. I wondered if that was the temptation for my sinner-gossip, to feel that daily life was less ordinary. And where could the sin be in that?

Presumably, in the reduction of a human being to something as marketable as a designer watch. Like the tins of tuna being unloaded from the van, anyone can become a product, with a good or bad brand. And we can be wrong about anyone, even those we know well, as my other sinner's confession to envy of my 'perfect' life demonstrated.

I shivered. The wind, *a-blowing all day long*, was piercing my T-shirt, and my first coffee was still ten kilometres away.

We hoisted our packs onto our shoulders. The ladies of the *pueblo* waved.

'*Ellas tienen hambre*,' Herr Theologie remarked. 'Oh, I apologise, my dear. I forget. English, not Spanish … They hunger. For company.'

'Yes,' I said, facing away as I adjusted my pack.

'It is normal. The natural thing is for a person to want his own kind.'

I resolved to give myself over to the natural thing, and so we set off together between blossom trees and low stone walls, single file on narrow sections, pairing up as the road widened. We avoided barking dogs and greeted those with wagging tails. We spoke a mash of English and Spanish. He was curious about Australia. He knew of its 'excellent walking' and would have liked to visit, but it was 'so very far'.

I asked about his studies. My time in Rome had hardened me against Pope Benedict, but his student went to great pains to tell me that, once upon a time, *il Papa* was not so 'conservative'. He had been a free thinker and an inspiring mentor. *Provocativo. Herr T* also spoke of his own *vocación*, of the continuing call to serve God, and described life at the university where he worked.

We were less than an hour from day's end in the town of Alcalá la Real. I decided it was probably time to own up to my reason for making the walk.

I told him about my curiosity about faith and the idea of walking for others, about gathering the sins, and all the while he nodded, saying, 'Yes, of course, I see, I see.'

But clearly he didn't.

Every time I mentioned the sins in my *mochila*, his brow would furrow.

'But it is not without,' he said. 'Your pack is full.'

I apologised, explaining I was speaking metaphorically. Yes, my *mochila* was indeed full of my walking necessities, but conceptually, I was carrying a load of sin.

Several times we came to versions of this stumbling block and the conversation tripped itself up. Finally, I decided I had to be impolite.

'Do you know what sin means?' Ridiculous question to ask of a theologian.

'Sin? Yes, of course,' he said.

'So can you understand that I am carrying the sins of other people?'

'No. No, this I cannot understand,' he said. 'How can you carry without?'

Now he made no sense to me.

'Carry without?'

'Yes. Of course. *Sin*. Without.'

Finally, the nub!

His English had let him down on the most basic word of a theologian's toolkit. He was translating the word 'sin' into Spanish, where '*sin*' means 'without'!

Through our entire conversation, he had assumed I was carrying 'without'. Did he think I was embarked on a Zen exercise about emptiness?

I mimed sins, stabbing at the air with my walking poles and stamping my feet while repeating the word 'anger'. He watched, amused.

I decided to attempt Spanish, asking if he knew the phrase '*sin pecado*'.

'Yes, of course,' he said, his laughter stopping.

'In English, that means "without sin",' I said.

'Without sin?' He stopped in the white dust road. 'Without sin.'

He was silent a moment, then chuckled.

'I see. Yes, I see. But, of course! Language. It is such a problem! You are trying to be *SIN* SIN, yes? *Sin* sin. Without sin. Do you understand?'

He laughed again, waiting for me to share his joke.

I managed a smile. It had taken such effort to reach understanding that my funny bone had turned to mush. As we walked into the commercial hub of Alcalá la Real, towards another Moorish castle, he was still chuckling.

'*Sin* sin, without sin.'

My hopes for insight into the Seven Deadlies appeared doomed.

The main boulevard, with its multi-storeyed buildings and post-lunch bustle, was a culture shock after a day in the fields. We were hunting for an *albergue* when my telephone rang. Leonardo. Checking in.

I told him about my companion and he was tickled that I found myself so close to the Pope—only two degrees of separation. He insisted it was fate. I must consider *Herr Theologie* a blessing.

I battled to see *Herr T* in that light as he followed me in and out of possible lodgings awaiting my decision about where best to sleep. I was mired in just the kind of guilt one of my sinners felt about her aged parents. Her *endless stream of comforting understanding* was a long way off.

After locating a cheap but clean *hostal*, I closed the door and sank onto the bunk. Silence. Even hand-washing in my miniature in-room basin was enjoyable, conducted in the bliss of solitude.

My mind wandered back over its struggle for equilibrium through that day of constant company, and with my hands turning blue in the freezing suds I remembered the most practical definition I'd ever heard of the words extrovert and introvert.

It was a psychologist, his name lost in my personal mists of time. He was speaking on radio, his Brooklyn-accented voice explaining that an extrovert is someone who is nourished by contact with people, whose energy is restored by company. An introvert is someone who is nourished by solitude, topped up by time spent alone. It's impossible to tell by meeting someone whether they're an introvert or extrovert. It's totally reliant on how they fill their tank.

When I heard that, it made sense to me. I don't appear introverted. I forge connections easily, have worked in the collaborative environment of the theatre and relish my sprawling circle of friends, but if I don't get some solitude I can't manage any of it.

I'm an introvert.

I'm not sure if that was self-justification, selfishness or a white lie, but I promised my sinners I would try to commit less of their sins and be a more personable pilgrim. Then I took myself out to explore *sola*!

In Spanish, the word for heaven is *cielo*. It's also the word for sky. It was easy to imagine Alcalá's evening sky as paradise.

A billboard displayed *necrológicas*—obituaries—for Doña Antonia, Doña Maria and Doña Mercedes. It featured crucifixes, Madonnas, and requests for prayers for the repose of the dead women's souls. Were they *sin* sin?

In the old part of town, roads narrowed and shadows deepened. A tiled plaque proclaimed the birthplace of Juan Martínez Montañés, *el portentoso imaginero*. The portentous imaginer? It turned out he was a sculptor. *El Dios de la Madera*. The God of Wood. He had a high forehead and an imposing moustache, and glared at me as though he knew the contents of my heart.

I sped away.

The street opened onto trees and a square in front of a church. In the forecourt were girls in taffeta dresses—electric blue, lime green, lipstick red, ruffles, corsets, corsages. They clustered around an older woman swathed in magenta silk, her coiffed hair dwarfed by the towering black lace mantilla she wore. The mother of the bride. I told her she was *magnífica* and that I would like to photograph her. She smiled, inclined her head and posed.

Inside the church, Madonnas in black brocaded robes stared into space, tears streaming down their cheeks. Candles flickered, still burning from the wedding. I remembered being a little girl, racing to find candles when the generator failed or storms came; an adolescent, telling spooky stories with friends; the erotic charge of a bedroom with shadows flickering on bare skin; birthday cakes and time passing; 'Light a candle for me …'

Palimpsesto.

But all my wishing, asking and thanking in churches and chapels never answered my burning question: is there anyone listening?

I dropped coins into a metal box and lit a candle for my sinners, just in case.

Across the square, among sunglasses, scooters and non-essential oils, the Hiperbazar China offered a plastic figurine of Christ wearing a thorny crown. He cried red tears. Another depicted the saviour holding a palm frond in one hand and a grinning pet rock in the other. Behind him was a four-slice toaster.

The fortress peered down over town matrons clustering around fountains and stone crosses, watching their grandchildren at play. Bartenders waited for cheer squads to arrive for the big clash between Barcelona and Real Madrid. There could be no question about my loyalties there.

Other loyalties were less certain.

Back in my quarters, I stared at a postcard from the Caravaggio exhibition. It showed John the Baptist alone in the wilderness, his skin pale and luminous, his red robe no protection from predators. He was self-focused, brooding, melancholy. But he believed.

'It's easy for you, John,' I whispered. 'You're alone.'

John didn't even have the grace to squirm under my gaze. He had sermons to give, sinners to save, a message to deliver. He had certainty.

I picked up my pen and scrawled on the reverse of the broody image.

'It's hard to be *sin* sin. Today, I failed.'

I rolled onto my bunk to watch my washing dry.

9

REHAB

BEFORE TURNING IN, I'D told *Herr T* I might meet him at seven, to walk out together. I woke in plenty of time but lurked until he was gone.

I lied.

I'm not even sure it could be categorised as white. I told a black lie. I wanted solitude, so selfishness won out.

Two sins before breakfast. I was going well.

Worse, I'm ashamed to report that I was rewarded with intense pleasure. Yes, there were miles more olives, but the walk through them was ecstatic. The groves were ordered and kempt. The day was mild. Workers were out, pruning, burning, singing and laughing. Their chainsaws called to each other in a mechanical symphony, punctuated with a cuckoo-like birdcall and a repetitive bell sound that followed me down the road, challenging me to find lyrics to sing along. I was belting out my rendition of Van Morrison's 'Bright Side of the Road'—probably completely unrecognisable to Van!—when I turned a corner and walked smack into a group of men piling olive cuttings onto a fire.

'*Hola!*' they chorused.

They asked where I was from, where I was going. As smoke rose in dense plumes, I told them I was from the bottom of the world and I was walking to the stars. A tall man wearing a red bandanna said I had *duende*.

It was a new word for me.

'*No entiendo,*' I said.

'*Es una fuerza,*' he said. It's a force. A force you can't see with your eyes, but a force you can feel.

Another chimed in to tell me that it's like when the olive leaves move without wind. That is *duende*.

'And you, lady kangaroo, you have this *duende*,' the first man said, shaking my hand. I thanked him, and stepped out again onto the path, invisible forces swirling around me.

Duende.

It may have been the most beautiful word I'd ever learned. It was certainly a memorable classroom.

A city of caterpillars crossed my path, moving calligraphy against the white dirt. They were determined to cross from left to right and I was equally determined not to squash them. I didn't need murder on my conscience.

Roosters spruiked business for cafés. '*Boc-a-dill-o,*' they crowed, conjuring images of overstuffed bread pockets.

Palest fruit blossoms inclined towards me and wild hyacinths poked through cracked clay underfoot. Yellow arrows appeared to show me the way but my feet seemed to know it. *My eyes already touch the sunny hill ...*

I made a pitstop after fourteen kilometres at Bar Manolo in Ventas del Carrizal, downing a coffee under a low-hanging grapevine while two boys delivered the *Páginas Blancas*—White Pages—along the opposite side of the road. The *pueblo* was in full market mode. Stalls crowded the main square, selling everything from plumbing supplies to skeins of lace. I bought dried figs and mixed nuts, and talked with locals and stallholders who wanted to know why I was alone.

'*Hola, Rubia!*' Hey, Blondie!

It was a greeting I would hear constantly over the coming weeks.

'*Sí, sí, siempre camino sola ...*' Yes, yes, I always walk alone ...

Okay, not always. But a small lie. Very pale. And it was definitely my intention.

Leaving town, I was stopped by a woman on a ladder scrubbing her windows. She wanted to know where I was going.

'*Santiago? No, no. Muy, muy lejos* ...' Yes, I know, it's a long, long way!

'*No es posible.*' It had better be possible.

She said her name was Lucia, that she would like to go with me, but she was too old now and her back was bad. But one day. In a car or bus, maybe. But never alone ... never ... but perhaps I could say a prayer for her in Santiago?

I promised I would as she kissed my cheek in farewell, wishing me a walk with God. I turned to go but she ran after me, dragging me back.

'*Venga conmigo, peregrina,*' Lucia insisted. Come with me, pilgrim.

In her kitchen, I smelled bleach and effort. She wrapped two large salami-type sausages in foil. A loaf of fresh bread sat beside them on the bench, cooling.

'*Regalos!*' she said, advancing on me. Gifts!

Before I could protest, she pushed the sausages into my pack's side pockets and was attempting to undo the top buckles for the bread. I backed down the hall, laughing, thanking her, trying to explain there was no space.

At the door, I asked her to pose for a photograph.

Her black eyes regarded the world from under lids wrinkled by care and laughter. She wore a pearl stud in each ear—a little vanity, even for window cleaning. Her curly hair was red-tinted above greying eyebrows and her lips compressed in a smile that held back tears.

She kissed my cheeks. I kissed hers. We both laughed.

'*Gracias, gracias,*' I repeated.

And I walked, my heart and *mochila* both close to bursting.

I was convinced that Lucia had made me a better person by her charity. I felt rehabilitated from my state of 'sin', and was sure I could meet up with *Herr Theologie* and offer him companionship and grace.

My steps quickened.

Seven kilometres later I stopped, unable to resist the temptation of a high stone wall in the shade of a sprawling tree. To my left was a yellow and white villa surrounded by olives and palm trees. To my right, more olives. And above, the twittering, hooting, cheeping and squawking of birds.

I had killed no caterpillars, told no lies and wished no evil.

That said, my journal reflects that I berated myself long and hard for not giving Lucia anything in return for her gifts. I thought of my first donation, of my friend's vehemence. Of my pride.

'Don't think. Just say thank you.'

If humility was the Contrary Virtue I needed, I still had a way to go to find it. I whispered 'Gracias, Lucia' to the wind, and vowed not to turn the act of receiving into a negotiation, ever again. Then I lay back to survey my realm. Pleasure outweighed pain by a country mile, and I knew what a country mile felt like. I dozed, and dreamed.

The haze of Australian summer creates mirages, and although I hadn't seen any in Spain, I sometimes felt as if I saw a kind of mirage self when I walked. She was up ahead, stronger and sin-free, with the real me in her wake, trying to tidy my mess. Then she was behind, grimacing and whining, while the real me floated above, trying not to laugh.

Walking changes our perspective, enlarging aspects of self and highlighting dark corners. It's a magnified microcosm of a life. Magnified, because experiences are writ large. So much is intensified by the up-close-and-personal nature of it, by placing yourself literally on people's doorsteps or in their path. There's no hiding in the bubble of a car or the anonymity of public transport. It's a microcosm, because it compresses all the aspects of self and demands they be examined by that same self, even when not hauling sins. It's almost impossible to walk long distances without getting a wake-up call about foibles or weaknesses. Physical challenges can provoke emotional ones, and they arrive close together, affording little recovery time.

The camino roads serve many purposes for pilgrims: meditation, vacation, provocation. One of the most fascinating, though, is a service to the wider community: rehabilitation.

Going right back to the Middle Ages, pilgrimage to holy places has been used as punishment for sins. In 1283, John Pecham, then Archbishop of Canterbury, visited a parish priest who had reportedly been fornicating with women, then repenting of his sins, then fornicating again. The Archbishop ordered him to go as a pilgrim to three shrines: Santiago, Rome and Cologne. I don't know if walking dulled the priest's lust or if pilgrimage cleansed his immortal soul, but he must have had some impressive blisters.

Along the Francés I was repeatedly told of a man carrying a full-sized cross to Santiago. I was sceptical. It seemed like a performance rather than a private contract between a man and his God.

Herr Theologie and I talked about the idea of penance and *camino* rehab when we met at day's end in Alcaudete, another town with a fortress watching over its entrance, this one still intact from the tenth century.

He found me writing in my journal. Pointing out the chunky red plastic of the Crocs I was wearing, he laughed, saying my feet looked like a clown's.

'Yes,' I agreed. 'They're as ugly as sin.'

If he was annoyed that we had not walked together, he didn't show it. He beamed at the prospect of Lucia's *salchichas*, so we ordered a salad and settled in. He told me that when he walked the Camino del Norte, along the Bay of Biscay in the north of Spain, he had seen a group of young delinquents with a guardian, walking in lieu of a prison term. They slept in tents and carried their own cooking equipment. *Herr Theologie* thought it a bad idea because they were likely to escape and make trouble; they shouldn't mix with ordinary people walking the road; they should not be placed in a position where they could affect others or, presumably, be affected by them.

I thought it an inspired solution, particularly for those whose crimes were minor and whose 'sins' might have been exacerbated by circumstances such as poverty, lack of education or peer pressure. It might encourage offenders to become reliant on their internal resources rather than what they could take from others, a chance to formulate new visions of themselves and their possibilities.

Herr T was unconvinced.

'There are some who cannot be rehabilitated, my dear. Some are born bad.'

'Surely you don't believe that?'

Herr T didn't blink. 'Of course. Some people have evil. It is in them. They cannot be changed.'

'I don't agree. It's education, opportunity. Yes, humans have tendencies, good and bad, but we can learn to override them.'

'You are too soft, Miss Pilgrim. Too sentimental. Perhaps it is where you grew up. In my country, we have had to look into the darkness of the human heart. Evil exists. That is fact. And some cannot be taught the difference between good and bad.'

'I'm not soft,' I retorted. 'I believe we have instincts, like animals— to eat, to make shelter, to protect our territory, to procreate. But we can be educated to get those things without hurting people. We can learn morals and ethics. This is nurture.'

'But where is your evidence that we learn? Not history, dear girl. Of course good and evil exist, and they are always at war.'

'That makes it sound like it's outside of us, outside of our ability to change. I think that if we offend, it's because, somewhere, society has failed. Whether it's parenting or schooling, government or community, we can learn to make better choices than the ones we make purely by instinct.'

Herr T broke open a bread roll and smiled.

'I think you have some way to go to understand human nature, my Australian friend. How might you explain two brothers, like Cain and Abel, raised in the same circumstances, and one is good while the other offends?'

'Free will, perhaps? I don't know. I'm not saying that—'

'Believe me, there are those who do not want to learn, who cannot. There are those who are simply evil. And yes, of course, as a species we must learn. We must learn to see these people. It is our duty to recognise them, my dear. To be strong enough to face them.'

I wanted to say that I believed goodness would assert itself if we gave it more of a chance. 'Look at Lucia,' I wanted to say. We were eating her food, given for no reason other than kindness, the Contrary Virtue to envy. But they were emotional arguments, and I was attempting to keep myself on track.

'Then ... if we don't believe in the possibility of rehabilitation, what is the point of repentance?'

Our salads arrived before *Herr T* could reply. I joked with the waiter, who gave us instructions about the best way to leave town the next morning. *Herr T* passed olive oil across the table. We ate.

'It's good, isn't it?' I said.

'Yes, delicious,' he said, but his eyes didn't meet mine.

When our conversation resumed, it was about the birds that had called to me on the road. *Herr T* said they were indeed cuckoos, and the bell sound was made by frogs. He also told me that farmers were spraying to kill caterpillars. I didn't mention my efforts to avoid them.

After dinner, I went out into the twilight. Alcaudete was deserted save for two elderly *señors*, seated on a stone wall in the *plaza* at the top of the hill. They stared out over the plain, sniffing the breeze and inhaling the evening cool. As I passed, they called to me to stop and asked why I walked alone. When I answered, '*Estoy siempre sola*'—I am always alone—they shook their heads. No, no, they could change my mind about that.

'*Siéntese aquí*,' they said, patting their knees. Sit here!

I resisted their charms and continued my *gira* of the town.

I found a church, but it was closed, so I picked up a leaflet asking for prayers of intercession. An image of the Virgin adorned it, a weary, middle-aged Virgin holding the body of her lifeless son. Her oversized crown could do nothing to offset the well of grief into which she had plunged. Her boy, her son, slaughtered. What comfort was it to her that he would save all mankind? Too much had been asked of her. Even her clothes were tired. The blue and white robes were gone, and she wore brown and beige. This was not what she imagined at the Annunciation.

In the main street, a shop window boasted a range of saviours in robes of many colours, with varying quantities of thorns and blood. A Jesus in midnight blue staggered under a black cross. Red drops fell from his crown, over his flesh and onto the supporting gold-plate plinth.

Images of suffering seemed vital to the Catholic faith. Perhaps that's why we have come to associate sin with intense pleasure, because the opposite, intense pain, is associated with virtue. Could a life of pleasure be virtuous, then? Could a life of pleasure exist without sin?

Other shops displayed white First Communion outfits—miniature soldier and sailor suits for the boys, wedding-gown cut-downs for the girls, and extreme expense for the parents.

The façades of buildings were faded. Tiling chipped at the corners. Ornate exteriors hid abandoned interiors. Ochre paint peeled to reveal aquamarine underneath.

Palimpsesto.

I wondered about the layers, in that place that went back to the tenth century. The current residents were keen to proclaim their piety, if shop windows were any indication, but there were also doof-doof cars and flirting teenagers near the castle ramparts. Healthy young residents doing what healthy young animals do everywhere. Instinct asserting itself. Pleasures of the evening.

I walked back to the *hostal*, vowing to rehabilitate myself.

'*Mañana,*' I whispered to the first star. 'Tomorrow, I will walk with my theologian, and I will do better.'

10

ROAD TESTING

THE *CAMINO* GODS DIDN'T give me a free ride with my new resolve.

We missed a turning after only an hour and had to hike across more olive groves with nothing but faith for guidance. Finally, a worker who was burning prunings pointed the way. We stumbled in ploughed ruts that seemed specifically designed to torture the ankles of pilgrims. We crossed a swollen river that was meant to be a dry creekbed, and as I plunged in I almost lost my guidebook. Not that it would have mattered, it was so out of date. We lunched on Lucia's *salchichas* and dried figs. *Herr T* drank his litre of milk. We circuited a broad lake, after we realised the 'path across the flat swamp' would have entailed walking on deep water. We had no delusions of grandeur!

We endured a seemingly interminable stretch of white gravel under a threatening grey sky. We persisted along kilometres of asphalt past farms and factories. An olive-processing plant, with its pile of foul-smelling tailings, almost finished us, but we kept up our spirits by sharing the road's wonders.

See there, the fields of solar panels, sunshine being farmed like wheat. Oh, smell the olive smoke from the bonfires, so bitter on the back of the throat. How clear, the reflection of those mountains in lakewater. Over there, an entire field of white daisies and yellow mustard flowers. Listen! The cuckoo. So faithful.

After covering twenty-seven long kilometres—more with detours!—in six hours, we stopped before tackling the suburbs of Baena, resting on a lone piece of flat stone outside a machinery rental business. We nursed knees, feet and ankles to the sound of roaring engines.

Herr T's face furrowed and his shoulders curved in on themselves. He slumped. Not from physical exertion; his fitness was impressive. No, there was an interior hollow that he sometimes inhabited. Whenever I stopped to chat to a local, he would hang back, watching, smiling and nodding. He said that I 'make people good', and that he was not able to do that.

I didn't understand, but I think it had something to do with his reasons for not choosing the priesthood. He spoke of the difficulty of genuine connection, and of wanting to be a 'priest to the people' as opposed to a 'priest to Rome'. When he talked of religion, the furrows reappeared.

I reined in my emotions throughout that long day. I kept my euphoria in check, just as I managed to keep my temper from flaring. When we stopped for lunch I re-read the reflections of one of my sinners from my journal:

> I want to support you to carry 'anger' on behalf of the wider world. I fear anger. It is such a destructive, negative emotion. It's a natural, impulsive reaction which can lead to ugly words and deeds, irrational behaviour and pain … all of which is usually deeply regretted when the anger subsides.

Words on a page helped to prevent me from committing the sin. I'd experienced regret the previous day. It tasted like the pungent smoke from the olive fires, and I had no wish to sample it again.

In Baena, our stop for the night, we checked in at Pension Rincón and I took first turn in the shared bathroom, where the hot water softened my violin-string muscles. I saw a ninth-century castle (they were getting older with each town), an olive oil museum, a modern brick church with a high-pitched bell, and locals chatting without their esses.

Somewhere, I thought, there is a cave where the wind whistles 'ssssss' all day and night. The cave of lost esses.

I was tired. Clearly.

There had been no ugly words or deeds that day, and I hoped I had given no pain by silences or lack of consideration, but the effort to be good had exhausted me. Alone, I could channel my inner saint, but company tested me and my resolve to do better. With clean washing hanging over my head, I went to sleep pondering words from William Shakespeare:

> *If to do were as easy as to know what were good to do, chapels*
> *had been churches, and poor men's cottages princes' palaces.*

Next morning, breakfasting on *café con leche* and *tostada* while the man next to me downed a beer, my ritual reading of sins was interrupted by the news. An airliner had crashed in Russia, killing ninety-six people, most of Poland's political and intellectual elite, including the president and the chief of the armed forces. Even more tragic was that they were commemorating the Katyn massacre of spring 1940, when Stalin ordered the execution of twenty-two thousand Poles. It was an episode that had remained covered-up for generations. In 1984, when I'd workshopped a play about Katyn, I was staggered to find no evidence of it in history books.

I tried to decipher the Spanish newsreader's rapid-fire commentary. It seemed unthinkable that a nation could lose its best and brightest twice in the same place, seventy years apart. Coincidence or curse? The commentary from the newscaster hinted at the latter.

In the same bulletin, there was a report on the paedophilia scandal at the Vatican. No one in the bar looked up. I wondered how the Spanish faithful felt about it. The previous evening, they'd gathered at the block-brick church, kitted out in Sunday best on a weekday. They welcomed me with smiles and embraces, arthritic hands patting my cheeks. No mention was made there of the sins of the *Padres*.

Maybe their faith was not connected to *il Papa*, but was about community and service, and consistency. Turning up.

It was time for me to turn up. Time to walk.

With only twenty kilometres to cover, I'd told *Herr Theologie* I would make a late start and catch him down the road. Such a short distance between two *pueblos* was rare on the Mozárabe—another reason why so few walk it. On the Francés, villages with *refugios* are close together, meaning ten- or fifteen-kilometre stages are possible for those who are not accustomed, or addicted, to walking, and there is no need to carry weighty quantities of food and water.

I left Baena under open skies as children were farewelling mothers at school gates and shopkeepers were sweeping the pre-opening pavements. The morning was a blur of sunshine, breezes, wildflowers and solitude.

And olives.

This was extra-virgin terrain, they'd informed me at the olive oil museum. Contorted trunks twisted out of unforgiving ground. Spilled drops from my water bottle disappeared in seconds. My feet marked time to snatches of mis-remembered songs, and I drifted out to the end of my kite string to fly above my snail-self. Sky-surfing.

Time stretched and contracted.

I grounded myself to watch two hawks circling for what seemed an eternity. Then, from nowhere, a smaller bird launched itself like a fighter jet, targeting the black monsters again and again. Eventually, its precision dive-bombing paid off and the hawks left. It landed on a wire to preen its peachy-red and blue plumage.

'You've got *duende*,' I called to it. '*Mucho duende*.'

At my feet, fire-engine-red poppies and butter-yellow daisies offset each other, the colours more intense for their proximity. I murmured more lines of Shakespeare emailed to me back in Granada:

> *And this, our life, exempt from public haunt, finds tongues in trees, books in the running brooks, sermons in stones, and good in everything.*

Will must have been a walker. He certainly knew about goodness.

It was a challenge to see the good in asphalt, but I distracted myself from the heat underfoot by meditating on the sin of gluttony, which is defined as the over-indulgence of food or intoxicants to the point of waste. While I love my food, and have a formidable appetite, I was using every bite of it in service to the kilometres I walked. I did wonder if it was possible to be gluttonous about the act of walking itself. Walking is an intoxicant for me and there were definitely times when I over-indulged in it.

Perhaps, rather, my walking was a symptom of greed, a deadly sin that no one had nominated, defined broadly as 'an excessive desire to possess wealth or goods'.

But no. I decided I couldn't possess walking, even if I could be possessed by it. I admitted to myself that I was greedy about solitude, and words, particularly when they shaped themselves as poems, but I didn't see too much harm in either of those. Not that morning, anyway.

I wondered if there was harm for my sinner in defining himself as a glutton. It's a harsh word; a harsh thought to have about oneself. I didn't know if he consumed 'to the point of waste' but I could imagine there might be a lot of guilt in his ownership of that sin. I wondered if it was possible for him to freely enjoy the food he ate.

All I knew as I beat along the pavement was that walking gave me pleasure, even on broiling tar and with burning soles, and that food did too; and while I was sated for steps, I was hungry for my daily bread.

Castro del Río was my destination, and I reached its blossom-lined streets by lunchtime. I located a bar for coffee and a *bocadillo*, and removed my boots to rest the toes. *Herr T* found me and told me he had taken a room for the night. His knee was swollen after the asphalt.

Santa Cruz, the next town, was another twenty-two kilometres. I felt strong and there were hours of daylight ahead. To walk on to Córdoba would place me a day closer to news from home, and possibly, reports of how my sinners were faring. Should I continue or stay the night?

I waited for a sign.

Mind you, I was in no position to ask for intervention, having exhausted my quota of wishes for the day. In the last couple of killer kilometres, I'd prayed for a lift, and immediately, a man stopped in a van and asked if I wanted a ride. Perverse *peregrina*, I then told him I must walk.

The bar was emptying. I poked my head out the door. There were clouds in the distance and the air was cool. Walk, I decided. Walk on.

Six hours later, I was in Santa Cruz, devouring beans, bread and a red wine, or *vino tinto*. I'd walked a marathon over hills, highways, clay and bitumen. My feet throbbed. My knee creaked. But the grin wouldn't leave my face.

Over my hermit's dinner, I recalled the afternoon.

Wild blue irises, so expensive at home, grew like weeds out of the rocky ground at my side. Highways and byways of asphalt and concrete made my breathable Merrells into mini-saunas. Trucks and cars passed hard and fast.

Smaller roads soothed me. Hillier, but deserted, they invited speed. Fields of green crops waved me past and ranks of olives monitored my moves.

... but what we feel is the wind in our face ...

Slow down, *peregrina*. Remember the snail.

A mirage farmhouse became real, and it even had shade. Boots off. Figs. Water.

From nowhere, a brown dog appeared. She snuggled, wagged and nuzzled. She plopped beside me and licked my toes. I gave her a morsel of *salchicha* and made a friend for life. We panted together into the silence.

My phone beeped, making my four-legged friend race for cover under a farm truck. There was a message from my husband, who had tried to call. Somehow, in all my dipping and winding, the signal couldn't locate me. In danger of plummeting, I booted up and walked on, leaving dog and melancholy behind.

I sang to the sky, a noisy dot moving along a ribbon of shimmering black, and eventually I rose to observe myself traversing wide river flats, but somewhere around the thirty-kilometre mark, I crashed to earth again, sore and spent. And alone. Tears threatened with each burning footstep. Hot tar and thistles abounded. No one gave a damn. No one even knew.

I remembered my iPod. I'd debated bringing it, telling myself the music of the road is always enough; that the songs that find me are the right ones; that I remember what I need to hear. But at that moment, an external rhythm seemed a very fine thing, so I clipped in the earbuds and clicked Play.

A heavy-husked voice and a chiming guitar kicked in, along with an insistent drumbeat I knew well from other walks: miles and years of walks. The music was a hand in the small of my back, propelling me with a hymn to home and places beyond imaginings. It was a shot of walking *palimpsesto*. It was U2 singing 'Walk On'.

So I did.

Off road, on a track so untravelled I wondered if I was imagining it.

In fact, I was off the *camino*. The recent flooding had meant detours. A man stood by a river far in the distance, his binoculars trained on me, tracking my progress. I waved. He lowered his glasses and climbed into a four-wheel drive.

The track became a path. The path petered out, eroded by rain and rabbit holes. The guide was no help but a yellow arrow gave hope, which was promptly dashed by the steepness of the next incline and biting briars at my ankles. I knew from the sun's position that my direction was correct but I didn't want any extra kilometres. All I wanted was to get somewhere. I was driven by the push of an inner voice, chanting 'on, on'.

I recognised that voice. Both friend and foe, it urges me forward, but it can also do damage. Just in time I heeded the lesson of the snail and slowed for the final kilometres. When I hobbled into Santa Cruz, its streets bordered with flowering lemon trees, my left foot was bruised and screaming, my trousers stained, my shoes muddy, and my hair stuck out like straw.

'Buenas tardes, Rubia,' an old *señor* called. Good afternoon, Blondie.

The man with the binoculars! How had he passed me? Where was the road? It had been three hours since I'd seen him in the distance, the only other human all afternoon. He was like a found friend, chatting in the square with his *amigos*. He offered me a lift to a *hostal* in his four-wheel drive, and although it was less than a kilometre from one end of town to the other, I climbed aboard. His gentlemen friends waved as we cruised down the street.

'Descansa, niña,' were his parting words. Rest, child.

I had walked over forty-two kilometres. An all-surfaces marathon. I asked for olive oil when I checked in and mixed it with eucalyptus from home. I rubbed my aching limbs with the fruit of the two countries.

And I did rest, kind *señor*. Long and deep.

Next day, I walked through another world. No olives.

For over a hundred and forty kilometres they had been my companions, and now they were gone. I was in farmland, ploughed chocolate earth and vivid crops. Fences delineated solid blocks of unbroken green or yellow crop. White farmhouses broke the abstract shapes at irregular intervals, but mostly it was just me, snailing across the landscape.

Deep erosion confronted me, the track a series of gullies and washaways. Ants lugged twigs, working harder than me. Flowers swayed. Clouds sailed high into the swimming-pool blue.

Endlessness.

Somewhere the hum of a tractor.

A hill to climb. A descent to beware.

A bend in the track. Another hill. A yellow arrow.

An Andrew Wyeth painting with an Australian intruder in it.

A *meseta*.

No wonder my pace picked up and I began to sing. I made the day a particular offering for my slothful sinners and stepped out the miles on their behalf. Sole proprietor of all that space and light, I forgot body aches and let myself soar high, exploring perspectives—of the landscape below, of the landscape ahead, of the relief I wished for my sinners—all the way to the hilltop where I first spied Córdoba.

The city appeared as if conjured.

Córdoba. Ancient capital of the caliphate, city of arabesque and picturesque and the famous cathedral–mosque, the Mezquita.

Delicious words.

On the outskirts (never as inviting as the inskirts) two men stopped to chat. A lawyer and an engineer, they were inspecting the area for a developer.

'We admire your prime minister's policy on immigration,' the lawyer told me.

I remembered my sinner's anger at that policy and her equally passionate support for refugees, but said nothing. These men had Romans, Moors and Celts in their history. African faces were prominent in all the towns I'd passed. I had no knowledge of Spain's policies and was not going to initiate an argument about Australia's detention centres with two gentlemen who insisted on placing my pack in their car and allowing me to ride up front to the Roman bridge spanning the river Guadalquivir. Another delicious word!

As we parted they shook my hand, telling me that their kindness was nothing; everyone, even a pilgrim, needs a lawyer! I was glad that for once I'd paused before giving an opinion. I was in another place with different complexities based on other histories.

I stepped out onto the bridge, ancient Rome under my feet. A stone angel greeted me mid-way across and on the other side the Mezquita waited.

Behind were six days and 164 kilometres of walking through landscapes of tough wonder. Ahead lay another 1036 kilometres in an optimistic thirty-six days.

But for now, there was a city of over three hundred thousand people, and a rest day with all its possibilities.

11

CÓRDOBA

NEROLI, THE SCENT OF spring, drew me to the centre. Blossom dusted the tops of orange trees and petals lay thick between cobbles on streets that had been trodden by Arabs, Romans, Jews and gypsies.

And now me. The Aussie influx.

The window of Residencia Marisa's room 109 with shower opened onto a souk-like lane. I inhaled spice as I peered down on bargains being sealed, and a candle-decked shrine to the Virgin on a wall of the Mezquita.

I unpacked everything. I washed everything. I showered. Everything!

By early evening, I was ready to wander, a tourist and not a pilgrim.

I found a *ciber* and tried to gather thoughts for my home village.

The Spanish have been kind, I typed. *The road has been kind. Leonardo and Ricardo still call every day, yet we don't even know each other's surnames.*

A friend mailed back: *Don't ask. Angels don't have surnames!*

Others reported pain.

Sin-telling had become psychological warfare: a determination to locate the source of envy that threatened a friendship; a request for me to make *a small aspiration on the wind from a sacred spot* because acceptance of the past would not come; fear of having nothing to offer without lies or gossip; guilt at turning away from a homeless person who requested money for food ...

That sinner wrote that she had thought of me out on the road, and walked back for ten minutes to give, only to find the beggar had moved on. She felt she had become blunted by selfishness, unable to give unless there was a tax donation attached.

I was not sure what to write in reply. I'm not a psychologist and had no advice, and presumably the mediaeval pilgrims on whom I was modelling myself had not had any contact with their sinner-employers. I could only report on my experience. I told how people walked with me if I looked lost or uncertain, across creeks and eroded tracks.

'*De nada*,' they said. It's nothing.

It was something.

'You're a pilgrim,' they said. 'It's important work. *Muy importante*.'

More kindness than I could report with a queue waiting to use the *ciber*.

My elation was partly due to the thrill of arrival. Having reached Córdoba, I began to believe I might be up to the task.

Then there was Córdoba itself.

The bridge, the river, the winding streets of the Jewish quarter, horses clopping on cobbles, patios spilling geraniums, and that neroli … like an opiate.

Herr Theologie appeared. His knee was troubling him, so he had ridden buses. He looked smaller without his pack and checked constantly for his wallet among the jostle of holidaymakers. He'd booked into another hotel, but felt he was paying too much, so decided to move to Residencia Marisa.

'You always find a good place,' he said.

I'd traipsed around for an hour before locating it. The city was overflowing with tourists and rooms were scarce. *Herr T* told me there was an airline strike and all these people would not be able to go home.

But it wasn't a strike. Over dinner we learned a volcano was erupting in Iceland. Clouds of ash swirled above Europe and planes were grounded indefinitely. People battled to book trains and buses. One man had hired a cab to drive him all the way to Germany!

We ate *pisto*, like a *ratatouille*, with crusty bread and olive oil. Between bites, *Herr T* remarked that, once, people might have thought they'd offended the gods in some way to cause the eruption— that the wrath of gods was feared, and so people were more mindful of their actions.

'So … people were good because they were scared?'

Herr T stopped refilling our glasses and exhaled.

'No, of course. That is not what I said. But it is like a child. Respect, and yes, a little fear of the parent, can make a child choose to be good.'

'But if we're only being good because we're afraid, or worse, because we want something from our parent, then that isn't truly good, is it?'

'No, but it is better than having no boundaries at all.'

'But how do we know what's good, *Herr T*? What if we haven't been well educated by this parent? What if I just take your bread now because I want it? I mean, if I've never been told that's stealing, where's the offence?'

'Ah, well, surely you can see that if you take the bread from me without my permission, I may go hungry. I may starve. That is not a good result. I may be sad, or angry. Surely you would see that this is not good. You will realise for yourself, it is bad what you have done.'

'Not if I have three children who haven't eaten for days. It's easy for you and me to obey rules. We have homes and food and families. But if I had no roof over my head? If my children's bellies were empty.'

'You would do better to ask me for help for them.'

The waiter cleared our table.

'Do you think, then, that something is good because the gods say so?'

Herr T smiled.

'So you have read Plato down in Australia? Is an action good because God loves it or does God love it because it is good? Yes? It is a favourite question from my students. An excellent question. Fair.'

'And what do you answer them?'

'Of course, I don't answer them. I encourage them to find their own answer.'

91

'Then what is your own answer?'

He shook his head. Smiled.

'You are very persistent, Miss Pilgrim. It is like the way you walk. You go and go, when sometimes I think you should learn to slow down. To stop.'

I may have had the good grace to blush.

'It's true. But it's natural for me. I try to slow down, but it's hard.'

'Yes, to go against our nature is difficult. Surely that is the point of the struggle to be good. Sometimes it asks us to go against our desire. But you could be a little kinder to yourself, I think. Your sincerity, it is clear. Your effort is clear. And if I can see it, I am sure that God can too. And that he loves it.'

'How can you know that?'

'I can't. Of course. But I see you. I see what comes to you. I say it before: you always find a good place. We are told that we will know them by their fruits. I am sorry. I see I embarrass you.'

'No, no, it's just …'

My face burned. Any moment he would see that his assessment was flawed.

'I don't say that you are a saint, dear girl! Only that I can see the fruits of your actions and I think you are good. Or your intentions are. God sees that. You need have no fear.'

'I have no need of fear, *Herr T*, because I think that what I seek in any god is the possibility of my best self.'

The thought surprised me. Sometimes it's only in the give and take of conversation that I get to learn what I've been mulling over.

Herr T placed his glass on the table. He raised his eyes and smiled.

'Go on, Miss Pilgrim. I listen.'

'Well, perhaps no God made us. But rather … we "made" God. An idea of something perfect. A way for us to … to … aspire to perfection.' My words came in bursts, like crossing creeks on stepping stones. 'I think that religion gives us forms and shapes. Traditions. Ritual. And some useful laws. But I think that the spirit—soul, if you prefer—is utterly unconnected to religion. I think it's connected to …'

My stepping stones petered out.

'… aspiration?' *Herr T* whispered, nodding his head.

'Yes, exactly. Aspiration to goodness. We yearn to realise our full potential, so we invented the idea of perfection so we could aim for it.'

Herr T said he believed that not only was there a God, but that he was all-knowing. That God knew, when he created man, that everything, yes, even wars and disasters, would happen. Psalm 139: *All the days ordained for me were written in your book before one of them came to be.* It was not easy or fashionable to believe it, but believe we must, if we are to live in God's love.

'If goodness is loved by God,' I said, 'He or She has a funny way of showing it. Bad things happen to good people all the time.'

My thoughts went to my brother. The discussion was getting personal for me.

'My dear, you cannot know the workings of the divine or of people's hearts.'

'No. But I also can't reconcile abuse and wars with love. Your God is like a parent who decides to conceive a child, knowing it will be raped or tortured. How do you love such a parent?'

We wrangled further, over flan. Then coffee. He remained patient and steadfast, but we weren't going to resolve those questions over dinner.

Herr T said that he loved to be out in the world, being challenged. He spoke of his surprise that people on the *camino* liked him. I told him the surprise for me was that I liked myself, and that I was enough for myself, for days on end.

'Yes, I also feel that,' he said, but I wondered if he did. I wondered why he had taken the bus into Córdoba, rather than have his rest day in Castro del Río. Admittedly it was a *pueblo* and had little entertainment, but my experience of the smallest places was that they could offer deep peace and rich exchange. More so than cities.

I told *Herr T* about a meeting I'd had on the Camino Francés.

At the end of a long hot day's walking, I had arrived in El Ganso, a *pueblo* my guidebook called 'hauntingly crumbling'. It was dozing, and yes, perhaps a touch melancholy, with its Cowboy Bar at the entrance decorated in saddles and cowskins.

El ganso means 'wild goose'. I didn't chase any.

I wandered out of the *albergue* as the sun flirted with the horizon. A lone dog barked and a bird fluttered among the beams of an abandoned adobe building behind me. To my left was the handful of houses that made up the town. To my right was the road out. Opposite was a narrow dirt lane between two tumbledown buildings, and walking towards me up that lane was a man with broad, open features. His eyes were surrounded by deep lines. He leaned on a walking stick and waved with his free hand.

'*Buenas tardes, peregrina,*' he called, his face creasing into a grin. That smile was my introduction to Domingo. We stood in the main street, talking about the weather, how far I'd walked and where I was from.

Australia got a good response.

He held out his free arm and suggested a little walk—*un camino pequeño*.

We set off at Domingo pace, stopping to sniff the wind, to look and listen.

He gave me the grand tour of El Ganso, where he had spent his entire life. We saw the houses of his brothers and sisters; a big two-storey house, not so nice as the low ones; the vacant land, just waiting for a nice lady from Australia to buy it and build a new home; the abandoned houses, falling into disrepair and back into the ground; the edible rosehips; and the scratching chooks with their scrawny chicks.

Stories everywhere. The house where he was born. The families who went away. The home that waits for his son. The flowers he planted for his sister. The figs, so good, so good …

Then he took me to his house and ushered me inside. He showed me his kitchen, and the kettle his wife favoured; their bedroom and bathroom, both modern and cool; the guest room—for next visit? Then his shed, with its tools and folding garden furniture. His back-yard, where he picked for me white roses tinged with softest pink, and two perfect pears. He had sons in Seattle and Madrid, he told me. They made a lot of money but they didn't come home much.

The whole tour took maybe an hour. Details, affection, the wonder of his almost-abandoned town ...

'*Te gusta mi pueblo?*' You like my town?

I did. I still do.

As the sun set, he walked me back along the empty main street to the *albergue*, where he left me with a stiff bow and a sweep of his free arm, saying, '*Esta es mi pueblo.*'

This is my town.

I watched him walk away, the scent of pears and roses wafting in the warm air as the church steeple turned orange. All around his retreating figure, the stones of the houses glowed. His home was radiant, radiating. I saw how full it was of loves and losses, and how much richer I was for him having stepped into my life to tell me of them.

I took my fruits and flowers to adorn my table at the Cowboy Bar. Cowboys were a disappearing breed and I wondered about the future of those *pueblos*. Would they survive the rush of the young to the cities and beyond?

'Perhaps they will,' *Herr Theologie* said, 'if you and this Domingo keep telling his story.'

I laughed. For a time I'd left Córdoba and *Herr T*, and indulged in the memory of that other road, and of Domingo's gifts, given not to get a result but simply because he was kind. Like Lucia. They weren't buying eternal brownie points. It was natural impulse, not fear of a vengeful deity.

As I walked the twisted alleys back to Residencia Marisa, singing partygoers overtook me. The waiter had said the girls of Córdoba were the most beautiful in Spain and I saw nothing to make me disagree as they swished past, certain of their attractions. Children raced to hide around corners, and parents linked arms with their parents, the generations at play.

My last thoughts, before sleep, were of other pilgrims, in other places ...

An American *peregrina*, hiking a trail called Wilderness of Rock in the Santa Catalina Mountains. She'd emailed she was walking in solidarity with me. I imagined her legs and heart pumping in clear desert air.

My husband, planning a road trip to see the newly flooded inland rivers of our drought-afflicted land.

My *compañero*, who had sent words to carry me:

> *courage, ailsa,*
> *you do not walk alone*
> *i will*
> *walk with you*
> *and sing your spirit home*

Next morning I rose early to attend Mass at the Mezquita, a Catholic cathedral inside a Muslim mosque, built on Visigoth foundations, around the corner from an ancient synagogue. Misty rain was falling and I stepped with care across the cobbled courtyard's slick of squashed blossom.

On entering, a forest of ochre and white striped columns greeted me. There were no icons or adornments. It was a mysterious, lofty space, inviting contemplation—a place to drop you to your knees in wonder.

The Mezquita began its life around 600AD as a church dedicated to St Vincent. Then, after the Islamic conquest, work began in 785AD to re-fashion it as a mosque. For several hundred years, Córdoba was one of the most enlightened cities in Europe, with the Mezquita at its heart. Now, at the heart of the Mezquita lies a Catholic cathedral. It was inserted in 1523 after the Christian reconquest.

I took my place in a pew near the front; carved mahogany choir stalls to my left. A tiny, white-haired woman sat beside me and shivered, pulling her cashmere cardigan closer. We whispered greetings. From Australia. *Madre de Dios!* A pilgrim. *Verdad?* Yes, truly.

Others filed in, perhaps twenty. Then came the priests, twelve of them, some in purple robes, some in red and gold, and the smiling central celebrant wearing embroidered grape leaves. Twelve for twenty, arrayed around a gilded altar. They sang the mass, including the much-needed prayers for *il Papa*. My body remembered all the ritual movements, and my new friend squeezed my hand as she trilled responses in a wobbly falsetto.

When Mass was done, she gestured for me to bend down.

'*Me alegra*,' she said, kissing my cheeks. You lift me up.

I thought of Domingo.

Those ancients. *Ancianos*. They struggled up hills to recite the rosary, walked through rain to polish candlesticks and arrange flowers, and battled rheumatic pain to bestow kindness. What made them keep the faith?

I craved their belief. I longed to feel that reverence, to feel devotion and awe, and to have a relationship with the source of that awe. But it can't be manufactured. Wishing will not make it so. Is envy a sin, I wondered, if what you envy is faith?

It felt mean to envy my diminutive friend. I watched her totter into her day, and wondered if that meanness was what my sinner experienced when she thought of me. I also tried to imagine, as I'd done many times, what my mother would have been like had she grown old. I couldn't see Sue as a grandmother either. *Forever young ...*

The Mezquita opened to tourists. Cameras flashed and tour guides brandished flags. Silence was dispelled. I left, grateful I'd had an opportunity to experience the place for the purpose it was intended.

The rain had stopped and sun released the neroli scent. That, combined with humidity, spices and the tumble of red and pink geraniums, made sightseeing irresistible, so I set out to explore the streets of the Jewish quarter—*La Judería*—a maze of narrow, winding lanes.

In the Middle Ages Córdoba was a centre of science and intellectualism and the wealthiest city in Western Europe. The Jewish population was established there in Roman times and there are remains of a synagogue that dates from 1315. Now a tourist attraction, it contains fragments of its past life: teachings, frescoes and tiles. On its south wall was a psalm: *I will sing unto the Lord because he hath dealt bountifully with me.*

The Jews were expelled in 1492 by Ferdinand and Isabella.

Nearby, a statue honours Maimonides, the Jewish philosopher, born in Córdoba in 1125. He wrote much about charity in its different forms, famously saying: *Give a man a fish and you feed him for a day; teach a man to fish and you feed him for a lifetime.*

A stone's throw from him is a statue of Seneca, another son of Córdoba, who went on to become tutor to Nero. He wrote: *I do not distinguish by the eye, but by the mind, which is the proper judge.*

Córdoba's history of tolerance and its intellectual and civic achievements overwhelmed me. Yes, they were lost to prejudice and violence, but when I hear the name, I'm reminded of the possibility of something remarkable: peaceful co-existence.

I wandered. I pondered.

Above me, a woman shrieked. A passerby whispered, '*Scandoloso.*' Looking up, I saw no trace of scandal, only potted geraniums and lines of verse.

I'd lucked in on a festival of poetry. Banners hung from balconies, bearing snippets of poems by Miguel Hernández, who must have written many of the words over my head as he languished in jail, sentenced for anti-fascist sentiments. Wherever I looked I saw heart and soul—*corazón y alma*; earth and sky—*tierra y cielo*; love and flowers—*amor y flores*. His verses fluttered free in the breeze.

In an Arabic *salon de thé*, tiled tabletops were piled with copper bowls of flowers, fruit, Turkish cakes and sweetmeats. A fountain tinkled amid palms, ferns, orchids and mirrors. I ordered a peach tea and two almond cakes, and opened my journal to copy a quote from the wall:

Amor es mi credo y mi fe. Love is my creed and my faith.

I looked up, and there was *Herr T*.

He perched on the edge of a child-sized chair, ordered tea and clicked a photo. We talked about the city sights. He told me he too had been at Mass that morning and had seen me there. Then he began to sob.

I put an arm around him and waited, afraid of what had happened. His shoulders shook, tears fell, and he tried to apologise. I hugged him and that made him cry more. He avoided my gaze, opened his mouth and then closed it. He sipped tea. And finally, he spoke.

He said how empty he had found the Mass, how the priests lacked spirit, how broken he felt. He said that our conversations of the previous days had made him question his faith. He whispered that this 'breaking' frightened him. Previous *caminos* had never made him feel like this, he said.

'I am so afraid,' he repeated.

I suggested that perhaps it was fatigue, after the long walking stages, or an excess of solitude. Maybe he should consider staying on a day or two to gather strength, or take a bus to Mérida and join the Via de la Plata, where there would be other walkers and a convivial pilgrim community.

No. He would continue this road he had begun. This is the experience he must complete. He gripped my hand. Perhaps we could leave together tomorrow morning?

I nodded. Yes. Of course.

We finished our tea, and he returned to the hotel to rest. I left the ancient part of town for the 'real' world of post offices and supermarkets, and to put some distance between the two of us. I was in my own turmoil after our meeting.

I had a load of sins, and my physical and mental health to consider. I didn't want to nurse anyone else down the road. Selfishness surged as I bought candied fruit, stamps and a phone card. I texted Leonardo and Ricardo to ask their surnames and address, then bought them a card, handmade by a man called Fernando, who asked me to make a prayer for him in Santiago.

Santiago de Compostela.

That impossible destination, still over a thousand kilometres away.

One of my sinners emailed a question about 'simony', which he described as the sin of asking another to take your penance. Was I enabling sin? I googled the word and found a host of answers.

It was paying for holy offices or sacraments. It was trafficking in money for 'spiritual things'. It was the buying or selling of ecclesiastical pardons or offices.

Was I a sinner by carrying sin?

Was the Church a sinner when it sold pardons and relics?

Walking through the darkening streets, I examined my intentions. I knew I wasn't undertaking the walk for any ulterior motive, though I still couldn't answer for myself exactly why I was doing it. There are many more pleasurable ways to spend the days than walking thirty kilometres with a pack, only to sleep in lodgings that are worse than a boarding school dorm. There are far less painful things to do than meditate on transgression and failure all day long, particularly your own. Whatever I was doing, I decided it wasn't sinful. It was too difficult and demanding.

Why, then, did I want to continue?

Well, I was following an intuition. Maybe even, if I dared use the word, a vocation. And I was doing a job, keeping faith with my sinners, who believed in me, even those who didn't believe in absolution from the Catholic Church. I did notice that I hadn't confessed my sins to them in my email report card and wondered if that was pride again, but I decided my sins were not the point. I was in service, and whatever the purpose of confession might be, it was not meant to be mutual. I was paid to receive and carry.

My musing led me to a courtyard, where I sat with spiced vegetable soup and a *vino tinto*, to compose words in fractured Spanglish for the card to my Barcelona angels. *Tomorrow I walk again*, I wrote. *I have a companion on the road. He is a kind man. I walk with you, too. In my heart.*

A bell rang out. And another. Different pitches.

I thought of Domingo.

I wondered if the bell in the ochre steeple in El Ganso was tolling. How many times had it rung out for Domingo's clan? How many more times would it call to them? Christenings, weddings, funerals. Rosaries, communions, novenas. All of the village, turning up. Day in, day out. Year in, year out.

Rewards flow from that. Belonging and connection. Deep communion.

Pilgrimage is faith in motion, I wrote in my journal. *You just keep turning up. Whether you want to or not. Whether it is the way you pictured it, or not. Keep walking, and the spirit flies, even if you don't know where. Keep turning up.*

In the perfumed night air, as bells tolled, I gathered myself for the days ahead.

Faith, sins and simony would have to wait.

I had a *mochila* to pack for the road to Mérida.

12

WEATHERING STORMS

IN THE MORNING DARK, I was cold and crotchety. I didn't want to be meeting up with *Herr Theologie*, travelling together and making plans. I did not want to be responsible to or for anyone else, or to do their crying.

This from the sin-carrier!

I thought of my sinner's impatience and frustration with her elderly parents.

But this is different.

I thought of the two people who had asked me to carry selfishness.

But this is different.

I thought of all the variants of anger, and knew I was on dangerous ground.

I thought of the sinner who had acted on lust, and knew that at least was not a possibility.

Then, when *Herr T* asked if I was certain I did not mind his company, I told a big fat white lie and said it was fine.

The streets were shiny and slick after rain. We sat on an icy metal bench waiting for a bus to take us through Córdoba's suburbs. *Herr T* had found a brace for his knee and was optimistic it would hold. That's what he said, just before he dropped his head into his hands. I couldn't tell if he was crying. He was backlit against an illuminated mascara advertisement. An airbrushed movie star smirked down at us, her impossibly white teeth just above *Herr T*'s huddled form, making his sadness seem inappropriate. Unseemly.

I wanted to get off the bus before I even got on. What I needed was a dose of patience, the Contrary Virtue to anger.

Contrary. That was me.

The bus travelled past one-euro shops, smokestacks, raincoated shift-workers and Caracol Express—a restaurant offering speedy servings of snail. By the time we'd alighted and strapped on our packs, there was light in the sky. I hoped it was a sign.

Our first coffee stop was over twelve kilometres away. Rain came and went, along with my plastic outer layers. The wind, the wet and the protective clothing made conversation impossible, so we walked apart, which was probably as well for *Herr T*.

The trail was soggy and strewn with litter. I sidestepped the skeleton of a goat, its skull flung back, its jaws gaping. I picked up plastic and paper, irritated that the soldiers weren't detailed to do it.

Yes, soldiers.

For several kilometres, signs advised that I was walking through a *Zona Militar*. Privates scrubbed rows of tanks, emergency vehicles screamed past with sirens blaring, a marching band paraded, flags raised and lowered, and a garrison of strutting recruits watched me from behind wire fences. I should have felt safe, but all that military hardware made me conscious of how vulnerable I was.

In El Vacar, the coffee-stop town, I saw not one of the ninety-six residents. Sensible folk, they were all tucked up inside. I peeled off my plastics outside Bar Laura and found *Herr T* inside. We nursed hot mugs and watched the TV news.

Dark volcanic ash was blanketing Europe. In Poland they mourned. In Málaga there was unprecedented flooding; and in Madrid, the *presidente* was grim-faced about budget cuts necessitated by the financial crisis. We slumped in silence.

Leonardo called.

Was he hot-wired to my moods? He always rang when I was low, and I always said I was fine. Hearing him, and saying it, I was. Fine.

I wished *Herr T* dry walking as he loaded up. I wanted to stay and write. By the time I stepped back outside, the clouds had cleared, and although there was a chill wind *a-blowing*, the sky was blue.

The road threw me about. There were hills, which were good; and flooding, which was not. There were mis-directions, which were infuriating; and footprints, which gave hope. There were rocks and washaways, and slushy slopes; lavender and rosemary, and a perfumed musk rose.

There was a phone call from home, a rare occurrence as friends and family understood that contact could throw me off my emotional course, dragging me back to my other life. They respected the difficulties of staying spiritually upright over long stretches of tricky terrain! Nonetheless, this was special. My husband, sister and best friend were together at dinner, and when I told them my circumstances, they roared with laughter at my fury. They knew that if I was railing I was safe. I knew that if they were laughing, all was well.

Still, as I slid down the face of a muddy bank, I heard myself shouting.

'Why am I here? I didn't want to walk another *camino*. Why? Tell me.'

Brushing sludge from my pants, I heard a reply.

'It's called free will, you idiot. No one made you come.'

No, it wasn't God speaking. Just me talking to myself. Things really were going downhill.

Actually, they weren't. There were climbs ahead. Plenty. And puddles. And mud.

I straggled into Villaharta to see *Herr T* plodding towards me, his pack still on and his head down.

'There is no accommodation,' he said.

He was making for a motel down on the highway. I decided to go up into the village and sit in a warm bar with the locals before following him.

Waves and *holas* met me from all sides, so I decided to try the *ayuntamiento*. My luck was in. Juan-Claudio stamped my *credencial* and walked me to the *polideportivo* (sports centre), where he unlocked my quarters high above the town in splendid isolation. Mine, all mine.

A changing room next to the basketball court. Concrete floor, wooden benches around the walls, two plastic-covered gym mats for a mattress, two showers, a handbasin, a toilet and the luxury of a row of hooks on the wall.

I shook Juan-Claudio's hand too hard, said *gracias* too often, and removed my sodden boots.

Standing at my door, I looked over terracotta rooftops to the mountains. No question: a storm was coming. I unpacked my sleeping bag and all my clothing. That concrete floor would not hold warmth. I texted *Herr T* to tell him I was staying in the village and went out to explore.

At the bar, I found hot coffee, toast, oil and tomato sauce. Not tomato sauce as we know it in Australia. This was puréed tomatoes from the garden, poured over local oil on freshly made bread, salted to taste. Zero food miles.

I could have indulged in a glass of snails. Locals lined the bar, downing gastropods by the glassful. The barman told me it was peak season and they were delicious, but I resisted. Between cigars, he also told me the weather for the coming days was very bad. *Muy malo.* The TV backed him up. *Muy muy malo.* Very very bad. *Tormentas.* Lots of rain. Big storms. Rivers rising.

The next stage was thirty-nine uninterrupted kilometres through forest trails, a day I'd been anticipating as reward for all the walking on *carretera*—literal translation, highway; pilgrim translation, purgatory. My day in the woods was sounding like it would be a day on the high seas if the barman was right. *Agua. Mucha agua.*

I went to the stationer's and treated myself to two pens and two postcards. At the grocer's, I bought dried fruit and nuts for the day to come, and dinner: a tin of tuna, a tomato and capsicum for vitamin C, sheep's milk cheese and bread. All the food groups.

Back in my change room, I laid out my purchases. Such bounty.

Then I opened the door again.

O wind, a-blowing all day long …

Wind buffeted me, buffeted storks as they flew home to precarious nests, buffeted antennas, buffeted basketball hoops. It whistled in wires. The sky turned from indigo to purple. Rain fell. I grabbed my washing, brought my boots in and slammed the door.

O wind that sings so loud a song.

It was as though I was in an orchestra pit and the wind was tuning up the instruments. Even if I got warm I would never sleep in the cacophony, so I located an elastic bandage given to me by my osteopath, ripped off strips and patched all the holes in the walls. The symphony sounded less like Mars and a little like Venus. More bandage, around the gaps between windows and frames, and the symphony became a solo flute line. Bandage over gaps between door and lintel and the room was a patchwork of beige strips but all was silence.

Then it hit. Thunder, lightning and sheeting rain.

It was barely 8 p.m., but day turned prematurely into night. I pulled on every article of clothing I had, wrapped my rain jacket around my head for warmth, rolled up my plastic pants for a pillow, and slept long and deep. Villaharta was one of my happiest nights on the road.

The next day began with a text from *Herr T*: he was waiting for me in the bar.

Damn. We had made no agreement to walk together and I wanted that forest walk to myself, mud or no mud.

Selfish? Big time. Sinner? Guess so.

I ripped off the room's bandaging and opened the door to drizzle and a stork wading on the basketball court. The world was waterlogged and the bar was populated by blokes with smokes, hunkering down. Seeing my *mochila*, they were appalled.

No, no, you cannot walk today.

'*No pasa nada*,' I said. No worries. I'll stay put and walk tomorrow.

No, no. Tomorrow will be worse. The rivers in the forest are already waist-deep. This rain won't stop and the rivers will rise. You must take a bus or a car today, because it may be many days before the waters subside.

What about the road?

No, no. There would be no visibility. *Muy muy peligroso.* Very very dangerous.

What finally convinced me (because I protested and requested second and third opinions) was the uniformed man who said I would risk other people's lives if they had to come and save me.

Australians regularly hear of travellers in need of rescue from remote places. We shake our heads and ask how they could have been so stupid as to ignore the advice of locals, to walk out alone into the desert, swim in those floodwaters or ignore signs about crocodiles.

I told *Herr T* I would catch a bus to Alcaracejos.

'Of course,' he said, downing his hot chocolate. 'I come too.'

Weatherproofs crinkling and boots sloshing, we made our way downhill, battling to stay vertical. The landscape was blurred, all its edges dripping and dissolving. We sat in chill wind for over two hours, watching busloads disembarking into the motel dining area and trying to believe the barman each time he insisted our bus would come— just another fifteen minutes.

When it arrived, we each paid our two euros and I claimed a space by a foggy window to peer out at steep oak-wooded slopes, rolling hills dotted with ruins and paths criss-crossing emerald sward.

And rivers. Honesty demands I report that the landscape streamed with red water. All the mud in the province had turned liquid and was descending. There was a torrent at every turn. Walking those paths would have been lunacy, but still I mourned the lost climbs.

We got off the bus into more rain, but I was not trekking around to find accommodation when I could be trekking across level country to Hinojosa del Duque. *Herr T* said he would walk too.

We set out on a farm track populated with barking dogs and scratching chooks. I hung back to create some distance between us.

Since Córdoba, *Herr T* had spoken little. I don't know if he was embarrassed or afraid to engage in the kind of conversations that might prompt more distress, or if he felt my frustration, but I hadn't tried to draw him out. I berated myself for my selfishness, telling myself I should be walking with him and wondering if I should have stayed in the motel the previous night to allow him more access to me. I thought of my sinner's confession to shallowness and how he still carried guilt about his friend's suicide. Should I be intervening more in *Herr T*'s internal life?

I did nothing but plod. It was wet. It was cold. My boots were soaked through and the path was dotted with dung of infinitely varied perfume and texture. I felt like excrement myself.

One 'stream' had swollen to a river. The path led straight to the water's edge and took up again about twenty metres away on the other side. No bridge was visible. No people either. Cold had frozen me from my saturated boots right up to my brain and the only solution I could imagine was to strip off and wade across. The rain stopped, so I clenched my teeth, peeled off damp trousers and knickers, and stuffed them into the outer pockets of my pack. I tied my sock-filled boots in place around it, tucked my T-shirt up into my bra, hoisted pack and walking poles over my head, and walked towards the shallows, singing 'Waltzing Matilda' as loudly as I could.

Tadpoles and green fronds swirled about my toes. The current was not fast, so I stepped towards mid-stream, my lower body naked and goose-bumped. Frogs croaked in alarm while turtles swam close for a peek. I stopped looking down after I'd counted six of them, concentrating instead on not cutting my feet on any hidden stones in the icy mud that felt like custard between my toes. When the water reached my pubic hair, I let out a screech, but Matilda's swagman didn't desert me and, still singing, I advanced until the water reached my hips. I stumbled, shouting something most unladylike, but righted myself, and clambered out through slime and long grass.

There were no whoops of triumph. I was shivering so hard I could barely unclip my pack to get my handkerchief-sized towel. I dried off as best I could. My damp undies gripped my damp thighs before settling onto my damp bottom. My trousers stuck to my shins. Wet feet went into already-wet socks and boots. I pulled plastic outer layers on for warmth and looked back.

I was an idiot. It was only then that I registered the risk. I could have been swept away, could have slipped and drowned, could have lost my phone or my camera or my pack. But I didn't, and there was no time to berate myself. I had to get moving before hypothermia set in.

Ten minutes later, a text came from *Herr T* telling me there was a bridge just past the place where I'd crossed.

Serve me right, I thought. Every squelching step was punishment for my selfishness, my gluttony for solitude, my impatience towards an older person. All I needed was a hair shirt to be in masochism heaven.

Occasionally the sun came out, lighting on poppies and mauve blossoms and fields of suddenly golden wheat. On a clear day, with dry boots, I would have marvelled at the cultivated green framed by distant mountains. But that day was grey and blisters threatened from walking on soles like overfull sponges.

Herr T texted again, saying to *rest on the road* because *down on the fields is an inondation.* I obeyed, and my penance continued. Highway 422 had no love for pedestrians. Semis sprayed water and fumes.

Pilgrim purgatory.

Leonardo called, the archangel of antipodeans, lifting me out of myself. I tried to make my steps an offering, though I still had no idea to whom. I thought of my sinners, of mediaeval pilgrims without rain gear. I trudged on.

Past a hermitage surrounded by parked cars and tents, where families huddled around fires as music blared. Past a doll strung up by the neck in a fig tree. Past the big hotel on the highway, where there was no room—the *fiesta*, don't you know? Past factories and deserted industrial parks, into Hinojosa, where rooms were impossible and the *ayuntamiento* was closed. Just as I was in danger of slumping in total defeat, I was sent a miracle.

A group of plastic-clad hikers rushed toward me like I was a prodigal, overwhelming me with hugs and rapid-fire questions and congratulatons. With the help of a perpetually smiling Spanish–Australian called Monica, I figured out why.

They were the *amigos* from the Camino Association in Córdoba, one of the *camino* support groups. They'd been out in all that rain painting yellow arrows, a true act of faith when so few walk that road. To see an actual pilgrim was vindication.

I was a drowned Aussie rat with scarecrow hair grinning amid a sea of altruism. We talked of Gore-Tex and rain ponchos, and visited the Church of San Juan Bautista to get a *sello*. It shows a horse, or maybe a lamb, wearing plumage and resting on a large book. I'm yet to understand the symbolism.

Herr T appeared. He, too, had been unable to find a room. The *amigos'* president located a policeman who could open the *polideportivo* for us. *Herr T* had no sleeping bag, so the *policía* said he would find blankets and return to collect us. More miracles.

Herr T and I waved off the *amigos* and settled onto the steps of the town hall to wait.

And wait.

And wait.

The town was empty. The wind was ice. The elements were indifferent.

The priest came out of the church, waved and drove away.

Herr T shivered. I made for a bar.

On TV, footage of flooding and volcanic ash confirmed my sense that the world was upending. Behind the bar a Romanian beauty called Adriana—an outsider with excellent Spanish—explained that the next town was thirty-three kilometres away, impossible in freezing darkness. No, there was no bus and no taxi. And yes, there was only one policeman, his first duty was the *fiesta* at the hermitage, and no one else could open the *polideportivo*.

We waited another hour.

Nada.

Adriana said I could stay at her place, but her *hombre* would not want another man in the house. *Herr T* was a huddle of plastic on the steps of the *ayuntamiento*. I couldn't leave him. Could Adriana suggest anything else?

She rang friends. She petitioned the men at the bar. She said we could come in until closing time to be warm, but she was not the boss, so couldn't offer us the floor for the night. I said she was kind. She said kindness cost nothing. She knew what it was to be without a place to sleep. She kept calling and eventually she located a man with a car who'd take us to the next town, for a price.

Herr T was transformed. 'I pay, I pay,' he said to me.

No. I wanted my slate to be clean. Maybe it was pride but we split the fare.

The headlights lit up yellow arrows along the entire road; the walk would have been all asphalt. Still, it was the exit from the province of Andalucía into Extremadura. I loved the idea of crossing that border on foot. I'd missed two stages. I still think of them, still hope to go back and walk them one fine day.

The car pulled into a darkened village and nosed its way along cobbled streets to a square of light. Was there ever such a welcome sight as the glowing Hostal Vaticano in Monterrubio de la Serena?

Yes! In the bar were four German pilgrims.

I wanted to sing. I wanted to dance. I wanted to drop to my knees and give thanks to that mystery listener in the *cielo*. In spite of my hard heart, I had been delivered. Other walkers! Company for *Herr T*!

Over a late dinner, and wearing blissfully dry clothes, *Herr T* detailed our day to them. Released from the strain of speaking English and Spanish, he smiled and held court. The others nodded and poured *vino tinto*. They made plans for the morning, inviting me, in English, to join them.

'I'm not sure,' I said. 'I'd like to spend a Sunday in a village.'

Herr T smiled. 'Of course. Some time for your own self,' he said.

We wished each other good rest. I would catch him up, he said, squeezing my hand. We would meet in a day or two.

The last image I have of *Herr Theologie* is of the smile under his bushy white brows as he ducked into his room down the corridor.

'*Buen camino, peregrina,*' he called. Good walking, pilgrim.

'*Igualmente, señor,*' I replied. Equally, sir.

Our paths didn't cross again.

13

PEREGRINA SOLA

IN ROOM 102 OF the Hostal Vaticano, I woke at six to pounding rain.

I rolled over.

I woke at eight to *Herr T*'s footsteps in the hall. He was late.

I rolled over.

I woke at nine to silence.

I breakfasted in the bar on toast and tomato and considered walking. My back screamed. My legs throbbed. Over my second coffee, the *señora* said there was to be a big celebration that day.

Decision made.

The teenagers of the *pueblo* were making their Confirmation, where they become adults in the Catholic faith, responsible for their choices and their sins. In the sixteenth-century Church of Nuestra Señora de la Consolación, the girls wore very big hair to balance their very short skirts. The boys wore American hip-hop gear. One tall *niño* sported a white suit over a peacock-blue silk shirt. Elvis lived!

Pews were packed with fussing parents, smaller siblings and camera-toting aunts. At the sign of peace, when the congregation turn to each other and extend hands and cheeks, I experienced a mixture of inclusion and isolation. I was glad to be welcomed, hugged and kissed, but I knew I was not truly a part of the community. I had no right to be there, enjoying the fruits of the faith of others.

I watched the teenagers kneel to receive the sacrament. As the priest placed a wafer on each tongue, my thoughts drifted to a communion I'd experienced on the Camino Francés, on a day when the only clouds were art-directed wisps in a Hockney-blue sky and the road led through terrain that spoke of the toil of generations. A *palimpsesto* road.

Around noon, I'd met a group of workers who had downed tools for a picnic of cheeses, cakes and fruit. They invited me to share it with them. On learning I was Australian, they asked for 'Waltzing Matilda'! I sang a few lines and they danced around me in blue overalls and yellow fluoro vests, spinning to the song of the swagman. We broke bread in the field and they offered me tastes of everything. Communion in the best sense. I sipped wine as sweet as honey, toasted their generosity, and stepped back out onto the road. Then, from nowhere, forgotten words flooded back: *Behold the handmaid of the Lord …*

In Catholic primary school, we little ones were taught catechism and prayers. I particularly loved the Angelus, recited daily at noon, and the idea that workers all over the world stopped in factories or offices to contemplate the angel announcing to Mary that she would be the mother of God.

It was an honour to be chosen to ring the Angelus bell. When it was mine, I'd gallop across the playground, past the Virgin's grotto, and into the cool silence of the wood-floored church. I'd cross myself with holy water and tiptoe down the back to tug on the thick rope, relishing the delay between the action and the sound of the big bell.

Then I'd race back, the only moving creature in the midday stillness. In the classroom all heads would be bowed as the Hail Mary was recited and we pictured the towering angel with his outsized wings telling Mary she was going to have a baby.

Miracles. I was instructed in them. Certain of them.

At home, things were not so clear-cut. My mother's childhood playmates had been Aboriginal children and she could recall her first sighting of another white girl when she was about six—astonishment and mild resentment! She believed in different miracles, wrought by the Aboriginal spirits. Things that confounded me. How could a bone kill someone, just by pointing it? How could a person be 'sung' to death? I never asked her why she sent me to a Catholic school when its teachings were so remote from her own beliefs. It also never occurred to me that the miracles she believed in were no less plausible than a Virgin birth.

Regardless, those Spanish workers feasting on the Camino Francés took me back to my little girl's devoted heart, her head tilted to receive the body and blood of the saviour. The pleasure of certainty.

In the wooden pew in Monterrubio, that pleasure felt more and more remote. Growing up had taught me about contradictions and ambiguity and led me to the conviction that certainty is the only thing that isn't possible. Perhaps the teens making their Confirmation needed certainty in order to navigate adolescence, but in time they too might find it didn't tally with day-to-day living.

Storks wheeled overhead as we exited the church. A simple man of about fifty, with three teeth and a milky eye, told me that the priest had put a hand on his head, too, just like the Confirmation kids.

'Yes, I see him,' I said, unable to remember my past-tense conjugations.

The simple man nodded, then put his hand on my head. I waited for him to remove it but he stood a long time, looking into my eyes and grinning.

'*Confirmación*,' I said. He nodded again, his hand firmly in place.

Finally his mother, a stooped woman with tight grey curls, came and led him away. He was still smiling, still touching his own head.

Duende fled. I wept all the way back to Hostal Vaticano, undone by his gaze. He had seen inside me, but still gave me his benediction.

Card games were in full swing in the bar. It was a communal living room. The floor was littered with peanut shells, the air thick with smoke and stories.

Leonardo phoned, saying Ricardo was stressed. I had no idea of their family, health or financial situations, but longed to help.

I listened to the TV news, searching for words I knew.

Espero … I wait, or I hope …

Tormentas … storms …

Inundado … flooded …

The volcano, the weather, the skies, the destruction. Interrupted flights, ruined rail lines, house walls collapsing from water damage. Were the gods unhappy after all?

I put on my plastic jacket and went out into weak sun. Storks settled deep into their tub-sized nests at the church, and seeing them tucking in, I felt consoled. White-haired Lorenzo invited himself to stroll with me, recounting stories about when he lived in Germany many years before. I was aware of the whole town observing us, and when finally we separated, two matrons enquired if he had been telling me of Germany. I nodded.

'Aahhhh!' they said. '*Siempre!*' Always.

I didn't mind. The stories were new to me.

In another bar, six men played cards at a window table. They waved as I passed, hands full of hearts and diamonds. Dogs flopped from one doormat to another. Women looked to heaven and crossed themselves.

The next day's walk to Campanario was thirty-six kilometres and every step had spring in it.

The morning was cocooned in fog. Under my feet: red soil. At my sides: lavender for buttonholes, wrists and hat. Poppies, margaritas and lupins appeared as the sun broke through. Swallows and wagtails got up close and personal. And welcome, most welcome, were my old friends, the olives. Distant mountains rose with the fog. Cobalt sky. Stone outcrops. Dogs. More dogs. And a wide white road bounded by flowering mimosa leading me towards Castuerta, where grey asphalt hurried me through its industry and suburbs, and cobbles stepped me through its heart at lazy lunchtime.

Back onto asphalt again and out of Castuerta, I stepped across the train lines, singing up to a bird on the wires. It tilted its head, its eyes ringed with orange liner. I broke into McCartney's 'Blackbird', raising my volume as a tribute, but the bird only winked an exotic eye and lifted off. I sang on.

Singing releases endorphins. It gives the lungs and heart a good workout, too. It pumps the intercostals and diaphragm, because we're sucking in more oxygen, energising ourselves. I can certainly vouch for the benefits of singing aloud into a Spanish sky. Sin is unimaginable.

Into Campanario I warbled, to find the *pueblo* dozing in sultry late-afternoon air. The owner of the first bar directed me to a house where a lady rented rooms. I rang the bell. Nothing. Rang again. Silence. Knocked. Nothing.

'Hola, Rubia!'

Across the empty main road, two *ancianos* in three-piece suits patrolled, their walking sticks tapping in unison. After interrogating me about where I was from and where I was going, why I would do such a thing, and where was my husband, they told me the lady was not home.

Okay, the *ayuntamiento*? No. *Cerrado*. Closed. Too late in the day.

Hmmm … time to consider the church porch?

A police car pulled up and a man of about twenty-five emerged, in a navy and fluoro uniform. He wore metal-rimmed glasses and a wide smile. On his chest was the word *Policía*. His name was Angel. A policeman called Angel.

I showed my *credencial* and explained my plight.

'No hay problema,' he said. No problem.

He directed me to a park bench and told me to sit. He would find me a bed.

I sat. I read sins and poems. I journalled and wrote postcards. I sent wishes winging to *Herr T*, hoping he was safe on his path. I visited the church to light a candle, and the gracious Antonia stopped her sweeping to show me her favourite saints and to offer me a bed if Angel couldn't find one. I watched teenagers pouting at each other in a *plaza*, oblivious to the plaque inscribed with the words of their famous writer, Antonio Reyes Huertas:

117

> *... my heart, filled by my village, sun, sky and fields, longs for*
> *a noble, simple life ...*

Angel found me, copying the Spanish words into my journal.

'You have a bed,' he said, ducking his head and grinning as I hugged him. He had been gone for over an hour—to the *polideportivo*, back to the woman with the room for rent, asking in bars, knocking on doors, making calls. He told me this as we drove out through town.

Eventually, he'd found the manager of the town's closed *albergue*. He convinced her to open for one pilgrim for one night, and to provide dinner. We drove further, into fields. Where was this *albergue*?

At a railway line, a girl called Amalia emerged and handed me a set of keys. It took me some time to understand that the old railway station behind her had been converted into a refuge of two peach-coloured storeys with a white balcony and tall pines around it. I held the key to a mansion.

I didn't know whether to kiss Angel or Amalia. Angel repeated that it was only his job, his pleasure, his responsibility. It was nothing. *De nada.*

They always said that as they did something remarkable.

Amalia showed me how to open the heavy doors and double locks, and left. I crossed the threshold. The room could have held forty of my closest friends, if only they had been there. Its gold walls glowed in the late sun. There were sofas and standard lamps, and a table with six chairs should I decide to invite the ladies of the village for cards.

Upstairs were the bedrooms, each with four or six colonial-style beds sporting checked coverlets and access to gleaming bathrooms. I chose a bed on the railway line wall, next to a door that opened onto a terrace. I photographed myself grinning at the countryside, which grinned back at me, knowing how gorgeous it was. I washed clothes and grinned. Rubbed my leg muscles and grinned. Watched a train pull in to the new station and grinned.

At dinner, I couldn't stop grinning. Amalia presented me with salad, bread, olives and a glass of wine, and when the meal was over, she handed me a thermos of coffee for the morning, because I was so far from the village.

Apparently she had converted the railway station, but because there are so few pilgrims on the Mozárabe, it was not worth opening except for pre-booked tourist groups. Amalia said many people, even residents, still didn't know there was a pilgrim trail through these parts. She wanted to know how people made a go of it in *albergues* on the Francés. When I explained the pilgrim numbers her eyes almost popped.

As I bedded down, I thought of *Herr Theologie*, who had texted the previous day to say he'd taken the train because there was no accommodation in Campanario. He must have stood on the platform, not knowing paradise was over his right shoulder. I wished him good rest, wherever he was, and snuggled in as the last train swept past.

Next morning, I soared.

Deep-pink sunrise, deep-red roads, deep-green sward. Storks in lakes, dipping and scooping. Storks in the air, gliding and soaring. Shoes off to wade. Shoes on to walk. Flowers and wheat shimmering to the horizon. Granite amid grass. Swallows and swifts. Swift swallows.

Far below, a pilgrim walked on a winding dirt road. Sometimes she wept as she grinned. High above, I was tethered to her but never felt chained—that airborne sensation for which I may never find words.

After ten kilometres I came to earth on approach to the village of Magacela. Three old men waited in the middle of the road, one on a mule.

'*Hola, Rubia,*' they croaked, roaring with laughter at their joke.

'*Hola, señores. Qué día hermoso.*' Beautiful days demand acknowledgement.

They asked where I was going. 'Santiago? No! Alone?'

Yes, yes, yes. A thousand times yes.

'Then you need my mule, *Rubia*. Very cheap.'

The mule in question swung his head around.

'Yes, little mule. Wouldn't you like to go to Santiago with this lady pilgrim?'

The mule stamped his feet and the ancients laughed again. There was not a full set of teeth between them.

I thanked them and walked on, chomping the apple they'd insisted I take. When I looked back, the mule curled his lip at me. Too late, I realised the apple was his.

Workers harvested asparagus, bent low over the thin stalks. They shouted encouragement as they straightened to stretch their lower backs.

Ahead was a lung-busting climb.

Magacela perched at the top of a pyramid-shaped hill, the only interruption to miles of flat green. I'd watched it looming for over an hour. The ascent to its centre was reminiscent of my first day's climb to Moclín. Vertical torture.

Near the top, red-faced and panting, I passed two women exchanging the news of the day. I became a headline.

'Going where? From where? No husband? Mother of God, so brave. So crazy!'

'Here, you need this. Fruit. Yes, take it. And this juice. It will make you strong.' Hugs, kisses, encouragement and laughter.

Downhill, singing a medley of 'sunshine' songs in time with the feet, the walking poles and the sway of grasses, I felt guilty that I couldn't fix on sin. All I could feel was happiness. In a surge of gratitude, I decided to say 'gracias' as I walked. I called my thanks to the powder-blue sky for health, rescue, beauty, space and time. Then for my home village.

I wanted to thank everyone I'd ever loved. But how?

The Organiser stepped in. Alphabetically, of course.

I recalled each person, beginning with Aarne, moving on to Abbe, and so on. I considered what they had taught me, their particular gifts, and I thanked them. Talked to them. Conversations I had always meant to have. Sometimes I backtracked. An 'S' reminded me of an associated 'B' I had neglected, who sent me to the linked 'D'. Twice I got lost on

120

backroads and had to turn back, so deep was I in conversations. No matter. The road slid by in a refrain of thanks, my village walking with me across mushy fields and flinty roads. Kilometres vanished.

I should have kept watch on my body. I was speeding again, and when I landed in the village of La Haba, my feet were throbbing and my map had deserted me. Somewhere out there in the land of *gracias*, the pages that were to direct me to Mérida went walkabout.

De nada. Yellow arrows were leading now, though there were times when they felt like weapons, designed to wound.

Bitumen. Highway. *Carretera.* Each fiery step threatened blisters on the soles.

Cars. Trucks. Buses. Every one that roared past was a punch to the stomach, and there were many.

Plod on, pilgrim, and hope for drivers with eagle eyes. Hope for softer paths. Hope for road's end. Plod under power lines and over ditches. Plod through endless, heartless, characterless outskirts. Plod and hope. Plod for sinners. Plod.

Restoration came in the centre of Don Benito, where shoppers promenaded, grandpas chin-wagged and purses opened. Grace, elegant proportions and prosperity were the order of the evening, despite the For Sale signs I'd seen walking in. The Church of Santiago was closed, but I did sight some angels: skipping children chanted rhymes, a backlit fountain sparkling behind them. Their mothers murmured encouragement as jumping heels clicked on stone. No matter how hard the yards, sitting for an hour in a Spanish *plaza* in golden sunlight will ease cramps and soften any callous.

So I did, before sleeping the sleep of the virtuous.

Rain on waking. Rain on walking. Rain on the highway. Rain on the pilgrim.

The rain it raineth every day.

To Medellín. Roman, mediaeval, modern. Castles, churches, history. And closed bars in the early morning.

On I went through sodden fields, the squelching of my socks and rustling of my plastics unable to cover a plopping sound that followed me. What was it?

Looking down, I saw hundreds of frogs flinging themselves into irrigation channels at my approach. I sped up but still they leapt. Storks clacked their beaks at me like jackhammers. Tut tut tut.

There were no snails though. Had they all been rubbed into the skin of the women of Don Benito, where I'd seen moisturiser made from them in a *farmacia*? Poor little *caracoles*, mixed with aloe and vitamin E.

Trucks thundered down Highway 430, laden with groceries and goodies, spraying and buffeting my plastic-clad frame. Head down, I forged on, wondering if they were punishment for neglecting sins the previous day. The rain sheeted and the wind swept.

A lorry approached at warp speed. Close. God, so close. No. No! Too close!

The force of its slipstream flung me against the highway's metal guardrail like a crash-test dummy, a tangle of walking poles, pack and pilgrim. Wet steel and bitumen met soft flesh and fabric, resulting in searing pain. I picked myself up as cars sped by, and when I found my feet I screamed after the long-gone driver. You want to know anger? I'll show you anger.

Along with obscenity, blasphemy and, yes, the wish for vengeance. Bring it on.

Let me pin him to the asphalt with my walking poles while I dance on his bones in my waterlogged boots. Let me scrape his hands on stones until they bleed, and see how he likes it when he tries to pick himself out of the mud with ten kilos on his back.

Rage kept me upright, but eventually I cried. Tears mixed with rain as I put one foot down to test it. Yes, okay. Then the other. Only just okay. I gathered my treasures. Hiking poles, mobile phone, camera, water bottles. All accounted for. Stamina? A bit damaged. Pride? Returning.

I limped. There was nothing else to do but keep on walking, off the freeway, into fields and onto farm tracks. The rain stopped, the sun peeked out and the earth was made over in primary tones. A wide sky of vibrant blue was bisected by white jet trails and a yellow balloon floated above me dodging clouds, weightless, as I longed to be.

I stopped. At my feet, a trail of ants crossed the path. Seen from that balloon, I must have looked like an ant. From the jets above it, the balloon and the monster trucks would have been toys. And from space … from farther out?

The ants didn't stop to wonder. They just got on with their job.

Perhaps it was perspective that lifted me but I shouldered my pack and tramped on, body throbbing and steps slowing. Heart sagging. Hips nagging. Suburbs looming. Traffic booming. Boots drying. Still crying …

Rational thought must have been left on the road where I crashed and I kept walking long past sanity or safety. I kept on past the sad-eyed girl in the empty bar at Torrefresneda, where cigarette butts piled up with peanut shells at her feet. I kept on past the closed *albergue* at San Pedro de Mérida, and the truckstop on the *autovía*. I kept on walking with nothing in my stomach but toast, juice, coffee and trail mix, because it was the one thing I knew how to do.

For forty-three kilometres.

It was after six when I hobbled into Mérida, where the Mozárabe meets the Via de la Plata. Four hundred kilometres in thirteen days. A third of the way to Santiago.

Mérida.

Ancient city of Roman marvels and the end of my solitary road.

Crushed from the marathon and from pounding the streets to find room at an inn, I checked into the fourth *hostal* on the tourist office's list, paid a whopping twenty-five euros, signed an agreement and took the key.

Mould and bites finally broke me.

It was a concrete cell with a steel door. The bedding was damp and stained and I swear the fungus in the bathroom moved. The fleas on my ankles certainly did.

I had walked too far, too fast, and had not paid attention. I should have looked at the room before handing over money. You don't always find good places, I told myself. You have to stay conscious.

Praying the bites were fleas and not bedbugs, I picked up my ten-tonne *mochila* and left. I'd learned a big lesson. A hard one. Trust must not be given carelessly and not everyone is an Angel.

But they were out there.

In case I needed reminding, Barcelona called as I closed the door.

'*Estoy segura,*' I heard myself say. I am safe.

'*Estoy en Mérida.*'

I'm in Mérida.

INTERVAL

14

MÉRIDA

LEAVING THE MOULDY FLEA *hostal*, weary and teary and fretting about my lost euros, I wandered among crowds, hoping to be led. I had no guide for Mérida, having lost those pages back in the fields of *gracias*. A road opened into a sunny square, the Plaza Constitución, planted with fruiting orange trees, and bordered on one side by a pristine white edifice. Flags flew along the façade and a stork nested in one of its turrets.

The *ayuntamiento*.

I stumbled in, filthy and tear-stained, to find a tall, suited man behind a dark wood counter. Showing my *credencial*, I asked if he could help me find a bed.

'*Por qué no aquí?*' he said. Why not here? '*Es muy agradable.*'

I looked around. Yes, very nice. Clean, silent, smelling of polish and luxury.

But there were no desks. No municipal offices with room dividers. This clearly wasn't the Town Hall. To my left, I saw a rate sheet. Then I saw a name. Parador de Mérida.

I was in one of Spain's famous state-run, five-star hotels!

'*Muy caro,*' I squeaked. Very expensive. '*Gracias, gracias. No es posible.*'

I backed towards the door.

'*Señora,*' the man called. '*Un momento.*'

He rounded the counter, took my pack from me and extended his hand.

'*Soy Angel,*' he said. I am Angel.

He ushered me forward, inspected his ledger, and then said he could find me a room and it would cost sixty euros. It was a huge discount, but still a fortune by pilgrim standards—five nights' accommodation costs, when I'd already squandered good money at the Mouldy Flea.

He raised his eyebrows. '*Sí, peregrina?*'

There was ample credit on my phone and I would just eat less.

I handed over my passport. '*Sí. Muchas gracias.*'

Angel led the way up a staircase, along a corridor and around two corners. The building had been a convent and I wondered if my legs could carry me to my distant cell, but I was happy, so happy, for thick walls and carpet. Finally he stopped, opened a door, placed my pack down and handed me a key.

'I am Angel,' he said again. 'Call me if you have a problem.'

I stepped inside.

Room 110 was vast with a vaulted ceiling. Twin beds boasted precision-ironed coverlets. Armchairs nestled by a marble coffee table. A window framed by curtains and shutters let in a glimpse of pink sky. Chocolates beckoned from a bowl. The in-house magazine featured a pilgrim on the cover.

I bent to remove my boots, joints creaking like a crone's, and tiptoed over tiles to a wooden door. Behind it was a gleaming full-length tub, polished tapware, two sinks, bath-towels, hand-towels, face-towels and bathmats. And toiletries! Spice-smelling conditioner, shampoo, moisturiser and even cologne, for a woman who had been relying on olive oil and a cake of soap.

And there was a mirror.

I looked. Looked again. I turned on a light and looked closer.

My eyes belonged to someone else. They stared, perplexed by the strange creature with raw red skin and straw hair looking back at them. Slumping onto the edge of the bath, I saw the creature in the mirror grimace in pain at the tenderness of her bruises.

Then I cried. Really cried.

I had walked over one hundred kilometres in the preceding three days, in all weathers, and on testing surfaces. Sins had weighed on me—mostly my own.

But the tears were not for any of that.

They were for kindness and beauty; for the miracle of a hand-towel, like those at home; for the pleasure of shampoo, taken for granted in my normal life; for surfaces cleaned with care; and for plump chairs in a room all my own.

A home.

I undressed. My body was a patchwork of blues and purples, cuts and scrapes—and there would be more coming after the battering by the lorry.

No matter. Get on with it.

I laundered every article I had in twin sinks and chose hanging places from an array of possibilities. I doused my boots in peppermint and ti-tree oils and bid them rest. I tipped unguents into the tub, said a prayer to the water-gods asking forgiveness for my excesses, and turned on the taps. I let my numb feet linger under hot water as the bath filled, and finally I lowered myself into deep, bubbling water, taking up residence as the sky turned black outside the square window.

Mérida cranked into life while I wallowed, oblivious to the fact that the city had been overrun by thousands of partying teenagers for the European Festival of Greek–Latin Theatre. I lay in watery silence, skin wrinkling, remembering words from a poem by my compañero, sent before my departure:

> they talk about arrival
> i think they mean that it
> feels like when you
> walk in your front door
> and smell the feeling of home in
> your bones ...

When at last I moved, my steps were like an invalid's. Snail-slow to the toiletries. Slow to the novelty of a hair-dryer. Slow, slow to complete the marathon to bed, to pull back the cover, to slide between sheets so tightly tucked I was barely able to insert myself between them.

I was, however, able to sleep. I dreamed of home, on the other side of the world, where it would have been four in the morning. Still and silent.

Home.

It's my favourite word in the English language, even if sometimes I feel confused as to where it is on the planet.

I love the house where I live. It holds years of dreams and striving, the best and worst of me. It overflows with colour and sunshine.

I love Melbourne. I grew up in the west of Australia, and lived happily in Sydney for a time, but Melbourne was a home-coming: instant and deep recognition.

My love of Australia is visceral. The bush of my childhood is both real and mythical for me. I know it in my bones, but these days I only meet it as a visitor, like most Australians. Yet I never cease to be overcome when I return, flying over the continent to my lower right-hand corner, with all those dot paintings below me. How did Aboriginal artists know what the landscape looked like from above, thousands of years ago?

It's a land steeped in mystery, exposed by sharp, white light.

A friend once said that in the beginning, we love 'because of', but in maturity we love 'in spite of'. That's true of my feelings about Australia.

If home is where we locate those we love, then I have many homes. I am 'at home' all over the world, whenever I am eye to eye with an intimate. As my *compañero*'s poem also said:

> ... *arrival is the interaction between*
> *your deepest self*
> *and mine* ...

My most profound experience of home is internal—the home of the self.

At home with myself. At home in myself.

It's an interesting conundrum, linguistically.

Spanish, Italian and French don't really have an equivalent way of expressing those sentiments. Most of their expressions for home revolve around the idea of an actual house. *Chez moi. Mi casa, su casa.* There seems no single word that encompasses heart, belonging and soul in quite the same way as 'home'. There's no word like it!

Regardless, home is where my heart is, and part of my heart will always be in Mérida.

It was founded in 25BC as Augusta Emerita, a retirement village for the Roman emperor's soldiers. It has more Roman ruins than anywhere else in Spain, probably more than much of Italy. It's an open-air museum where history is alive and throbbing in mint condition.

The Puente Romano embodies grace and glory. One of the longest Roman bridges in existence, it spans the Río Guadiana as though it were a trickle.

The aqueduct is called Los Milagros—The Miracles—and it does look like divine intervention was involved in its design and construction. There is a *circo romano* outside the city and sections of Roman road in the pavements of the centre.

In the first century BC amphitheatre, adolescent girls posed as classical heroines, unaware they were as beautiful as any goddess. Tourists ambled over millennia-old stones clicking digital photos, and lovers smooched in an archway where gladiators had waited to fight before crowds of up to fourteen thousand. An elderly Japanese couple picnicked in the stands near me as I did battle with a few of my own beasts.

Was I a bad pilgrim for sleeping in a Parador? My intention had been to experience the road in the manner of a mediaeval pilgrim, reliant on humble lodgings or charity. Was I a real pilgrim if I slept between starched sheets?

Not one of my sinners would have begrudged me my luxury. None of them wanted pounds of my flesh. It was my own rigid rules that weighed on me. On the Camino Francés I'd turned up my nose at *peregrinos* who stayed in hotels, used phones to book ahead or had their luggage transported. Tourists. Not real pilgrims like me.

Pride again.

Now I was having my fall.

And what did it mean, anyway, to be a 'real' pilgrim? How was it possible to have a 'mediaeval' experience when trucks could run me down, I wore fancy hiking boots and applied factor-thirty sunblock?

Did it even matter?

Why not just accept that the road had led me to Angel and the Parador just as it might have led a mediaeval pilgrim to a soft bed? Why not let go of an expectation or two? Be grateful I could afford to accept the treat?

I wasted a good hour grappling with being the recipient of kindness. I forgot the lessons of Lucia and of my first donation, and my journal was a litany of futile, ungrateful ramblings, rooted in my unbending nature. In pride. Yet again.

Eventually, gales of laughter from the nearby theatre distracted me from pilgrim penitence. I strolled on a carpet of pink blossom to the Roman theatre, two storeys of columns, intact walls and detailed statuary.

What a thrill to enter an auditorium packed to the non-existent rafters with an audience captivated by a Greek comedy! Aristophanes would have been agog to see kids pocketing mobile phones to laugh at jokes that were millennia old. The theatre holds six thousand and it must have been nearing capacity. I squeezed into a place near the back, unwittingly observing the original rules that people be seated according to rank, so women and slaves belonged on the high, narrow seats at the top.

It didn't matter. The view and acoustics were perfect.

With enormous spongy breasts and a white afro wig direct from a seventies disco, the best of the players flounced about as an overbearing queen on sky-high platform shoes, dwarfing the cuck-olded mini-king.

Poor little king. He panted helplessly, his skinny red-stockinged legs trembling as the queen's nubile slave girls whipped him into a lather of desire, only to leave him gasping and unsatisfied. His queen, mean-while, shook her considerable booty at a handsome cuckolding villain.

An age-old story. A perennial. There were double- and triple-takes, pratfalls during chase sequences, and laments as infidelities were discovered. There was remorse from the queen, and glee from the audience when she winked at her next potential lover. We all wanted the sinning to continue. It was much more fun than the pros-pect of virtue.

Performances enlivened the stalls, too. The jet-haired boy in front of me slipped his arm under his girlfriend's T-shirt as she played with the band of his designer underwear. Little *chicas* dressed as slave girls in filmy apricot raced up the central aisle after their dance, giggling at their triumph. To my left, a bloated Nero clapped too vigorously and had to adjust his laurel wreath. I saw him later, walking the main street, still in full costume, parading like a time-traveller.

Palimpsesto.

Sun shone. Birds flitted. The crowd laughed and roared its approval.

I was home.

The theatre can be fickle, but it also unites people. It's relentlessly, deeply present. Performers, audience and technicians all breathe the same air at the same time. We tense up, sweat and gasp together. Skin tingles with excitement, guts knot with fear. It is belly-aching, heart-stopping and breath-taking. It is a place of union: a broad, welcoming church crossing time, space, race, religion, sexuality and sensibility. It's where we tell stories to remind ourselves of our shared humanity.

And wasn't it a story that brought millions of pilgrims to walk the *camino*? True or false, in some ways it didn't seem to matter whether people believed there was a saint or relics or miracles. A story of dis-covery and hope drew us to walk, a story written by millions of slog-ging feet and seeking spirits. In Mérida, I sat among kids from all over

Europe. We didn't share language, history or experiences, yet we were connected by story.

The final act came to a close and after ten minutes of curtain calls and encores I returned to the Parador's silence, opened my emails, and went home to my village.

The sinner who'd confessed to sleeping with her friend's husband was doing it tough. She was bedridden, forced into days of *convalescence and recuperation, repatriation and contemplation*. She wrote of being forced to surrender. She had set her clock to Spanish time so she knew when I was walking. In that coincidental way of Spain and *camino*, she and another sinner both sent me the lyrics of 'You'll Never Walk Alone'!

One of my sloths sent quotes from the famous sons of Córdoba:

Seneca: *It is not because things are difficult that we do not dare; it is because we do not dare that they are difficult.*

Maimonides: *The risk of a wrong decision is preferable to the terror of indecision.*

I thanked Rodgers, Hammerstein and the Córdoba lads equally.

My brother wrote: *Like you, we keep putting one foot in front of the other.*

Fungus and fleas seemed miniscule concerns when I read that.

There were snippets of domestic lives ... *we have spent the day pottering in our garden weeding and planting some winter flowers. I was lying on my bed reading and realised I felt utterly happy.*

I wrote to them of my losing battle with the lorry and of my trepidation at joining the pilgrim-populated eight hundred kilometres of the Via de la Plata.

I didn't admit I was writing from a Parador.

It wasn't strictly a lie but was definitely a sin of omission.

Finally, I asked if they'd like to walk with me on the coming Sunday. I loved the idea of joined dots in landscapes, a walking village.

I went to rest under a thick blanket. It was nearing midnight in Australia. I tried to picture their faces but, mostly, I failed. It's an intimacy to watch another in sleep, reserved for lovers and family.

And even then, their dreams are secret. No matter how well we know someone, there'll always be something unknown. We're puzzles to each other, and more beautiful for it.

The spice and amber scent of the Parador smelled like mystery, like the faces of sleepers I couldn't see. I dozed.

When I woke, it was late afternoon. At the Roman bridge, teenagers flirted on its footings, joggers ran over and around it, and one long-haired sylph did a Fred Astaire impression with an umbrella in the fading gold light.

The town was jumping. Costumed performers jostled for café tables, disputing which ice-cream flavour was best, oblivious to signs asking them to join an anti-nuclear demonstration. They swarmed past the Temple of Diana, racing instead into souvenir shops and the instant-photo booth. Four toga-wearing nymphs crowded in, their sandalled toes visible behind the curtain as they shrieked at the images they were making.

In the town square, tots kicked a football between palm trees while parents sipped aperitifs. Grandmothers held hands with mini-matrons decked out in patent leather and petticoats. Watching over them was the real *ayuntamiento*, three storeys of municipal spectacle presiding over the plaza like a Roman general. It made the Parador look like a foot soldier.

Throughout the town, the scent of neroli tracked me again. On the Camino Francés I had smelled figs everywhere. Citrus was the signature of the Mozárabe.

Returning to the hotel, I found Angel. He asked if I was better.

'*Soy una nueva persona,*' I said. I'm a new person. '*Gracias, gracias.*'

He would have none of it. It was nada.

'*Un turista hace las demandas para muchas cosas. Un peregrino da las gracias por nada.*' A tourist makes demands for many things. A pilgrim gives thanks for nothing.

I scurried upstairs to note down his words, wanting to live up to them.

Before leaving home, I'd copied down the Seven Corporeal Works of Mercy from the mediaeval catechism. Snuggled in my armchair, I read over them:

> *Feed the Hungry*
> *Give Drink to the Thirsty*
> *Give Shelter to Strangers*
> *Clothe the Naked*
> *Visit the Sick*
> *Minister to Prisoners*
> *Bury the Dead.*

I'd received many of them during Act One of my Mozárabe. I hoped I wouldn't need the final one, but I felt sure that if I did, it would be taken care of too.

I wrote a postcard to Leonardo and Ricardo. I wanted to tell them that Mérida is listed by UNESCO as a World Heritage site, and that it was my third on the trail, after Granada and Córdoba. That I was on a walk of wonders.

Vocabulary failed me. I wrote of love and of beauty. I can't remember if I wrote of home, but I should have. Mérida restored me. Mérida, and its Angel, earthed me, reminding me that, sometimes, home feels like a hand-towel and sounds like an audience cheering a villain.

ACT TWO

15

PILGRIMS

I LEFT LATE THE next morning, around nine, for a seventeen-kilometre saunter. The three-storey Roman aqueduct sprawled beside me, storks nesting among its arches and tut-tutting me on my way. A new cycle path led to a new road, which led to a new entrance to a Roman dam.

I was a new pilgrim!

The interval in Mérida had readied me for Act Two.

I smelled of Parador unguents, laundry detergent and peppermint oil. My strides were long and even, in spite of the bruising from my tussle with the lorry and the tenderness of my feet. Too much highway walking had taken a road toll on my soles.

Still, I wasn't convinced that Act One of the Mozárabe had conformed to the tradition of the Francés. Undoubtedly there had been lessons from the body, but coping with *Herr T*, reading through the sins each morning, then scrutinising my actions in the light of both, had proved painful and exhausting. My mind was a punishing instructor. My intention for Act Two was to try to carry my own sins in the way I was carrying those of my sinners. View your failings with compassion and distance, I told myself. They are done and can't be undone. Try to understand and improve, but not to flagellate.

My Barcelona angels called to wish me *'flores en tu corazón'*—flowers for my heart. They were celebrating the feast day of St George when, according to a Barcelona tradition, men give women roses, and women give men a book. By day's end, four million roses and eight hundred thousand books will have been sold. *Viva Sant Jordi!*

I told them I was now walking on the Via de la Plata.

I wanted to explain that purists insist *'plata'* doesn't refer to the Spanish word for silver, but to an Arabic word that means 'broad-surfaced road'. I didn't have the vocab for that. Instead, I told them the Via followed a Roman road from Seville to Santiago and that there would be other pilgrims about.

'Bueno,' they said. *Sant Jordi* was already looking out for me.

They talked me all the way through the graffiti-tagged industrial fringes of the city to the Embalse de Proserpina—Proserpina's Dam. The path around the reservoir was blocked by excavations that had uncovered the Roman foundations. All yellow arrows had been demolished but the workers kept me on track. I was skimming along a bank when I saw a figure loping ahead, a wooden staff in his right hand. Pilgrim alert!

Over six feet tall, he had a full beard and wore a lime-green scarf around his head like a turban. He was lugging a bulging backpack and carried a circular object that might have been a drum.

Two hours was a respectable first leg. I parked myself on a wall by a Red Cross lookout so he could put some distance between us. Despite the physical challenges, I had been much more peaceable within myself after *Herr T* left, and was in no rush to share the road again. Momentary connection was fine, but I didn't want the responsibility of a fellow traveller.

Hello selfishness.

Looking out over the choppy surface of the *embalse*, I reminded myself of the story of Prosperina. I'd read it as a child, turning the pages of a book of Roman myths and legends, during a baking summer holiday. The exotic names and northern hemisphere landscape, rendered in vivid watercolour, beguiled me. Proserpina was the daughter of Ceres, goddess of agriculture and crops; and Jupiter, god of sky and thunder. For an Aussie country kid, that sounded pretty fine.

Proserpina was picking flowers and playing with some nymphs at a lake, when Pluto, the king of the Underworld, emerged from a split in the ground, in a chariot pulled by four black horses.

My mother rode a stallion no one else could mount and we'd recently had a major shake-up from an earthquake, so I recognised Pluto's world. He stole Proserpina from her friends, so she could live with him in the Underworld.

Ceres looked for her daughter in every corner of the earth. Grief-stricken, she stopped the growth of fruits, vegetables and grain crops. She roamed the wide world, leaving deserts wherever she went.

Children lost in harsh bushland are part of Australia's mythology and I could hear my mother's anxiety in Ceres' cries.

Worried about humans starving on a barren Earth, Prosperina's father Jupiter, the boss-God, ordered Pluto to free Proserpina. Pluto obeyed, but before he let her go he made her eat six seeds of the pomegranate, or *granada*. Those who ate its fruit could never return to the world of the living. By forcing the seeds on Proserpina, he compelled her to live six months of each year with him.

My grandmother had a *granada* tree in her front yard, so I understood why its bitter-tasting fruit were considered the food of the dead!

The myth was an illustration for children of the changing seasons. Ceres welcomes her daughter back and the earth blossoms. When Proserpina returns to her husband, cold creeps in and trees are bare. The spring flowers of the antipodes took on new significance. They were Proserpina walking the earth. We called them everlastings, but I knew their life was short.

Even back then, stories explained my world to me.

Sitting by the Embalse de Proserpina, I tried to imagine Roman legions building it, making eternal spring by conserving water for the good citizens of Mérida. Thousands of years later, a woman who had read their myth on the other side of the world sat on their handiwork, watching Spanish engineers and labourers refreshing it.

Palimpsesto, palimpsesto …

The wind was cold. My turbaned *peregrino* would be way ahead. Time to boot up.

A black-and-white bird played tag with me, appearing and disappearing. Three cyclists sped past, Lycra blurs shouting, '*Hola, Rubia!*' The creek to my right dawdled, trying not to disturb the white flowers on its surface. A yellow arrow on the roadside caught my attention just in time to direct me onto a dirt track through fields of *encinas*, the evergreen oaks that were just beginning to sprout their yellow catkins. The track became a walled lane edged with wildflowers in baby pink and duck-egg blue. My wagtail bird hopped among them like a Disney animation. Proserpina was surely about.

Then the cartoon turned to a horror movie.

At my feet, a metre-wide pilgrim shell had been etched into the path, with the bleached skull of a cow at its base. Everything raced. Pulse, mind, breath. Who could have made it?

Not the cyclists; there were no tracks. The turbaned one?

I heard an engine noise and gripped my hiking poles, preparing to meet the worst. A scooter came around the bend. The rider looked ordinary enough, but then aren't most serial killers just 'average guys'?

He stopped. His eyes were wide and his speech rapid. He opened his scooter's hold. For a second I expected to see—what? A knife? A gun?

No. A muddy bag.

He put a finger to his lips and glanced over his shoulder. I could see no one. From the bag, he produced a dirt-covered tuber. A potato? He pushed it under my nose and I inhaled. It smelled of earth.

'*Muy bien,*' he said. '*Muy, muy bien.*' Very, very good.

He kissed the mud-covered root, wrapped it again, and tucked it back into place with as much care as if he were cradling a newborn. And off he went, singing to the air.

I had barely walked twenty paces when another man stepped over the hip-high stone wall to my left as though it were a kerb. He greeted me with a stream of rapid-fire Spanish, waving his arms, laughing and slapping my *mochila*. When I recovered from the shock, I saw he had a staff, a shell and a guidebook.

Pilgrim alert two!

I explained that I wasn't a fluent Spanish-speaker, so he fell into step beside me and we began a conversation at foreigner pace.

My *amigo* had a treasure—one of the tubers. Scooter-man had shown him where to search for them and he'd found a beauty. It was wrapped in a tissue and secreted in his vest pocket. For later. Wink. Nudge.

His age could have been anywhere from late twenties to late forties. He smiled so readily it was impossible to tell. He had a brown birth-mark on his right cheekbone and black curls framed his surprisingly blue eyes. He worked in the financial sector, but the economic crisis had upended his world and he was giving himself six months to reassess his priorities. As part of that, he was walking the *camino*. He was delighted at the prospect of company and, in spite of my reservations, we walked together through flowering paths into El Carrascalejo …

And out again …

At a wayside cross honouring Santiago, we met the turbaned *pere-grino*. My *amigo* whispered that he was a *moro*—a Moor. He was sitting on the base of the cross and smiled when I greeted him. A cautious smile. I'd have liked to ask what made him walk a Christian pilgrim trail, but I recognised his reticence to chat. He carried all he needed so he could sleep in the fields; the 'drum' was his tent.

We left him there. Perhaps he would make camp under the cross.

It was then, on the downhill into our destination, Aljucén, that my *amigo* confessed it was he who had made the image of the skull and shell. He thought it amusing that I'd been frightened, quoting a favourite poet, Antonio Machado:

> *Late, corazón … No todo*
> *se lo ha tragado la tierra …*

> Beat, heart … Not everything
> has been swallowed by the earth …

My *amigo* told me the words were from a poem that had been written after the death of Machado's wife. They took me to my brother. Blunt and emphatic, they were like the skull my *amigo* had placed so precisely within his etching of a shell. It was a physical depiction of what I sometimes felt: that death was right in the centre of the *camino*.

But there was no time for philosophy. My *amigo*'s phone rang. The woman who ran the Aljucén bathhouse was on the line. Would my *amigo* still like to keep his massage appointment?

Aljucén is a *pueblo* of two hundred and fifty people. There are two bars, a church and a *refugio* for pilgrims. How could they possibly sustain a Roman bathhouse? Apparently, it operates as a *casa rural*, or what we call a B&B. Aljucén was a popular weekend get-away for the burghers of Mérida.

It was lunchtime. The *pueblo* dozed. When the bathhouse owner said pilgrims could take the waters for five euros, all hesitation vanished. There followed an hour of plunging from icy water into steaming water, with a tepid bath to restore equilibrium. Those Romans had life sorted.

My *amigo* appeared, so we averted eyes and folded tissue towels around ourselves as we moved through the silence from one pool to another. My bruises made an impressive abstract of purples and browns, but I figured the water could only help and my feet loved me like never before. Oil burners flickered. The watery soundscape was soporific.

Eventually I hauled myself out and dried off. There, waiting for me at the entrance, was my lemon-smelling *amigo*. We wound our way up deserted streets to the three-bedroom, twelve-bed *albergue*. Basic but clean, it was run by the same people who owned the baths. Yellow arrows, a Santiago cross, and a shell or three decorated the exterior. Chairs and tables filled the concrete back garden and sitting on them were pilgrims.

A Spaniard. Lean, fortyish and smoking.

Two Italian men. The white-haired *Capitano* talked like a bullet train, detailing how much rain he had walked through in the two hundred kilometres from Seville, oblivious to the fact that the others had sloshed through the same rain. His friend, *il Soldato*, listened in silence, a smile lifting one corner of his mouth. It would be difficult to surprise that old soldier, my *amigo* said.

The *albergue* world was instantly familiar, and just as I'd done on the Camino Francés, I offered foot rubs to the others after the day's chores were done. My *amigo*'s hand shot up. As I massaged, I reminisced with the Italians about a hermitage *albergue* we all knew at San Nicolas on the Francés. Each night, for the blessed few who get to sleep there, the Italian volunteers who run the refuge perform an extraordinary ritual.

Pilgrims sit in a semi-circle on a candle-lit altar as prayers are read aloud, wishing everyone a *camino* of humility, the Contrary Virtue to pride. A metal pan is placed at the feet of each pilgrim in turn. One volunteer bathes the feet, one dries, and when it is done, a kiss is planted on each arch.

I'd been seated at the end of the semi-circle and by the time my turn came tears were falling. Only days before, when I'd had to stop with knee problems in Burgos, I'd visited the cathedral, where I'd seen a painting depicting a Magdalene of lush beauty with long curls hanging in ringlets around her naked body. As my feet were bathed, I thought of Mary Magdalene washing Christ's feet with her tears then drying them with her hair, and understood the grace of her action as never before.

After that ritual, I offered foot massages daily. It seemed a small thing in return for the safe lodging, kindness and knowledge that was gifted to me along the way. It was also a privilege to feel the surrender of bodies that were working so hard in service of the spirit; to feel skin on skin, communication without words. If my *amigo*'s reaction was anything to go by, I would be rubbing feet all along the Via!

A German couple arrived later, when socks, jocks and a pair of women's knickers were drying on the lines. He was wiry and jovial. She was silent and weary. They moved in with me and we accommodated each other, despite having not a word of shared language.

The smoking Spaniard asked if I was English, and when I said no, he said he knew it because English girls have no teeth! He called me *guapa*, a word I came to regard with mixed emotions. It's used for men and women, and can mean 'handsome' or 'pretty' or 'sexy', depending on the tone. I hated it from *Señor Smoker*, blew hot and cold when my *amigo* used it, and adored it from the Barcelona boys. Perhaps it was a good indicator for my feelings about someone.

My *amigo* produced the tuber. They were called '*criadillas de tierra*'. We cut into it and nibbled it raw: earth, mushroom and nut flavours. *Señor Smoker* said they were an aphrodisiac and winked. There was a lot of laughing and nodding. Later I learned that *criadilla* translates as 'testicle'. No wonder a blonde woman nibbling on it was hilarious!

Up at the church, opened for us by the caretaker in the last rays of light, six baby Jesuses played in six cribs, and a life-size crucified Christ lay encased in glass. *Señor Smoker* demanded to be photographed delivering a sermon from the altar and then again as Jesus on the cross. I wanted wilderness and a garden of olives.

Back at the *albergue*, a mother cat had moved her kittens to my top bunk. I scooped them up and found another nest for them, then made up my bed. For our ten-euro tariff, we were given a sheet, pillowcase and towel made of the same tissue fabric I'd encountered at the bathhouse. Having seen bedbug bites on the Francés, I was grateful for every barrier.

I rolled out my sleeping bag, found my earplugs, arranged my belongings for a quick escape in the morning, and by 9.15 I was tucked into my top bunk writing my journal, marvelling at how far I had come from the Parador.

The Italians chatted in the next room. Or at least, *il Capitano* did. Before going to bed, the old soldier had told me he was looking forward to the coming walk through Extremadura, because he'd loved the silence of the *meseta*. *Il Capitano* went a bit mad out there, he said. *Pazzo*.

Señor Smoker and the Germans headed for the nearest bar. My *amigo* was relocating kittens, after the mother cat had resettled them deep inside his sleeping bag.

Day one of the Via de la Plata. And now we were seven.

Six too many, I wrote. Selfish pilgrim.

Selfish.

The first entry for it in my thesaurus is *egocentric*. It continues with *egotistic, egomaniacal, self-centred, self-absorbed*. Then it segues to *inconsiderate, thoughtless, uncharitable*. It really gets up some steam with *mean, miserly, grasping, acquisitive, opportunistic*.

I remembered my first response to the word, back in Rome.

Selfishness. Selfish. Self-ish.

If we say something is yellowish, we mean it's a version of yellow. If we say a person is tallish, we mean they are 'kind of tall'. Did self-ish imply that a person is only a version of their true self?

A Swiss student of English once asked me about colloquialisms. She was baffled by our use of 'fourish' and 'sixish'. What was this 'ish'?

I said it means 'roughly'. Like when we say we'll meet for dinner 'at eight-ish'.

She tilted her head and thought for a moment.

Then she replied, 'We don't have this "ish" in Switzerland.'

Maybe that's a good thing. A land with no 'ish'.

My *amigo* popped his head in to check if we might set out together next day.

'*Depende*,' I answered. I didn't want to push my luck.

'*No pasa nada*,' he said, full-force smile at maximum wattage. No worries. '*Hasta mañana*.'

See you tomorrow.

16

TENTACIÓN

IN DENSE, HEADILY PERFUMED fog, my phone rang. Barcelona calling.

I have an *amigo*, I told Leonardo and Ricardo. He is here with me.

Good, they said. Now you will be safe.

Every day they ring, I told my *amigo*. I said they were *llenos de fe*—full of faith—because I didn't know the Spanish for faithful.

Yes, I was in company. When I crept into the kitchen area of the *albergue*, snores thundering on all sides, my *amigo* was waiting for me, grin in place.

It was my mother's birthday. Had she lived, she'd have been seventy-three. I'd wanted to spend a solitary day remembering her and Sue. Not to be.

We loaded our packs with extra water because it was twenty kilometres to the next settlement. Visibility was almost zero as we picked our way along what we hoped was the path. As the fog lifted, I discovered why the perfume was so potent. We'd been walking between banks of rock roses—*jaras*—and wild lavender.

My *amigo* taught me new words.

Pájaros carpinteros. Carpenter birds. Woodpeckers!

They tapped furiously on the cork trees—the *alcornoques*. I repeated that word as I walked. *Alcornoque. Alcornoque.* Like percussion. My *amigo* cautioned me against singing my song in public because the Spanish also translate *alcornoque* as 'idiot'. '*Bruto como el alcornoque*,' they say. As stupid as the cork tree. I felt sorry for the maligned *alcornoques*. Our yellow arrows were painted on their trunks, and they proved totally reliable.

We played the Spanish version of a favourite childhood game, I Spy!

Veo veo. I see. I see.

Que ves? What do you see?

Veo una cosita. I see a little thing.

Que cosita ves? What little thing do you see?

Veo una cosita que comienza con … I see a little thing that begins with …

Little things. Walking triggers pleasure in things like language and rhyme. Poems don't have to be grown-up and games don't have to be complex, because landscape fills in the gaps. My *amigo* spent a good twenty minutes trying to guess my *cosita* that started with C. When I told him the answer was *cielo*, he protested.

'The sky is not a little thing,' he said.

And he was right. Not out there. Not that day.

The fog was gone. Mystery had been replaced by white light and true blue. Bells rang out from nearby sheep and cows. Distant hills called us on and the fields were a carpet of wildflowers sprouting from Extremadura's red earth.

Extremadura could be translated as 'extremely hard' but it gave me 'extremely sweet' walking along picturesque paths, which were made even more memorable by the fact that we had them to ourselves. Just two pilgrims, bright sun and a dirt track.

We stopped after fifteen kilometres at a wayside memorial to a boy who, according to the story, was eaten by a wolf while on his way to a *fiesta* for St John the Baptist.

El Cruz del Niño Muerto, the guide said. The cross of the dead boy. I pictured my postcard John the Baptist, with only his red robe to protect him from wolves.

When I told my *amigo* it would have been my mother's birthday, he offered me licorice, saying it was his younger brother's favourite treat.

'Where is he?' I asked.

'*Muerto,*' he said. '*Suicidio.*' Suicide.

He looked away to the hills, but his voice remained steady. He told me he had found his brother after a bullet ripped off the top of his head. My *amigo* said he could still see the traces of tears on the cheeks of his brother when he arrived, too late. And he still asked the same question, ten years later.

'*Fue este un pecado?*' Was this a sin?

I watched his back as he chewed his licorice. The sun went behind a cloud.

'This was no sin,' I said. No *pecado.*

He turned to look at me.

'No,' he said. 'This was war.'

I shook my head, thinking I had misunderstood. He continued.

'*Una guerra con desesperación.*' A war with despair.

He said it was good to remember his brother, there in the sun. And my mother. And my sister-in-law.

'To remember is to love,' he said, and for a second the smile slipped.

I thought of my sinner who had experienced decades of regret for not intervening to save his friend. I wanted to tell my *amigo* that failing to rescue this brother was not a sin either, but I'm not sure he'd have believed me.

The day got hotter. We walked faster.

The higher the temperature, the happier I walk. On through Alcuéscar where, in a *refugio* run by a religious order, pilgrims are offered food and Mass with their bed. It was tempting to stay in the cool, to sit with those kind men, but the day was a religious experience of another kind and I was going on.

My *amigo* came too.

We walked apart so as not to trample each other's songs. He played air guitar to Latina rock while I danced with my walking poles to Joni Mitchell. Eagles soared and storks hunted tadpoles in puddles.

We picnicked by the road, eating bread, cheese and dried figs, and harvesting a side dish of wild asparagus.

I learned the word for soul. *Alma.*

I'd been taught it before, but sitting with my back pressed against warm stone, collecting salad from the earth, it lodged. That's a language class.

We stepped in time down a Roman road, across a Roman bridge, the distance measured by Roman distance markers, *milarios.* We clicked photos of each other, and when I looked at them, I saw faces lit with laughter. There was no trace of the grumpy *peregrina* who didn't want company.

After almost thirty-eight kilometres and a full day together, our conversation was of *fidelidad.* Fidelity.

Yes, I was married. Yes, I was faithful. Yes, it was sometimes challenging to be apart. Yes, I feel desire for others. Yes, I take the vows seriously.

Good questions to answer, in the light of such a day.

Separations have always been part of my marriage and have never seemed odd to me, or to my husband. Some people are dubious about how it works. Have we remained faithful? Do we suspect each other of infidelity? In every language, my answer would be the same: I trust him. My world is built around that trust. Equally, I've never given him reason to doubt me.

Love consists of this: two solitudes that meet, protect and greet each other. That's what Rainer Maria Rilke has to say on the subject of love.

I'm with Rainer!

My *amigo* and I walked straight into a wedding in Aldea del Cano. Squeezing to the back row through lace and satin, we listened to vows of eternal love and *fidelidad.* A small girl hoiked her red party dress over her head and danced. We dragged our sweaty bodies to the six-bed *albergue.*

The Italians were waiting on the front step, showered and fresh, and wondering what had taken us so long. Decades older than us, they walked thirty or forty kilometres per day. Easy, they said. *Forza Italia!*

Inside, a bare-chested Nederlander smoked and upended a bottle of red. With him was a tall German woman sporting a shaved head. She pointed me to a double room off the kitchen, where she had the top bunk and the Italians had claimed the lower one for me. I removed my boots, rummaged for soap, and slipped through to the shower as *Mijnheer Holland* opened another bottle.

My roommate was resting when I returned. She'd been walking for eight weeks and was over it, she said. She was gay and found Spanish men confronting. They were not spiritual, she said. They watch too much TV, they are too noisy, too social and eat the wrong foods. In Germany, she said, she could close the door and get away from people. She just wanted to be alone.

I heard myself say, 'Why are you here, then? That is the *camino.*'

Take your own advice, *peregrina australiana.*

I offered to rub her feet, her shoulders, but no, she said, she did not like to be touched. But thank you. She rolled over and faced the wall, her feet dangling off the end of her bunk.

At the bar, the entire village watched football as we ate dinner. A full house of kids, families and visitors played cards, smoked, argued and laughed.

How not to love it? How not to feel happy when every chair is yours, every face is welcoming, every answer is yes. *Sí, sí, sí.* Even *Mijnheer Holland* couldn't get our waitress offside. She smiled and joked, never wilting under 'too many people'. I ate my salad, drank my wine, cheered for a team, and contributed stories in pidgin Eurospeak.

In the middle of the night, I had another visceral Spanish lesson, as I scanned my memory bank for the verb 'to snore'.

That's it. *Roncar.*

It came to me as the *ronc*-ing from the other room reached a shattering crescendo. I had a feeling it was Dutch-accented.

No matter. I lay in the darkness, thinking how Mum and Sue would have loved my *amigo*, the Italians and the crowd in the bar. They were both party girls and would have been in their element. They'd have approved of me living a full day rather than walking in solemn solitude.

Next morning I got away in darkness, before anyone surfaced. It was Anzac Day in Australia, when we remember those who served in wartime. It was also the day I'd suggested to my supporters they might like to walk with me in solidarity. As the sun rose, my husband phoned— a rare treat. He had driven through a locust plague as big as the area of Spain. It sounded Biblical, nightmarish. He sounded so familiar, so close. Surely he was only in the next *pueblo*, waiting with coffee?

But no. The next *pueblo* was at the end of an eleven-kilometre broadcast of wishes. I imagined myself as an antenna, transmitting at full intensity to my co-walkers and sinners. I recited John Donne's meditation:

> *No man is an island, entire of itself; every man is a piece of the continent, a part of the main. Any man's death diminishes me, because I am involved in mankind; and therefore never send to know for whom the bell tolls; it tolls for thee …*

I remembered how an earthquake shook Chile only a month before I left home. Waves had travelled to Australia at speeds up to seven hundred kilometres per hour. Our days are now shorter by 1.26 microseconds as a result of the planets shifting. We are all connected.

Leonardo called, as if to verify that.

'Tutti famiglia,' he said. 'Todos familia.'

'All family,' I agreed. In all languages.

At Valdesalor, with toes freed, I did my morning reading of the sin list as I breakfasted on toast and tomato in a service station on the N-630. Weekend travellers gulped their first hit of caffeine. They looked bleary of eye and vulnerable, smelling of vanilla and coconut, their hair still damp and clothes still pressed. Maybe they were en route to *pueblos* to attend church with their families, or to lunch and loll.

I stared into space, letting my mind drift to my husband in his locust-encrusted car, and my sinners who would be coming to the end of their Sundays. It was rare to have the opportunity to dream. Usually I was firmly present, my mind on the next footfall. But here it was, not yet ten—obscenely early by Spanish standards—and I had only twelve kilometres to Cáceres, where I planned to luxuriate in a hermit afternoon. I was spoiled rotten.

The doors burst open and *il Capitano* arrived, *il Soldato* bringing up the rear with badly infected blisters. They mainlined coffee while *il Capitano* pulled out maps, print outs and phone numbers. If they took a taxi, they could go to the emergency department, the foot could be rested for the afternoon, and they could still walk tomorrow and be on schedule. It was *molto importante* to stay on schedule. They were a two-man army on the move.

My *amigo* arrived. He was looking forward to reaching Cáceres, a city he didn't know. Another World Heritage site, he informed me, it was founded at the same time as Mérida. As well as Roman relics, it boasted a perfectly preserved mediaeval centre. It also had a thriving Jewish community until 1492.

That year, Boabdil surrendered to the Catholic kings on 2 January, and on 31 March they ordered all Jews to convert or leave Spain. In the same year they commissioned Christopher Columbus, and he 'sailed across the ocean blue' to discover the Americas.

Certain dates etch themselves into us. September 11, 2001 is the date for our generation, another that tells the story of a clash of ideologies.

There we were, on a road that celebrated unity and peace. An injured Italian soldier, an Australian remembering the fallen, and a Spaniard speaking of centuries-old conquest as though it happened yesterday.

A taxi pulled up and the Italians de-camped. I set off with my *amigo*. Just like that.

We took our time. There were conversations to be had and poetry to be shared. He enjoyed words and stories, and was able to recite favourite poems from memory. He asked me for the poem I loved best, but attempting to translate 'The Owl and the Pussycat' proved impossible. He was delighted to learn I was a writer, but amused by my attempt to carry the sins of others, saying I needed to make some sins of my own. He laughed, and he made me laugh.

He taught me the Hymn of the Centenary of the Real Madrid football team, which includes a lyric about a 'field of stars'. I taught him 'Waltzing Matilda', Australia's unofficial anthem about a sheep thief. I explained that we were like the hero of the song, an itinerant with a swag, or pack, on his back. I didn't sing the lines that describe the swagman committing suicide. I had no wish to make him do any more crying for his brother.

If *Herr T* was characterised by earnestness, then my *amigo* was his polar opposite. When he talked of his religion, it was connected to family gatherings and tradition. He said he enjoyed the silence of churches, finding them cool respite from the heat of his thoughts. He was going to walk the *camino* in sections during the Holy Year, in memory of his brother. When I asked him why the Holy Year, he said, 'Because it is special.' He never spoke of absolution of sin, but I wondered. Maybe the man of futures trading, iPhones and online market updates couldn't bring himself to verbalise such hopes.

A life lived among Catholic ritual, the year defined by saints' days, and transitions marked by sacraments, would be hard to release. I'd had only a decade of such rites and felt their impression on me still.

The sun was high when we arrived in Cáceres. We made for the *plaza*, where I satisfied my craving for spice with falafel. Families were weekend lunching. Children angled for extra dessert and grandparents indulged them while parents scolded. The vast *plaza* was a stage, and every citizen a player, costumed, coiffed and starring in their own drama.

My *amigo* had shared rooms with snorers all the way from Seville. He wanted to catch up on sleep. I wanted to freshen up and explore. We found an *albergue* and were offered a room with two beds, a balcony and a private bathroom. We didn't hesitate.

We were negotiating our way around each other in the room when I began to get uncomfortable. It was intimate. Too intimate. I didn't say anything, but I felt like I had entered a grey area, morally. An area of 'ish'.

Why? *Albergues* don't allow for coyness about bodies. Get over it if a flash of flesh is a problem. Deal with the smelly feet or farting of others. *Albergues* are life at its most basic, and that is both their challenge and their gift.

I realised that what had always made me feel free in them was the number of people. Being only two in a room implied intimacies of a different kind—sexual and emotional. Domestic even. I caught myself wondering if I should wash my *amigo*'s smalls when he threw his socks into the bathroom.

No. The internal voice was loud and clear on that.

We managed to shower and launder without stressing my moral compass further. We hung our washing on the balcony and it made a very cosy picture. Again, I baulked. What was going on?

We were adults. We had shared the Roman bathhouse with decorum. He was kind. I was not in danger. The Italians knew where we were. We'd seen them in the square, *il Soldato* limping, his toes bandaged. I had a telephone. Any sound could be heard through the walls. What was my problem?

We went out into the town together. I didn't protest when my *amigo* joined me, although I thought he wanted to sleep. I didn't want him to guess my thoughts, and jumping my bones was probably the last thing on his mind, given his reasons for walking.

Citizens filed into the Cathedral of Santa María, where the high altar was decked with flowers in celebration of the Virgin. Roses, carnations and lilies must have been trucked in from all over Extremadura. The Virgin looked overwhelmed.

The cathedral is in the old town. A forest of towers rises from within its sandstone walls and there is no sign of modernity. We had stepped back centuries, until a boy rounded a corner on a skateboard.

A lady selling cauliflower-shaped pastries told us that many films are made in Cáceres because it is *auténtico y verdad*—real and true. The crowd milling through to the cathedral didn't seem fazed by antiquity. They shouted greetings, kissed cheeks and embraced. In spite of its museum perfection, the old city was jumping. Preservation hadn't resulted in mummification.

In the cool dark of the Church of San Mateo, my *amigo* lit candles for us, then sat beside me and asked me my greatest sin. I answered 'selfishness'.

It was true. Had he asked me my greatest fear, I would have had to answer 'desire'.

Il Capitano called, crashing the silence, to invite us to dinner with *Mijnheer Holland* and *Señor Smoker*.

I fudged, whispering white lies ... maybe, *forse*, possibly, *un momento* ...

Being honest, I wanted to rest my head on my *amigo*'s shoulder and let him make the decisions, let him care for me, be strong for me.

What was I thinking?

I crossed myself, wondering if that was a white lie too, and left the church.

Back at the *albergue*, I decided to clear the air, even if I had to do it in Spanish. I asked how, on the *camino*, a married woman and a man can share a room, and it not be a sin.

He grinned. We haven't done anything sinful, he said. Why?

Ah, there it was. We hadn't done anything sinful, yet clearly I had something on my mind. And that is where it all begins.

I had thought the sin. I had imagined the possibility.

He indicated for me to sit, which was in itself tricky, given that the only surfaces were beds. He asked if I'd put the same question to the German woman in the *albergue* the previous night. She was gay, wasn't she?

'*Era lesbiana?*'

I nodded.

Why did I not have a problem being *sola* in the room with a gay woman, and yet I was worrying about sharing the space with him? Was it the bedding configuration? Side by side, as opposed to bunks?

We both laughed at that.

Surely the difference was to do with the possibility of desire, he said. I felt no sin sharing a room with a woman, because there was no likelihood of me feeling desire, whereas it's always a possibility for me to desire a man. He rested his case. *Sine qua non.*

I didn't challenge him about whether I could desire a woman. That seemed destined to invite a conversation that was way too difficult. And while I wasn't mad about it when he put a protective arm around me, or told me I was *guapa*, there was no doubt that I could imagine feeling desire for him, at least notionally, in the abstract …

So the sin, or the risk of it, lay in the temptation—in the mind—and the most perilous moment is the gap between thinking about a sin and acting on it, that moment when there is space to say no, even if the gap is tiny, as it might be in the choice to gossip. Take a breath. Consider. Lengthen the gap.

My *amigo* laughed. He smoothed the crease between my brows.

'*Hay mucho adentro aquí,*' he said. There's a lot in here.

He said we should go out for a drink and murmured a phrase I came to love, a great favourite of both Ricardo and Leonardo: '*Tranquilo. No te preocupes.*' Be still. Don't worry yourself.

And so I didn't. I let him lead and was grateful he led me out of temptation. We found a café to watch the evening promenade, he ordered the meal, and it was good. Marinated anchovies. Torta del Casar, a regional specialty of oozing sheep's milk cheese, tasting of earth and musk. Salad with perfect crunch factor. Our waitress flirted with him while I wrote postcards and journalled. Shakespeare visited me, whispering in my ear some words from Hamlet: *There is nothing either good or bad, but thinking makes it so.*

Thanks, Will. I'll try to remember that.

The other *peregrinos* joined us. I settled into their company, listened to stories of their days, and in the sultry air of a spring night in

Extremadura I was purely and simply happy. Perhaps confession had something going for it.

Back at the *albergue*, we tucked in, side by side. Not like innocent children. We were adults, fully aware of the possibilities in traversing the gap between our beds, and clear about our intentions not to. I'd be lying if I didn't admit that I enjoyed the whisper of his breathing and the sight of his sleeping face. They were unearned intimacies, making me feel simultaneously closer to home, and far, far away from it.

17

KEEPING COMPANY

I READ THROUGH THE sins, trying to skip over 'gluttony' as my *amigo* and I breakfasted on *churros*, deep-fried pastry strands dusted in sugar. They crunch on the outside and melt on the inside. High in fat and carbs, they launched us into the morning sun, past the bull-ring and the statue honouring the washerwomen of Cáceres, through the sleeping suburbs.

We overtook two Spanish *peregrinos*. It was their first day on the road and a conversation began, the three men chatting at Speedy Gonzales' rate. Pleading lack of vocab I sped off along the freeway's shoulder, racing ahead so I could sing at top volume. Wildflowers and wisteria marked the way, and two hours later I'd covered eleven kilo-metres, had a natter about merinos in Casar de Cáceres (home of the sheep's milk cheese I'd eaten the previous night), and stocked up on water and juice. I was sitting in a square of shade at the end of the main street, boots off, journalling, when my *amigo* caught me up. He asked if he could sit with me.

Yes, of course. Why not?

He smiled. You don't want company. I see that.

He was right. I didn't. Not his. His company was seductive. I'd had time alone and had owned up to myself fairly and squarely. I didn't want temptation.

He also came between the road and me. He stepped in at every café, every meeting, and made introductions, asked questions, did the talking, negotiating and deciding. He was caring for me, but as a result I became a 'passenger', and I didn't like it. Something had been lost by having an intermediary. I was not walking my *camino*. I was having our holiday.

Plus, I was working.

He made it easy for me to forget that I was an employee charged with a task, a pilgrim walking a spiritual road and not a hitchiker along for free rides. I was answerable to my sinners and myself.

I couldn't possibly explain all that when sun glinted on the marigolds by my toes, my *amigo* grinned, and the road shouted that it was running away from me. So I booted up and we walked together.

Hats off to willpower.

The temperature rose and my spirits went with it. The sky was new blue and the road was whitest gravel fringed by kilometres of smooth stone walls. Mostly we walked in silence, but when my amigo asked me for a poem, I tried to translate fragments of Rilke:

> *My eyes already touch the sunny hill …*
> *… So we are grasped by what we cannot grasp …*
> *… but what we feel is the wind in our face.*

He loved the last line, even in my second-rate Spanish, and in return gave me more of Antonio Machado:

> *Con el aroma del habar, el viento*
> *corre en la alegre soledad del campo.*

> Carrying the scent of broad beans, the wind
> rushes over the happy solitude of the land.

When we stopped, there were boulders for backstops and a downy grass carpet. The world opened wide and my Australian blood raced in the heat, reminding me of the poem that first spoke to me as a child:

I love her far horizons ...

That might have something to do with why I crave solitude, I said to my *amigo*, as we sat in noonday shade looking to a line of hills. The Australian relationship to space. We have so much, compared to Europeans in their close-quartered communities.

He'd finished his yoga salutes and I'd written and stared into the distance. He said he too enjoyed solitude, but not too much. I laughed. He was hard-wired for connection. A true extrovert.

I told him the definition I'd heard on the radio. An *extrovertido* is fed by company, I said. An *introvertido* is fed by solitude. They have different *comidas* for their *almas*. Different foods for their souls.

Translation is tricky. Language classes don't always give me the vocab I want for the conversations I enjoy. My *amigo* listened as I delved for words like *soledad, reflexión, tranquilidad, restauración*. I think we got there.

'*Sí, sí, entiendo,*' he said, and if the ensuing days were an indication, he really had understood. It made it possible for us to find a rhythm we could both enjoy: separation and reconnection. Like Proserpina, I could surface into company if I had spent time in the solitude of my own underworld.

The Spanish *peregrinos* had caught us up, so I set off alone into scorching sun. The heat was dry, like home, and I was in my element. I sang my way past fields of wildflowers, a multitude of tiny faces contrasted against a skyline of giant rocks. Opposites creating balance.

A farm dam twinkled at me, an oval of brown water in the middle of the Extremadura oven. I didn't think twice. I threw myself in, emerging among frogs and tadpoles. It was an icy pick-me-up and sped me on my way.

A walker. A road. Sunshine. Silence. Perfection, when I am that walker.

People sometimes ask me what I think about when I'm walking.

The answer is disappointing.

I don't think.

The great relief of walking, for me, is the silence in my mind. It is my meditation. When my feet achieve a regular rhythm, or when I am climbing hard with my pumping heart bursting from my chest, hours can pass without a thought. Days get lost.

No. Not lost. Never lost.

Days expand to something beyond self, beyond space. They transform into a kind of grounded timelessness. It's a conundrum. My walking is both physical and spiritual. It's through bodily effort that I achieve mental stillness, and that's rarely possible in company. It's what had made the walking with my *compañero* on the Francés so baffling to me. Effortless intimacy had been present in the first steps we took together.

One day, we were part of a pilgrim train on a stretch of Roman road. We had been walking in silence for kilometres when we both stopped, registering that for the first time the road was empty. We looked at each other.

'Who are you?' he asked.

'Your friend,' I said, though we were barely acquaintances.

Who are you?

A big question, like the ones in Mary Oliver's poem that had first made me set out to walk. Why am I here on the planet? What do I want to do with my allotment of time?

I want to live my life consciously, I told my *compañero*. To be awake for all of it.

As I am when I walk.

I remember the smell of thyme-like grass in the hot afternoon by a dry river bed, and telling him the story of my mother's death: of waiting for her to complete every relationship; of watching her uncertainty and eventual release; and of her promise that she would be with me whenever I saw a pink rose against a stone wall.

I remember how my *compañero* smiled when we walked past such a rose.

I remember silences measured by footsteps on gravel.

I remember sharing a sweet orange and salty green olives.

I remember hearing my *compañero* alternate between flawless Spanish and English, and feeling envy at his doubled capacity for understanding the lives of others.

I remember another day of walking in step for hours and hours—almost twelve by day's end. I don't remember much of what we talked about. Things that mattered. Some trivia. He saw a snake. We sang a couple of little songs to each other. We laughed.

I remember the days when I walked alone on that road. There were more of those, because we both craved solitude, but when the road threw us together again, I recall the joy, and that inexplicable familiarity.

Mystifying, but pleasurable to contemplate when I stopped walking at 4 p.m. after nearly thirty kilometres and found that I was walking on the Via de la Plata and not the Francés!

I could sniff day's end on the other side of a glittering *embalse*. It was an even bigger dam than Proserpina's and had been seducing me with glimpses for over an hour. I'd stopped to photograph the sun reflected in its surface when my *amigo* caught up with me and insisted we make a 'peek-neek'.

We were on the shoulder of a highway, our bodies sweaty and our water supplies exhausted. I wanted to get to the *albergue*, get washed and get into the water for another swim. We had four kilometres of road walking on the N-630 before I could achieve that dream and the temperature was soaring.

My *amigo* insisted. Please. *Por favor*.

He saw me waver.

'*No eres egoísta, mi amiga?*' You're not selfish, my friend?

He had me on a technicality.

We clambered down a rubbish-strewn bank. There was no grassy knoll, no spreading willow, but he urged me to have faith. Sure enough, we found flat rocks in the shade of a small tree and clear, sweet-smelling dam water. Its scent was too strong for an over-heated pilgrim. I threw off all but my undies and into the water I plunged.

Yikes! A turtle. And oh my Lord, now a snake!

'*No pasa nada*,' my *amigo* called from the bank. '*Es muy pequeño*.'

It might have looked small from where he was, but to me it resembled the Loch Ness Monster. I swam in to shore, ostensibly to see what he was doing, but mostly to leave behind the *serpientes*.

Waiting for me was fresh sheep's milk cheese beside a hunk of crusty bread, almond cakes and fruit. A half bottle of *vino tinto* was cooling in the shallows. He had carried our peek-neek twenty kilometres in all that heat.

Icy water tickled our toes, hawks circled, turtles stuck out their necks to gawp, and a cluster of poppies lorded it over the pastel daisies around them. The world was sharp focus. Every blade of grass appeared individually etched.

My *amigo* reclined in the shade.

'*Bueno*,' he said. And it was.

Words sank to the dam's bottom, down to where Pluto lived. Proserpina's spring carpet stretched for miles. In the land of *duende*, silence ruled.

Eventually we moved, and eventually my need for speed resurfaced. I sprinted the final kilometres of sticky asphalt, stopping only to accept water from roadworkers who had seen my red cheeks coming. I flung myself under a shower, my clothes into an actual washing machine, and my heart into my journal, giving thanks for unearned rewards from my day.

At dinner that night we were eight: Canadian twin brothers, an erudite Berliner, an Oxbridge gent, and two Dutch lady veterans. The conversation was in English, leaving my *amigo* in need of translation for once.

Only the Canadians were walking all the way to Santiago. The others were travelling the *camino* in stages.

Because it's not difficult for Europeans to get to a starting point, walkers from neighbouring countries often tackle *caminos* over several seasons or even years. Some repeat sections. My *amigo* had walked for a week from Cádiz to Seville in early March. He then did some consulting work for his old firm before commencing the Via de la Plata in Seville in mid April. He planned to stop at Salamanca before completing the leg to Santiago in autumn, arriving on his brother's birthday in October.

Although the pilgrim numbers challenged me after the Mozárabe, they were still low. Most days, it was rare to meet more than a handful of others on the road. For anyone seeking company, it probably seemed a lonely trail, particularly if they'd enjoyed the stimulation of the pilgrim numbers along the Francés. My *amigo* had spoken of the party-*camino* he'd walked there. He would probably stay with me to Salamanca, I thought. Even reluctant company was better than none.

And in fairness, we were managing each other, learning each other. I was not the grumpy *peregrina* who had battled for space from *Herr T* without ever being truly honest with him about my needs. Neither was I the peaceful *peregrina* taking synchronised steps on the Francés with my *compañero*. My *amigo* was another teacher, I suspected, but I was yet to grasp his lesson. At least I was trying to be frank with him.

He was watching me. I had drifted away from the conversation at the table, forgetting to translate the peculiarities of English for him. He was momentarily stranded, without connection, and in his blue eyes I could see something that might have been fear.

Perhaps company was the thing that took his mind away from the loss of his brother. Maybe it was his solace in just the way that solitude was mine.

Salamanca was less than a week away.

Surely I could be in company until then, with grace.

18

MAKING SENSE

THE NEXT DAY'S PATH wound up and down hills, through lavender and *jara*, the heat intensifying their fragrances. The *jara* was particularly potent. It's a rock rose, with papery white petals, maroon spots at its base, and yellow stamens. I later learned they're something of a weed and that the perfume actually comes from the leaves. To me, they were the scent of spring in the Sierras, replacing the neroli of Andalucía.

We walked and talked steadily.

Conversation shifted from the personal to the global, as our attention went from roadside lavender to the hills of the horizon. We spoke of the imperative of learning to be alone before forging a relationship. He had been married as a very young man but had not been 'ready'. They met at university, both studying law, but when the financial world claimed him, they split. Different priorities. They were, he said, still friends. They just needed to walk different paths.

We talked about the *camino* itself. He said that his ex-wife would never have walked one with him. Too hard. I heard myself saying, or trying to say, that *camino* is not hard, but rather, life is hard. *Vida real. Vida casera.* Real life. Home life. He looked perplexed, saying this was hard, this was hot, exhausting and lacked comfort.

For me, I said, *camino* is easier than real life because it's possible to be anyone you like on the road. You are the story you tell people.

I knew nothing of him, really. He may never have been married. He may have been rich or poor. He may have been a psychopath. All I had was his story and my sense that it was true. Instinct and a few pieces of information.

Also, I said, because there is no prospect of a future with most *peregrinos*, there is nothing owed, nothing required. Not even truth, perhaps.

Home, on the other hand, is the real *camino*. To walk thirty kilometres is not as difficult as to stay with someone for another week, a month, a year, when the days are *normal*, when there is grief, illness or loss, or in the test of ongoing honesty. Keeping a *promesa* is the real *camino*.

As we puffed our way up a steep incline towards a pine forest, I tried to explain the promises that underpin my marriage: to encourage each other to expand; and to allow each other to have individual, sometimes separate, lives within the framework of union. I think I managed to explain that I'd never looked for my husband to make me feel complete, because I don't believe we can ever be complete. We are works in progress. Pilgrims.

Finding a man who encouraged me to follow my own path was a gift. But it isn't easy. It's never easy to let the other go or to be left behind.

I struggled, inhaling hot *jara* and pine, to say that I believed pilgrimage to be selfish in both good and bad ways. It is for the self and it expands the self, but the only legitimate test is when we go home and discover how much *camino* lives on in us. *Camino* is not the big challenge because it is not forever. It can't be real. Or complete. *Verdad, auténtico* … true, authentic …

My *amigo* had listened, speaking only to help me find words, our feet in crunching synchronicity. I pondered what waited for me at home, in that real life. Family, friendships, commitment, routine, history.

Hard perhaps, but always beautiful.

Maybe that was why the *ancianos* asked if my *camino* was a *promesa*. They understood the importance of a pledge and the demands of it.

My *amigo*'s words wrenched me into the present.

'*Pero te quiero, amiga,*' he said. '*Para siempre.*'

But I love you, friend. For always.

Despite the body blow of the words, I managed to reply.

I said that we didn't know each other, that we were friends for today; that tomorrow might be different. I said that he was my teacher, instructing me how to be less selfish. He asked what I was teaching him.

'*No sé,*' I said. I don't know.

'You teach me about love,' he said. 'But love that is not easy.'

'*Estoy dura,*' I said. I am hard.

It was not right. We both knew it.

'*Soy difícil.*' I am difficult, I said, using the other version of 'I am'.

Spanish is tricky. They have two verbs that mean 'to be'. One is for permanent things like name and occupation, nationality and hair colour. The other is for temporal states. If I were to use the wrong verb, I could say that I am a cold person instead of that I am feeling cold. Initially, I had implied that I was being hard at that moment and then I'd said that I was always difficult.

Neither was what I meant.

Both were attempts to get around his use of the verb 'to love'. The Spanish say '*te quiero*', which can mean both 'I love you' and 'I want you'. I had no idea what my *amigo* meant, though I decided that 'for always' probably implied that he loved me, although in what way I couldn't be sure. Certainly, the notion of him desiring me for always seemed pretty far-fetched!

The silence stretched.

'*Es difícil.*' I said. It's difficult. Permanent use of the verb. Always difficult.

He said nothing, just walked ahead as I slowed to take in the fairytale meadow around me, emerald green and studded with *encinas*, where cows with flighty calves ambled through streaming golden light.

I'd meant that our conversation was difficult, but I'm not sure he understood.

To try to speak of feelings in a language not your own is thorny, but I was wrong in saying it was always difficult. Domingo had taught me that. Lucia had taught me, too. The language of the body can make the leap. Words create the problems. They're false friends.

Earlier, I'd had a baffling experience with language.

I was walking *sola* when I caught up to another loner.

'*Hola!*' I called.

'*Bonjour,*' he replied, grinning from under a battered straw hat.

Jean-Yves kept pace with me and we drifted into conversation in French. We chatted about pre-conceptions of nationalities (he said the French deserve their reputation for being well-pleased with themselves—after all, there is much to be pleased about!), colonialism, village life, industrialisation and the historical effect of the feminine on French political life.

We must have talked for half an hour.

He wanted to break for lunch, but my legs were still pumping so I bid him *au revoir*. It was only when I was down the road a way that I realised what had happened. I had not once struggled to find a word or asked how to say something or resorted to Franglais. We'd just talked, about things for which I didn't know I had a vocabulary.

What made that possible? I spoke the best French of my life, using vocabulary I'm convinced I'd never learned.

It was rather like the poems that surfaced, unbidden yet intact, when I walked alone. It was as if a parade of my nearest and dearest was striding towards me, confident I would recognise and welcome them.

The arrival of the poems and the French epiphany must have been side effects of walking. Perhaps hours of marking out beats with feet and walking poles triggered it, since poems are so linked to rhythm. Perhaps my brain was shaken up by the repeated footfall and all my under-used Gallic neurons fired. Perhaps it was just that my mind was not crammed with the usual day-to-day junk.

My *amigo* was waiting for me at a stream below the *pueblo* of Grimaldo. He watched me approach, his features unmoving, and I found myself clowning for him, dancing across stepping stones and pretending to fall in. When his smile re-appeared and he stepped across to join me, I was relieved. We strode uphill to the village through daisy-studded grass.

'You are happy to see me?' he asked.

Yes, yes, very happy.

'Then I am happy,' he said.

We installed ourselves in the cramped, overcrowded, sweat-smelling *albergue*, grimacing at the prospect of a night with the great unwashed.

Showered, laundered and late-lunched, we sat on a wall beside the bar for that moment of pause. What to do? The stream where we'd reconnected was about a kilometre below the village. The day was still hot. Water called.

We gathered his sleeping mat and my sarong, journals, iPods and unguents, and wandered downhill through orchards in blossom. When we reached the stream, my *amigo* stood under one of the trees and shook a branch. White petals cascaded to the grass.

'Now we sit on flowers,' he said.

We spread ourselves under the tree. Water tinkled. Birds chir-ruped. The world exhaled. We swapped playlists, clicked photos of insects and clouds, and translated fragments of the Miguel Hernández poems I'd copied way back in Córdoba:

> *of blood in blood*
> *I come like the sea*
> *wave by wave ...*

They were like Haiku, scrawls on scraps of paper.

> *The vocation of seeing*
> *What else matters?*

My sister had texted me titles of U2 songs to sing. They were a poem in themselves:

Beautiful Day
The Ground Beneath Her Feet
In God's Country
Tryin' to Throw Your Arms Around the World

My *amigo* knew the songs, but the lyrics meant nothing to him, just as Anglos hear 'one-tonne banana' when someone sings *'Guantanamera'*. As I copied them into my journal, my *amigo* noticed the words my *compañero* had sent to me: *I will walk with you and sing your spirit home.*

He asked me to translate them. I said it was *difícil*, but in truth I didn't want to try to explain my *compañero*. I wasn't sure I could. He'd belonged to me long before he'd even mentioned acupuncture, but that belonging was never confused with desire. He was a restoration of something lost.

Perhaps my *amigo* had been trying to express a sentiment like that earlier. Had I demeaned his offering? The vagaries of language meant I would never know.

He lay on the grass, his eyes closed.

I looked at the birthmark on his cheek. In conversation, I tried not to let my eyes linger on it, not wanting to embarrass him by drawing attention to it. And yet it was the part of him I liked best. His obvious flaw.

Like my sinners, whose decision to expose their flaws made me admire them more. I even loved the sins themselves, sometimes. Yes, they gave pain. But they had also forced the sinners to try to better themselves. To expand.

Sins ignored might be ugly, but sins addressed can have such beauty, I wrote in my journal.

So where did that leave my sins? My pride? My selfishness?

My *amigo* seemed to want nothing more than to walk and laugh with me. To love me, in his way. My first instinct had been to bat away his offering, to deflect and reduce it.

'*Estoy dura*,' I had said.

Was I hard? *Herr T* might say so.

I looked at the words I'd copied in the *salon de thé* in Córdoba: *Love is my creed and my faith.*

If I really wanted to live that, then perhaps I had to allow others to feel about me as they chose.

I headed for the creek, overcome with a need to get into the gush of water and wash away thoughts. I stripped down to knickers and T-shirt and tiptoed across the stepping stones until I was mid-stream, where I lowered myself into the torrent, letting icy prickles of water pound my flesh.

My *amigo* clicked photos and one shows me, back arched, hair almost touching the water's surface, with a grin wider than Andalucía.

Grimaldo.

Tiny *pueblo*. Bubbling stream. Endless sky. Happiness diluted to essence.

When I dried off, I picked up my journal. This poem, torn from a magazine in the Melbourne airport four weeks earlier, fell onto my feet.

Out beyond ideas of wrongdoing and rightdoing,
there is a field. I'll meet you there.
When the soul lies down in that grass
the world is too full to talk about.
Ideas, language, even the phrase each other
doesn't make any sense.
— Rumi

19

A SWAG OF SINS

THE ROAD WILL NEVER swallow you ...

I whispered those words as my *amigo* and I crept out of Grimaldo under an orange moon that would have made the owl and pussycat pirouette for joy. He repeated them as the moon dropped, twisting his tongue to cope with the difficulty of 'swallow'.

The quote is from Ben Okri's book *The Famished Road*, which was given to me by a stage manager when we were travelling with a play through rural Australia. As light flooded the Extremadura sky, my *amigo* asked what it had been like to be an actor. I told him that sometimes, particularly when on tour, it was very like walking a *camino*.

Uprooted out of real life, days are geared around show time. No matter where you are, or how far you've travelled, in the late afternoon you head for the theatre, community centre or bingo hall that will host the show. You might do a warm-up, test the acoustics or just walk the stage to get the feel of it.

Eventually, you head backstage, where you find your colleagues. If you haven't travelled between towns that day, you might discuss what you did with your free hours and if you had news from home.

You prepare: make-up, hair, costume, inner life. Everyone has their own ritual, some based in practicality and some in superstitions. There's an order to the process. It might make no sense to anyone else but it's vital. The rest of the world is discarded as the performance approaches. No matter what the day might have thrown at you—early starts, dodgy motel rooms, long drives, oft-told stories, roadhouse food—there's energy, focus and commitment.

I told him that I sometimes saw pilgrims in our *camino* village as a group of touring players. There were well-known 'stars' like *il Capitano* and his *Soldato*. They left messages for me, scratched in dirt roads or scrawled in *albergue* guestbooks, and other pilgrims were quick to relay sightings of them.

There were rituals, too. The most irritating took place before sunrise, as earnest pilgrims crinkled multiple plastic bags and metal cleats in a rush to be first out the door. It's not a lie of any colour to note that the majority of these dawn raiders were German.

There were favoured costumes and talismans. On the *camino*, as in the theatre, these were often reminiscent of childhood—the miniature pilgrim teddy bear, like Yogi with a scallop shell.

There were stage managers, those who facilitated for us in the *albergues*. The yellow arrows gave directions and there was always an audience, often captive. But, I said, the main difference was that on the *camino* there was no script. We were improvising.

My *amigo* reminded me of the three-act structure of the Camino Francés, and said that distance-wise, I was now well into Act Two of this *camino*.

The cast grew every day. More and more pilgrims were starting out, while others travelled at different paces, overtaking or catching up. Each night there would be a new face or a reunion. We were forming into a company, with all the associated alliances, curiosities and differences.

My *amigo* said that he would like to play out Act Three with me. That he was sorry he had planned to walk into Santiago later in the year. That perhaps he should re-write his story.

We were standing on a cliff edge, suspended in sky. Hundreds of feet below us, a wide river curved around on itself. Hundreds of feet above, an eagle caught an updraft. We were dots at a swirling centre.

I said nothing. I no longer knew what I wanted.

The heat increased, both actual and metaphorical. I thrived with the higher temperatures, but struggled with the growing population on the road and the increasing emotional proximity of my *amigo*. I repeated my road maps:

> *Through hope, through difficult ways, you'll arrive to the stars.*
> *… What we feel is the wind in our face …*
> *… The road will never swallow you …*

I was careering between intense pleasure and guilt about the pleasure. For hours at a time I was just plain joy-filled: when heat, sky and road combined to let me fly; when my *amigo* made me laugh like a child; when sins would not come to mind, no matter how I tried to focus on them.

Then I would begin the flagellation, wondering what the hell I was doing pretending I was on some *camino* cruise—if 35-kilometre days in thirty-degree heat can be called cruising.

When the guilt struck, I shut down. That's when I would punish my *amigo*, something I only recognised as a sin when we stopped for lunch in the walled town of Galisteo.

The *pueblo* was in full *siesta* mode, shutters drawn and doors latched. As we prowled the silence in search of a café, I wondered what was going on behind the closed curtains: eating, talking, laughing, sleeping, making lunchtime love after all other needs of the body were satisfied.

At Bar Emigrantes, we ordered *bocadillos*, removed boots and sprawled in the shade. Pilgrims straggled in. Conversation drifted. Could we pass a message to the Polish couple? Had we met the pilgrim who was begging along the road? Did we see the Belgian in the taxi?

Already uncomfortable with what felt like gossip, I realised that some pilgrims assumed I was 'with' my *amigo*.

With. Sly little preposition.

I laughed along. 'No, no … *amigos* … just friends.'

But something shifted because, of course, such assumptions don't come from air. They'd observed the shared smiles and miles. Could they see my thoughts?

For the rest of that long, baking afternoon, I withdrew into myself.

'You are like Galisteo,' my *amigo* said, as I pounded along scorching tarmac.

I said nothing, thinking I'd misheard him.

'You have walls all around you.'

I stopped. Made him repeat what he'd said.

He was right. I'd built fortifications around myself, and they were there to keep me inside as much as to keep anyone from entering. I was afraid that, just as other sins had defeated me, so desire would triumph. I'd had to watch myself fall to pride, selfishness, lies, anger, even gluttony, if one could be gluttonous about time alone. Was lust next? Desire doesn't stop just because we make vows.

There was nothing to say except to apologise and try to normalise the day.

We walked and walked, past waymarkers and roadworks, off-track and on, and beside the carcass of a newborn calf, half-eaten by the vultures that wheeled over our heads. I tried to describe the concept of collective nouns.

A wake of vultures.

A murder of crows.

An unkindness of ravens.

In return, my *amigo* told me the Spanish word for swallow: *golondrina*. The music of it went some way to erasing the image of the bloody corpse with its staring marble eyes.

But even language couldn't lift me. I was a babbling infant surrounded by a sea of deep Spanish water, unable to describe my emotional whirlpool.

I mentioned a wish to see the Roman arch at Caparra at sunrise, so we kept walking, foolhardy distances, as my *amigo* did whatever it took to lighten the day. We were both gutted when we staggered into Oliva de Plasencia.

The *albergue* was modern, with a television, a sitting room, doona-covered bunks and white-tiled bathrooms. I completed my rituals and fled. In the town square, I spoke with a German pilgrim. Statuesque and cultured, she was journeying alone. A young man had begun walking with her just before Mérida and she said she didn't have the heart to ask him to leave her.

'That is the *camino*,' she said.

I'd said those same words to another German girl only days before, in a town whose name I couldn't recall because I was so angry with myself.

Over and over, lessons repeated.

'You are so stupid,' I mumbled as I roamed the streets of the *pueblo*. I felt in real danger of being swallowed by the road and the sins.

I took out my journal and read poems aloud, all the scraps of verse I'd gathered along the way. I wrote four pages of thanks, to remind myself of all I had, of all my good fortune.

My eyes kept returning to a sentence I'd translated and copied down in Aljucén, the first night on the Via de la Plata, sitting at the *albergue* kitchen table with my *amigo* at my elbow, cutting up the tuber:

Shadows exist because we have light to illuminate them.

I don't think my translation did justice to the original words, but the sentence resonated. I was caught in shadows, when I had so much good light available to me. Why? Because of insinuation and innuendo? Gossip?

Or because of the fear that there was truth in that gossip?

After an *albergue*-cooked dinner for which I had little appetite, I lay on my top bunk, stewing in my own juices.

I will walk off your sins.

What kind of lunatic promise was that?

Who did I think I was? A new saviour?

I looked down on my near-naked *amigo*, lying on his bunk in a shaft of light from the street-lamp outside the open window. His sleeping sheet was thrown back, exposing sinewy legs and an almost hairless chest. The coffee-coloured birthmark on his cheek drew my eye. He called it an *antojo*, which, he said, also means 'wish' or 'craving'. According to Spanish folklore, his mother must have had an unsatisfied desire when she was pregnant with him.

There was no one else in the upstairs dormitory. Outside, the village slept.

Perhaps I should just give in and satisfy my own desire. Why not? I was thousands of miles from home. My *amigo* was free. No one need ever know.

He rolled over, threw his right arm off the edge of the child-size bunk, arched his back and sighed, before settling into the dip in the centre of the mattress.

I could climb down the metal ladder, I thought, and curl my body against his. Flesh on flesh. Intimacy.

But it wasn't intimacy I wanted. I wasn't lonely. I didn't want conversation or even professions of love. And if I simply wanted an orgasm, I knew how to deliver that, up there in top-bunk seclusion.

But masturbation would blind me, if not damn my eternal soul. Wasn't that the last word on self-pleasure?

Hell. Fire. Brimstone.

I'd forgotten so much. All the important rules.

I surely didn't want perpetual damnation and I most certainly didn't want to be unfaithful, to walk to Santiago with a scarlet letter on my heart. Even if it wouldn't be visible to others, I would know, and I wouldn't be able to live with that knowledge.

I didn't want to be the lusty queen from the Mérida comedy, or to make of my husband a cuckolded king. I didn't want to be like the fornicating priest, having to walk pilgrimages to atone for my lascivious nature.

What on earth did I want, up there in the warm air near the ceiling, watching my dreaming *amigo*? I felt like a perv, a voyeur of his most private life.

A fine frown formed. He looked older.

Then he smiled. Scratched his face. And he was a child again.

The boy is ever present in the man, just as, conversely, the woman is visible in the girl.

Good.

Stay with that thought a while. Expand on the differences between the sexes. Anything to take the mind off the possibility of sliding onto his bunk and touching that dark mark of unsatisfied desire.

He smelled of lemons and amber. He always did, unlike the majority of pilgrims.

Pilgrims. We are pilgrims. Remember that. Pilgrims don't have sex. They are pure. They don't fantasise about the deadly sin of lust.

Oh, God!

Was the fantasy sinful?

Remember Will Shakespeare: … *thinking makes it so* …

Was I committing a sin merely by imagining my hands moving over his body?

I vaguely recalled words from the confessional: *In my thoughts, in my words and in my deeds* …

Thoughts were the first cab off the rank.

My teal-blue *mochila*, the sin-swag, slumped in the corner, emptied of iPod, guide book, sins, sleeping bag and toiletries.

The iPod was another cause for recrimination. All day I'd wondered if it was sinful to wear earplugs, pretending to listen to music, in order to avoid conversation. Was that a white lie?

My *amigo* murmured something unintelligible.

Were I to launch myself onto his olive-skinned muscularity, what of the lies I'd have to tell to cover my actions? Lies that would dwarf iPod dissembling.

Or worse. Tell the truth. Confess and give pain. Murder something good.

One sin leading to another. And another. I was drowning in sins.

Had I imagined I was immune to the urges of my body?

Why? Because I was the righteous sin-carrier? Or because I love someone, am committed to him? Marriage vows can't keep our bodies from trying to perform the function for which they're made, I told myself. Remember your words to *Herr T*: 'We have instincts, like animals.'

My *amigo* slept the sleep of the innocent, looking for all the world like an advertisement for designer underwear. With each second, my overheated mind transformed him further. He was a slumbering god, a potent lothario. I imagined him attending to every inch of my body, stroking my skin, kissing my neck, sliding down my belly—

He snored.

A brief walrus of an inhalation, followed by a rumbling exhale.

I peered down at him.

He was flat on his back, his mouth open, with one hand cupping his genitals through the sheet.

Another snore. A lengthy trumpet blast.

Desire fled the building.

Roncar. It even sounds like a turn-off.

My *amigo* was a pilgrim again, and I was freed to concentrate on the tightness in my calves and the righteousness in my soul.

Call it providence or what you will. The road had not swallowed me and I was sin-free for one more night.

Unless, of course, *thinking makes it so* ...

20

GRACIAS A LA VIDA

WATCHING A FULL, FAT, setting moon, I stood under a Roman triumphal arch in company with my *amigo, sin* sin. That moon had set over that arch for centuries. Sandalled feet, warrior's boots, tourist espadrilles and pilgrim soles had walked that path, carved by the might and power of Rome. Stories had been written and rewritten.

Palimpsesto on an unfathomable scale.

I celebrated my own triumph as we watched the sun rise over the mountains, two pilgrim friends without the complication of adulterous sex to spoil the view. We inhaled silence as the two celestial bodies saluted each other, then we found a machine dispensing coffee at the nearby visitor's centre.

That's progress for you.

A day begun in such wonder could slide downhill fast.

Not us. We rose.

We talked all the live-long day. Different rhythms and a few rhymes. Out past the arch, into the twenty-first century, onto a long stretch of treed *camino*, stopping at a bridge for snacks and silence, on down the lavender-lined road, under tutting storks and past two orange-shirted diggers constructing a dry-stone wall. Roman techniques lived on.

Up to the freeway, over stepping stones, through mud, under scorching sun, along walled lanes, past a big-eyed *burro* in need of a scratch, through Aldeanueva del Camino, into the mountains, and all the way to a bar in Baños de Montemayor, where we sat with iced drinks, staring at each other, open-mouthed and dizzy.

We had spoken of devotion—of faith in a God, and of faith in others. About our most precious memories: for him, the birth of a son, when he said he had matured into manhood. For me, the death of my mother, when I vowed to live, not exist. I was reminded of that vow with every death.

About regrets. For both of us, moments of *adulterio*, adultery. In his case, the affair was with his wife's closest friend.

That stopped me in my tracks. He had spoken of fidelity with such urgency, and yet when he'd lapsed it was a double betrayal. I could scarcely believe I was walking with someone whose situation exactly mirrored that of my sinner's. I wished with all my heart that her circumstances were altering and that she was healing.

I asked my *amigo* how he could have been so careless of his wife, the woman he loved. As he was answering, I remembered my fantasies of the night before. No casting stones.

He said he was a different man then.

Why not? We can change. But we live with the regrets.

He asked me to tell him the sins I carried, and I said I couldn't.

'But I don't know these people,' he said.

'I made a promise,' I said. *Una promesa.*

We walked on, picking fennel-tops to chew and wild rosemary to sniff.

He said there was something he had never told anyone, and proceeded to describe events from decades earlier. I listened, but could make no sense. His casual tone didn't fit the words I was translating. I asked him to repeat. Questioned him. Eight? Yes, eight. Every night? Yes, every night. I had to ask him to show me what he meant, my brain was so unwilling to process the story. Finally, watching the mime I'd requested, I could no longer deny what I was hearing. Under an electricity pylon, I sank to the ground.

A man of the cloth had forced his penis into the mouth of my *amigo*'s then eight-year-old brother. Night after night.

His brother told my *amigo* one evening after they had been watching their sons play football. Then he swore my *amigo* to secrecy in order to protect their parents. *Una promesa.* It was never spoken of again.

My *amigo* sat beside me. His citrus scent mixed with the aniseed of fennel. After a long time, he apologised for speaking of his 'sin', as he referred to it.

'*No es tu pecado*,' I said. It's not your sin.

'*Es mi secreto*.' It's my secret.

I pictured that little brother, grown to manhood, and his fears for his sons. I tried to imagine the story my *amigo* had invented for their parents, and for his brother's wife and children. I wondered about the weight of all those lies. Lies told to honour his brother's wishes and to protect those left behind. How could they be a sin?

What I remember most is the anger. Like a tsunami.

And I absolutely do not believe that anger was a sin.

How could I not feel angry with the Pope, the bishops, the cover-up, the refusal to take responsibility for those little people, grown large, blaming themselves in stifling silence? And for those who loved them and were helpless to ease the pain? Anger seems a fitting response when hope is killed. Surely the theft of innocence warrants rage? I thought of *Herr T*'s God who could foresee everything and I boiled.

'*Tranquilo*,' my *amigo* said. '*No te preocupes*.' Be calm. Don't fret.

It was hard to hold onto calm or rationality. Hard to find compassion or to remember that the perpetrator might have been a victim himself. Hard to have any of those thoughts in the face of my *amigo*'s loss, his confusion about his own culpability and the Church's intransigence. It was hard not to wish for vengeance.

Distant thunder broke the silence.

My *amigo* held out a hand to help me up with my pack.

'*Vámanos*,' he said. Let's go.

No wonder we sat at the side of the road in Baños de Montemayor, nursing lemon drinks and staring into space.

That's how *il Capitano* found us.

There was laughing, kissing of cheeks, waving of hands, talking at full throttle, planning, directing, arranging. Within moments we had accommodation, dinner plans and an itinerary for the coming days.

Seeing *il Soldato* again, pieces of my fragmented internal jigsaw fell into place. He was like the Arch of Caparra. He allowed us all to fuss around him while he remained unruffled by life, or by pilgrims. He nodded when he first saw me, held my hand and touched my cheek. It was like a benediction.

Then Barcelona called, Leonardo and Ricardo completing my family. I crumpled.

Leonardo was instantly solicitous, volunteering to come, to help, to fix. I couldn't make him understand that it was relief and gratitude; that in the face of cruelty and sin, they were my daily reminder that love and compassion existed; that the teachings of prophets and poets, all the writings that urge love and unity, can be embodied in the actions of human beings; that he and Ricardo, two gay men in a relationship the Church would not acknowledge, seemed more Christ-like than many clerics.

Goodness is not pious. It is practical.

A Caravaggio painting came to mind, one I'd always wanted to see. *The Seven Works of Mercy.*

In it, a woman undertakes two of the Works, feeding the hungry and visiting a captive, by thrusting an exposed breast through the bars of a cell so a prisoner may drink. To some, it could appear a lewd or provocative action.

Not so. It's a woman grounded in reality, doing what she can to be useful.

Life is complicated. Angels do what is necessary.

A hermitage perched at the top of a hill in the centre of Baños. My *amigo* and I sat there in the early evening, watching columns of cloud progress around the surrounding mountains. Chestnut flowers drooped over our shoulders. We drooped under them. I asked him his deepest wish.

'*Paz,*' he said. Peace. For himself, he meant. Internal peace. Not for the world. Though that would be nice, but probably impossible.

He asked me.

'To continue to want nothing,' I said. 'As I do now.'

He asked if he could write a favourite poem in my journal. Written by Antonio Machado, it is also the lyric to a famous song, '*Caminante, no hay camino*'

> ... *Traveller, there is no road.*
> *The road is made by walking ...*
> *And turning, you look back at a road you will never tread*
>   *again ...*

The sky and the earth spoke to each other in hushed tones. A wagging dog barked at us, rightly possessive of his corner of paradise. The scent of spring blossom mixed with the smell of dry grass and manure. It was a slow night. Slow, slow, in that square above Baños.

And as lovely as any place I could recall anywhere.

Places are subjective. That's never more obvious than on the *camino*. One person will say they stayed in the most picturesque *pueblo* on the road and another will say it was a hovel. One person's Parador is another's Mouldy Flea. For me, Baños was heaven.

Clouds continued to rise like purified volcanic ash into the blue. I'd heard nothing more of the Icelandic eruptions, or Poland, or the financial crisis. A week had passed since I'd communicated with my sinners and supporters. I was glad Salamanca was on the horizon. Sin-fatigue was cutting deep. I was no longer sure who owned the *pecados* in my swag. My distance from them decreased with every kilometre I walked. I was capable of all of them.

Dinner was a rowdy affair. *Il Capitano* gathered people to him, and there were more and more pilgrims to gather. We were a dozen at table and everyone had a tale of another traveller who was ahead or behind, sending a message or receiving one. Notes were compared on towns, bars and guidebooks. I was glad when conversation rippled away in

German, Czech or Dutch. It gave me an excuse for silence. Perhaps a crowd was not such a bad thing. I could lose myself in it, walk away from it, slip ahead or behind, be alone, and no one would notice.

The next morning, I breakfasted with my *amigo*, but we walked apart for much of the thirty-plus kilometres. We were about to enter Castilla y Léon, the largest of the seventeen autonomous communities that make up Spain. It is their language, Castilian Spanish, that is the official language of Spain, though the Basques, Galicians and Catalans might rail at it. I'd traversed the northern section of Castile on the *meseta* of the Camino Francés, and was now crossing its southern border.

Another arrival. Another farewell. Extremadura's landscape and heat had sung to me. I was sad to be walking away from it.

But what walking.

As if to announce its importance, Castile turned it on. Under wisps of cloud, I climbed through walled lanes along the banks of the Río Cuerpo de Hombre—the Body of Man River—against a backdrop of snow-capped mountains. Cows, hidden in the woods, jangled their bells like a symphony from some secret orchestra. The sky was striped with jet streams, the ground soft underfoot. The scent from a sprig of wisteria in my hat carried me back to Rome. Each time I turned my head I inhaled the past. Present, past. Present, past. A time machine driven by perfume.

A thick-coated, erect-eared *burro* feasted on grass. Her owner said she was twenty-seven years old. She still had plenty of spring in her step.

A truck driver at the bar in La Calzada de Béjar offered me a lift.

'Venga, Rubia,' he said. Come on, Blondie.

What, go in a truck, when I can walk these lush paths? You're *loco*!

On, for another nine kilometres of winding roads, with fields of caramel cows on both sides. On, through Valverde de Valdelacasa— Green Valley of the Valley of the House!—with snow-capped mountains flanking me to the right. On, in the bliss of movement.

I was relieved, after the intensity of the previous day's conversations, to be alone and to let my *amigo* be *solo*, too. It was as though the intimacy had created a need for separation. We were making our ways to a *refugio* at Fuenterroble de Salvatierra, where *il Capitano* had promised to cook dinner. Italian pasta.

'Real pasta,' he said. 'Not this stuff that you all eat.'

I love nothing better than when someone prepares a meal for me.

My *compañero* had cooked for me on the Francés, after one of our chance encounters in the town of Hospital de Órbigo, where, in the fifteenth century, a knight is purported to have taken on all comers in hand-to-hand combat because he was thwarted in love.

Before we ate, my *compañero* had recited the words of his favourite song, *'Gracias a la Vida'*. It means 'Thank You to Life' and was written by the Chilean poet and artist Violeta Parra. Her death by suicide is inconceivable in the light of the lyrics, which are an anthem of gratitude to her body, her spirit, her friends, her lover, the physical world, the stars and the whole human race.

I had listened to my *compañero* whisper the words in the hiatus of evening's hush, under a timeless sky like that of childhood: *Gracias a la vida* …

Now, back on the Via, I was singing the song along the road towards my 'real' pasta dinner, when my *amigo* surprised me. He had stopped for a snack, and heard the song before he saw me. We sang it together, giving me a hit of *palimpsesto*. I was back on the Francés with my *compañero*, yet also present with my *amigo*. And *gracias a la vida*, thank you to life, his smile was back in place.

We sang past a tungsten mine, where a siren cut through the chorus.

We sang to a procession of jaunty *burros* being led to a *fiesta*.

We sang to the sky, our 'little thing beginning with C'.

We arrived restored, and an inscription greeted us at the door of the *refugio*: *I have given orders to my angels to guard thee on the way.*

On cue, Leonardo called!

That night, *il Capitano* triumphed. The pilgrim train was filling and the pilgrim hordes were filled with chilli pasta. Not to be outdone by Italian hospitality, Don Blas, the parish priest who ran the *refugio*, threw hunks of pork onto the open fire. They were set upon with gusto, though I can't report on them. I let others rip meat from bones in a mediaeval frenzy.

I was surrounded by good men and true.

To my right, *il Capitano*, bursting with delight at having fed the multitude on proper pasta.

To my left, Giovanni, another road-savvy Italian who spoke of the importance of maintaining personal boundaries while remaining available to others, as he topped wine glasses and cleared pilgrim plates.

Opposite me sat an Australian. Tall, fluent in Spanish, and with a slow-burn grin, Paul was the boss of the tungsten mine. He was staying the night in the *refugio* and walking to Salamanca the next day, to get a feel for the pilgrim road that circuited his mine.

A nomad with two-day growth and a Billabong T-shirt, he was irreverent, droll and quick-witted. His sleepy eyes missed nothing and his Aussie twang was music. I detected traces of it in his Spanish and liked the combination. We had spoken for barely ten minutes when he offered me a room in Salamanca, so I could wind down outside the pilgrim world.

My *amigo* flirted, laughed and told stories, the Italian contingent played beneficent hosts, and Don Blas opened bottles of lethal spirits to warm the communal cockles. It was a *fiesta*. *Gracias a la vida!*

The sleep that followed was deep, but was broken at 4 a.m. by the raucous rustling of plastic. Po-faced pilgrims, who had ostentatiously shushed us when we'd arrived the previous afternoon, were making their exit a retaliation: re-packing *mochilas*, stomping boots and waving torches. I drew my sleeping bag over my head and reined in thoughts of bloody vengeance as I re-closed my eyes.

Seven hours later, I was twelve kilometres down the road in company with my *amigo*, my Aussie and my Italians. We drifted in and out of pairs, trios and solos, talking of minerals and mushrooms, puppies and black pigs. The sniff of an approaching city and of stage's end spurred us on.

Somewhere, under the direction of *il Capitano*, we diverted from the main *camino*, and by late afternoon we were the only *peregrinos* in the picture-pretty but deserted *pueblo* of Morille, nineteen kilometres from Salamanca. The *sello* in my passport is from El Bar de Isa, where we stopped for beer and a breather. It shows a busty, long-haired beauty in profile—presumably Isabel, the patron, who was alone save for a near-comatose man in the corner.

Paul removed his boots to reveal blisters. Serious blisters.

He had covered over forty kilometres, much of it on dreaded *carretera*, having lost the trail at one point and been forced to backtrack. There was no way he could press on for three hours to Salamanca. His feet would be raw.

Paul didn't strike me as a man who liked to be beaten by a physical challenge, but it was clear that overnighting at the Morille *albergue* was not going to magically heal his feet so he could walk the next day. He called a friend to come and collect him.

The Italians walked on. My septuagenarians were not going to let nineteen kilometres stand between them and a restaurant.

My *amigo* was torn: to walk on immediately, to stay in Morille and finish the next day, or to come in Paul's car. He asked what I thought. Knowing the weight he was carrying, I felt he should complete the Salamanca stage *solo*. He nodded but I'm not sure he was convinced.

Paul's car arrived. That decided it for me. I would get out of the way.

I piled my *mochila* into the boot, hugged my *amigo*, and said I'd see him for a drink when he arrived.

Paul was an unlikely angel, and while he could never be accused of being sanctimonious, I thought him good. In a practical way.

The road had sharpened my instincts. He proved a generous host who let me find my own place in his modern white apartment. We talked about home, away, and everywhere in between.

And I was in Salamanca.

Renowned for architectural beauty, scholarship and a *fiesta* mindset, it had to party without me that night. I was happy to sit on Paul's couch, rub all four of our feet and sip sparkling Cava.

An indulgence of another kind.

INTERVAL

21

SALAMANCA

TURNING BACK THE HIGH-thread-count sheets of the queen-sized bed in my loft room in Paul's apartment, I remembered my sinner's warning about 'the seduction of easefulness'. I gave in to that seduction the minute my head touched the pillow in its pristine cotton casing.

I dreamed of walking.

I was with my *compañero* in pre-dawn darkness. A pale path reflected the light of the stars up at us as we surfed the air's temperature changes. It was like being in the ocean when you are unexpectedly bathed by a warm current, simultaneously luxurious and unsettling. We chased warmth to the centre of the road then followed it to the edge, trailing it back, forth, here, there.

I woke.

A field of stars dotted the square glass skylight above me. I wondered where my *compañero* would be now. He would have been glad I was remembering. The word 'remember' was a favourite of his. 'Re'— as in 'do again, repeat'. And 'member'—as in 'pieces, parts'.

'It's all we get,' he said. 'Just parts that we put together again.'

He taught me to love the word *igualmente*—equally.

'*Buen camino*,' a pilgrim would call to him.

'*Igualmente*,' he would call back, waving.

Equality, the wish for the world to be *igual*, was and is his personal quest.

193

Hermoso was my word, he said. Everything I saw was beautiful. My *amigo* made the same observation. Maybe I just needed more Spanish vocab!

My *amigo* taught me '*no pasa nada*'. Doesn't matter. It's not important.

He said it constantly. It became a joke between us. But maybe it was his motif for a reason; how else to live with such memories?

In the night, in my spotless room, I thought about his brother.

Abuse. It's just another word, after all.

Until someone tells you a direct experience. Then abuse becomes a racing heart and a cold sweat, as you taste the panic of a child, terrified of suffocating because his mouth is filled with an adult penis.

No pasa nada.

No wonder my *amigo* repeated the phrase.

I rolled over. The sheets smelled like lemons.

I woke late.

It was *fin de semana*. Weekend.

Camino, like my working life, doesn't always acknowledge the idea of a week ending. Days roll along and sometimes it's hard to remember which is which in the rhythm of the road.

Paul was on his computer, researching walking, perhaps to ease the sting of his blisters. He told me the greatest walker of all time was Robert Barclay Allardice, known as 'the celebrated pedestrian'. In 1809, in his most famous exploit, he walked a thousand miles in a thousand hours—one mile every hour for a thousand hours. Without Merrell hiking boots. As I tended Paul's feet, I gave thanks again to my boots and my New Zealand wool socks for my blister-free state.

And I gave thanks to Paul for my palace of dreams.

For a pilgrim, it was paradise. As was his company. He could produce a good story on call but never flaunted his knowledge or his travels. He reminded me that Australians are particular. I forget that when I see how much British tradition we have retained or how much of the American dream we have appropriated. Being with Paul, I saw the ironic, laconic Aussie humour and laid-back approach to life. He worked long hours in a testing job, yet retained a deceptive looseness.

No pasa nada. No worries, even as I sewed through his blisters to release liquid. I dabbed them with ti-tree and lavender oils, reassuring him this was not new-age mumbo-jumbo because lavender was used as an antiseptic in the trenches of World War I.

I opened my inbox to read stories from home:

People had walked with me on Anzac Day to the Aya Sofia in Istanbul, by the river in Perth, on trails in California and around the Manly Dam in Sydney. In Melbourne, they had walked with returned soldiers at the Shrine of Remembrance. They wrote of lessons they had been taught by their bodies, of transcending pain, of the pleasure of toil and the joy of silence.

I was learning a reverse lesson, I replied. The Via de la Plata has people on it. Strange creatures. Walking thirty-five kilometres in a day is nothing compared to negotiating with another human being.

Sinners reported in.

My 'adulterer' wrote that she was taking each step with me, *clinging on to the strap of your pack*. She wrote of the *insupportable loss* of friendship that had resulted from her actions, and that *self-forgiveness seems to be impossible*. She saw the walk as a co-creation and was working hard to keep up her mileage.

My sinner who had wrestled with anger at her parents told me she read one of my emails to her mother, and they cried together. *I think often of the fact that you're walking with my 'sin' and it reminds me to pay attention to myself, to take deep breaths—and just enjoy, for crying out loud!!*

Another spoke of seeing the walk as a chance to transform *poison to medicine*—a phrase from her Buddhist teachings. She wished me breezes on hot days. *They are the reaping of good karma*, she wrote.

I was relieved to hear from my procrastinator, who sounded tip-top: *I have been shedding and shredding 'marvellous much'*. Another hiked around Port Phillip Bay, her twenty-five kilometres an antidote to selfishness.

My brother told me he needed no crying on his behalf. He'd actually had a moment of feeling happy. It both scared and relieved him.

My husband wrote from our base camp that *all is well*. Three perfect words, when strung together followed by his signature.

I could have stayed all day on Paul's couch, pretending it was a normal weekend with my village just around the corner. Email gives that sense.

But Salamanca called. And breakfast.

I'd arranged to meet my Italians for coffee, so Paul and I strolled through mild morning sun into the sandstone centre of the old town. Architectural marvels lined the route, one after another, more ornate, more whimsical, more imposing.

Hermoso, hermosa, hermoso, hermosa …

She walks in beauty, all right!

Guidebooks can't prepare you for Salamanca's Plaza Mayor. It may be the most beautiful in Europe with its regal proportions, its stone, the carving, the shady arcades, the way the sky appears to incline towards it, helpless to resist.

It announces itself to you and beguiles you, simultaneously.

Could citizens ever grow accustomed to such loveliness?

Salamanca's nickname is *La Ciudad Dorada*—the Golden City. The sandstone of its buildings came from one particular quarry and the colour is ravishing. Of course it is a World Heritage city. No argument there.

Standing smack in the centre of the *plaza* were *il Capitano* and *il Soldato*. They showed no ill effects from their 53-kilometre day and intended to walk that afternoon to the next *pueblo*. It was only seventeen kilometres. Hardly worth loading the pack! They would be a day ahead of me, so it was unlikely our paths would cross again before Santiago, given their centurion pace and stamina.

Paul took us on a tour. Salamanca's university is Spain's oldest, founded in 1218. On the elaborate stone entrance portico, dominated by my old friends the Catholic kings, a tiny frog is carved into one of the panels. They say that if you locate him, you'll have good fortune and marry within a year. *Il Capitano*, a lifelong bachelor, said that didn't sound like luck to him! The frog, squatting on a skull high on the left side, didn't look amused.

Il Soldato was very taken with the Casa de las Conchas—the House of Shells. Dating from the 1500s, it was built by a knight of the Santiago order and its sandstone walls are studded with pilgrim shells. I photographed my knights there, before they went on their way, promising to text me, to leave messages, and to find me, their *libellula*.

'*Libellula?*' Paul asked, as we watched them disappear into the crowds.

'Dragonfly,' I said. 'It's what they call me.'

And they were gone. Just like that.

Paul took me for recovery by *tapas*!

I hadn't understood that you don't buy *tapas*. Rather, you buy a drink and are given a *tapa* to go with it.

Salamanca had some of the most elaborate *tapas* I ever saw, arrayed like jewels along sparkling glass counters. And variety? If choice is the great indicator of privilege, Salamanca is the lucky city. I wanted to photograph every bar, every morsel.

Around the Plaza Mayor, carved stone medallions adorned pillars: kings, dignitaries and heroes. One depicted General Franco. Someone had climbed up and drawn a Hitler moustache above his lip. He glowered at us.

Maybe a student had done it. They were everywhere, arm in arm, in groups, lolling in sunshine and cruising the bars. They come from all over Spain, because the university's reputation is high; and they come from all over the world, because Salamanca specialises in teaching the Spanish language. The city is enlivened by their vivacity, their curiosity and their beauty. The high-octane enthusiasm is infectious.

Salamanca had seen its share of upheaval and ugliness. The Inquisition and Franco both feature in its history, and the wealth and majesty of many of its buildings bear out a sense of entitlement and conservatism. To walk those streets now, among faces from all countries and bloodlines, it's hard to imagine the fear and bigotry that hid behind celebrations of the 'Spanish race' during the Civil War. The place is all light and bustling energy.

Salamanca was the third city I'd seen in Castilla y Léon, after Burgos and Léon on the Camino Francés. What a province, to produce three such magnificent examples of civic style.

It was Mother's Day. *El día de las Madres.*

Families feasted into the afternoon. *Madres* marvelled, as did we, in the Casa Lis, the Museum of Art Nouveau and Art Deco, and they kneeled in silence, as did we, in the airy interior of San Esteban's church.

Paul and I separated. I had pilgrim provisions to source in the commercial centre. I still hadn't fathomed Spain's shopping and eating hours, but I was grateful for the anomaly of Sunday retail in their Catholic culture.

Rather like legalised gay marriage. Spain, in spite of its Catholicism, recognises same-sex marriage as a fundamental human right. Their post-Franco culture constantly surprised me.

The twelfth-century, 'old' cathedral held more wonders, not the least of which was the climb over its towers. Up there among the sky and turret-tops, I looked back to the southern mountains. I was seven hundred kilometres from my starting point in Granada. I was simultaneously atop a cathedral and in nature. I was no wiser about faith, but I had given myself fully to the quest.

I met my *amigo* in the modern part of town.

In a city, in a restaurant with a starched tablecloth, with him in a new collared shirt, we were tentative, sipping cauliflower and almond soup with a local white wine. He gave me a perfect gift: words on a page. It was a card inscribed with the Spanish version of a prayer to St Teresa. It's a more formal version of '*no pasa nada*':

Nada te turbe
Nada te espante,
todo se pasa …

May nothing disturb you
May nothing astonish you.
Everything passes.
God does not go away.
Patience can attain anything.
He who has God within
Does not lack anything
God is enough.

We raised a glass to our journey. We had travelled almost three hundred kilometres together, on and off, and emerged as *amigos*. We wished each other *buen camino*, hugged, and said *adiós*. Goodbye.

The afternoon light was fading. Looking at his card, I was reminded to make one more prayer to the little thing starting with C: 'Please let nothing disturb him.'

A Salamanca matron in a camel coat nodded as I passed. More mad pilgrims, she was probably thinking. But she smiled, and murmured, *'Buen camino.'*

I had tired feet from cobblestone-walking and a tired heart from *amigo*-talking. When I looked at him now, I saw his smile as a mask and worried for his future. It wasn't just the financial crisis that had changed his life. His brother's secret was making demands on him and I'm not sure anyone could help him. I certainly couldn't do any of his crying for him.

Perhaps it was better to know him fully, but I wished I could still have believed him to be footloose and fancy-free. Something had been taken when he told me his story.

Abuse does that.

Anger does it too. It steals peace.

'But anger isn't all bad,' I said, and an elderly gentleman doffed his hat.

I had to watch my habit of voicing my thoughts in cities.

As I strolled to the Plaza Mayor to meet Paul, I grappled with the 'sin' of anger. Maybe it was time to look at it again.

'Anger reminds us that we care,' I whispered into the startled eyes of a Spanish bombshell in stilettos and tight jeans.

Change rarely occurs until there has been a bit of anger. Anger at the way things are. Anger at apathy. Anger at lack of compassion. And isn't the release of anger beneficial for psychological health?

I wondered how my *amigo* had arrived at such seeming calm. Was it faith? Therapy? Had he, somewhere, had a cathartic explosion of anger that had allowed him to wear that smile?

'I know,' I said, 'not all anger produces a useful outcome.'

But is that the fault of anger or of where we let it lead us? Shouldn't we learn to monitor our emotions? To recognise when they are leading us somewhere dangerous?

'It's about balance,' I said, as though I had stumbled on a cure for cancer.

An old man shook his head and backed inside his café door.

Some Buddhists say that evil is on the way to being good. I decided anger is on the way to change, and where we direct our anger tells us what kind of change will occur. Productive or damaging.

I was early into the *plaza*. I'd raced across town, leaving a trail of perplexed Salamancans in my wake. Cities are risky for pilgrims. All that sensory stimulation and all those people can overcharge the batteries. I sat on a bench in the centre of the *plaza* and exhaled.

Paul arrived and we watched the sky turn from deep turquoise to indigo to midnight blue. Gold lights came on in the square.

'Aaahh,' the gathered citizens sighed, applauding. As nightly rituals go, it's a beauty. Open-air theatre, played out to a guaranteed full house of appreciative patrons.

We wandered back to his place, drifting in and out of conversation. I was happy to be quiet with him, to laugh with him, to debate with him.

'Stay as long as you like,' he said. 'It's fine with me.'

It was tempting. A second rest day in that civilised city, in Paul's refuge, could be just what the pilgrim doctor ordered.

We said good night. Not goodbye.

ACT THREE

22

INTO THE WIND

I FAREWELLED PAUL JUST after dawn as he left for the mine. Waving him off from his apartment was unsettling. It felt domestic. Like a home.

I washed my clothes and hung them in the drying room. I wrote postcards, tended my feet and monitored the sky.

And I sat.

I couldn't go out because my trousers were damp.

I didn't strip the sheets from the bed, just in case.

Stay or go? Rest or walk? Resident tourist or itinerant pilgrim?

In the preceding days, I'd barely looked at my guidebook, letting others make decisions about roads, *albergues* and cafés. On the white sofa in Paul's white room, I scanned it. The directions were a foreign language.

Clouds rolled in. My clothes wouldn't dry. I had cold feet.

Stay or go? After seven hundred kilometres, why couldn't I decide?

Miedo. Fear.

It all seemed huge. Impossible. Exactly as it had after Sue's funeral, before leaving Australia.

Surely comfort wasn't leeching my courage?

That got me off the couch. I would not fall prey to softness. If I was going to be afraid, let me at least be staring into the eyes of a monster. I dressed in clammy clothes and shoved the rest of my near-dry belongings into the *mochila*. The first town was only seventeen kilometres away, after all.

Paso a paso. Step by step.

Into the wind. Into the cold. Into the fear.

I missed luxury the minute I dropped the key through the locked door. I missed Paul's humour. I missed my way. I missed my rhythm, which fled as the wind pushed against me, insisting I had made the wrong decision.

I missed my *amigo*.

Contrary creature! Now I had the solitude I'd wanted, I was sulking. The way was all mine—just me, the pea-green fields, a yellow arrow and the sky. Walk on, pilgrim. Thy will be done!

The road led on forever: straight, white gravel to the far horizon. I stopped and looked back. There was a city there. Just out of sight. I looked down. No shadow. Time held her breath.

'I'm no mirage,' I whispered. I took a step and looked back.

My footprint was clear in the gravel, its pattern a found friend.

I stepped again. The wind picked up, and so did I.

I walked.

Paso a paso. Step by step. That's how I got to Calzada de Valdunciel, a tumbleweed town, shuttered early, with not a soul to be seen.

After three attempts to find the *albergue* I located Carmen, who had the key. She opened the door to an eight-bed dorm, a sitting room, two showers, a kitchen, a place to hang clothes and a courtyard to corral the horses of riding pilgrims. A guestbook held a message for me from the Italians and an entry from two other Australians. I'd seen their names in previous books and hoped to catch them. A week earlier they'd been five days ahead of me; now it was only two.

When arthritic José arrived to collect my payment—a princely three euros!—we exchanged blonde jokes. He gave me a *sello* depicting a pilgrim shell and staff, then escorted me to the supermarket. Proffering his arm as though I was his *chica* and we were off to a dance, he showed me the modern sculpture of shiny windmills, the exterior of the locked church, and the library where the *niños* gathered to play on the internet. He told me I must have *vino* with dinner to keep warm. There was snow in the north of Spain along the Francés, and we were getting the full blast of the winds. He directed me to the best apples, complimenting me on my Spanish, my courage and my *alegría*.

And I was happy. Just like that. Dread to delight in seventeen kilometres.

Two German women arrived, Eva and Heike. It was their first day, after walking from Seville to Salamanca the previous year. Because I have no German and Heike had no English, we relied on Eva for connection.

She was sixty-two, with the vivacity of a teenager. Heike was perhaps twenty years younger and a foot taller. She was lean and blonde, where Eva was round, dark and constantly on the lookout for mischief. I was smitten by them and by the intimacy of their friendship. We had a night of graphic mime, laughter and toasty warmth. I was grateful I'd made it back onto the path, but my heart went out to the snowbound pilgrims in the Pyrenees beginning their first act. My sleeping bag was a cosy burrow.

Bring on Act Three.

The next morning was freezing. Literally.

Ana Balen Rey, the blonde weathergirl I'd seen on TV in every bar, told me over breakfast that today would be fine, fine, fine. And icy, icy, icy.

It was a twenty-kilometre uninterrupted haul to the next *pueblo* so I indulged in a second coffee before leaving the *Fräuleins*.

The wind was adamant I should not move. Head down in weatherproofs, with a hood and scarf around my head, I marched beside a four-lane highway, sloshing through mud on the service road and huddling in tunnels for warmth.

Scurrying past a penitentiary where a concrete tower loomed over a yellow-walled compound, I wondered if anyone inside had been given the option of walking the *camino* instead of serving time. Called Topas, the penitentiary was rated maximum security, for the toughest of the tough, and yet a monk from the Buddhist Liberation Prison Project taught meditation to its inmates. Surely *Herr T* would have admired that as faith in action, even if he doubted what it could achieve.

Remembering *Herr T*, the words of the Our Father came to me, as though for the first time. *Lead us not into temptation.*

Now, why pray that? Why would a father want to lead his children into temptation? And what did the words imply about the way the faithful viewed their 'father'? The Spanish version of the prayer asks that the *padre* does not allow the faithful *to fall into temptation*. It may only be a small linguistic difference, but it points towards a father who is protective rather than manipulative. Interestingly, their version of the prayer uses the word *ofensas* rather than *pecados*. Offences. Not sins.

Offence seemed to me a more practical word. We usually sense when we have given offence, or offended.

Pilgrim cyclists raced along the highway, shouting to each other over wind and trucks, shouting to me and waving; a blur of high-spirited, fluoro Lycra. Many walking pilgrims saw them as cheats or annoyances, not real *peregrinos*, but I enjoyed them. Most were Spaniards, which might have explained their tendency to travel in packs and party up a storm.

Wind battered my plastic layers. This was no breeze, no ripening of good karma. It was a full-force oppositional gale, but it energised me. I wondered if I function better with something to push against. Maybe an equal and opposite force makes me dig in, determined to vanquish it.

Pride?

My hands could barely uncurl from my walking poles when I made it to the bar at El Cubo de la Tierra del Vino. Twenty kilometres of snowy blasts had frozen me. I opened the door to be met by a warm, smoky fug. Card players sucked on cigarettes, their faces masks of neutrality. Cyclists fronted the bar in their riding slippers. They erupted when I removed my hood.

'*Hola, Rubia!*'

I was the only woman in the place.

'*Hola, hombres!*' I called, seating myself at a table in a far corner. I peeled off layers, ordered pots of tea and waited for warmth to seep into me. One by one, gentlemen of the village limped or sauntered over to exchange stories. They told me that many years ago, the phylloxera had killed their grapes but they were recovering. Days were not so bad. *Sola?* Surely not. *Australiana?* They'd seen two other *canguros*, only days ago. They said I was *valiente*.

No courage had been needed to move me through the landscape that morning. I had my own road, even if it was noisy and the elements taunted me. I had space and time. I was both selfish and self-ish. Pilgrim-ish. Getting back on form. A good reason to keep walking. The next *pueblo* was another fourteen kilometres, but even with the wind it felt do-able after my rest day.

Leaving, I spied the first of a series of terracotta marker plinths, erected by the Friends of the Camino from Zamora, the next major town. Each gave a snippet of history and reflected on the pilgrim journey. El Cubo's said that Hannibal visited with his elephants in 220BC. I pictured the parade of pachyderms and the Carthaginian conqueror.

Was there anyone who had not tried to take Spain?

My first few kilometres ran along a small-gauge railway line, through scrubby growth and past discarded sofas. The vines nearby were scraggly and stunted. The recovery I'd heard of was not apparent.

Then a turn and a hill.

Open country. Wide open. A shaggy brown pony trotted up. I ate an apple and gave him the core. His mane and tail streamed in the icy blasts as he nuzzled my palm and walked with me a while, a moving windbreak.

Cresting the next hill made the whole morning worthwhile. Sprawling to eternity were fields of brown, green and yellow. I clicked photos, my fingers like ice, and as I was replacing my camera in its holster I experienced an odd *palimpsesto* shiver.

My vantage point gave a mirror image of a vista I remembered from the *meseta* of the Camino Francés. In both places I was at the top of a hill, with a road before me winding east then west then east.

The difference in palette was stark. The Francés shots are golden, while the Mozárabe *meseta* was in its springtime show-coat.

I was looking across the valley of the Río Douro, a river that flows for almost nine hundred kilometres from its source in north-central Spain, carving a path through striated greens and ploughed red. It forms more than a hundred kilometres of the border with Portugal, before emptying into the sea at Porto. I would have stood and stared, burning the image of the valley into my mind's eye, but windchill made movement imperative.

The land rose and fell, and the *pueblo* of Villanueva de Campeán appeared and disappeared. Arriving at last, I walked the streets, trying to locate someone, anyone, who could open the door in the stone portico of the *albergue*. I could find not one of the inhabitants. Even the bar was shuttered against the cold. It was 4 p.m., usually a time when a couple of *ancianos* could be found nursing their spirits. On the marker plinth, I read Villanueva's message to pilgrims:

> *This town is an embrace of history … Walker, make of your life an embrace. In the embracing of history is tolerance. Tolerance is the peaceable fruit of love.*

I turned to find Isadora watching me.

She was short, dark of hair and complexion, and smiling. She had the keys to the *albergue*, and perhaps the entire town. Wind beat into our faces as we walked back up the main street, past her bar, where she said I could have dinner. She opened the *albergue* door and left me to it.

It was recently built, with shiny taps and all mod cons. In the kitchen, a guest book held a message from *il Capitano*, urging me to hurry up and catch them. I'd covered thirty-four kilometres against fierce wind. Although Zamora was just under twenty, there was no way I was pushing on, even for them. Besides, I had a ten-bed dormitory to myself. The mattresses were thick and firm, a primary-coloured blanket was folded on each, and plump pillows waited for me to choose where I would lay my head.

I laundered in steaming water and rubbed my back and feet. I arranged my nest with three blankets over my sleeping bag, two pillows for my head and another under my knees. I clicked a photo of myself grinning in the bathroom mirror. It was the third in a series that began in the Villaharta *polideportivo* before the storm and continued at the railway station in Campanario. Pilgrim bliss.

I rugged myself up in all my layers and scarves, took my journal and camera, and went out into the town.

And very quickly into the bar.

It was just after six. Way too early to eat, but way too glacial to explore. Isadora gave me a newspaper, turned on the TV, brought me a *vino tinto* and spicy olives, and left me to write. Outside, wind thrashed and the temperature plummeted. The olives took me back to the first day's walking out of Granada, the heat and the river crossing. Far, far away.

I thought how very good it was to be warm and safe.

I was the only pilgrim in the village. I had the bar to myself. I had the *albergue* to myself. And I had had the road to myself.

As Will Shakespeare wrote, *good in everything*.

On the television, a talk show wound itself up. Someone famous had deserted her husband for a younger man. She was *embarazada*, which I took to mean embarrassed but which, I discovered from Isadora, actually means pregnant!

Hands flapped and voices tumbled over each other as the commentators jockeyed to know the most or have the last word. There was *mucho* make-up for the women, gold jewellery for the men, and scandalised intakes of breath all round.

Gossip. That industry built on the travails of others.

Isadora appeared with food. She had fashioned a salad for me from every conceivable vegetable as well as the ubiquitous tuna. She had fried potatoes and spiced lentils. A pilgrim must have fuel.

I wondered about gluttony as I grazed. I was eating for Australia on the *camino*! Coffee and pastry at breakfast, a *bocadillo* at lunch, fruit between meals and usually two courses at night. And let's not forget the dried figs ... But I wasn't gaining weight.

The difference between fuelling and feasting is growing. Despite our 'great outdoors' reputation in Australia, the more we've learned about nutrition, heart disease and diabetes and their relationship to exercise and calories, the fatter we've got. In Spain, that seemed less of an issue. Yes, many people looked sleek and well fed, but I rarely saw the muffin-tops that are common at home. I re-read my sinner's meditation on apathy and food miles. Were Spaniards closer to their produce? I'd seen few fast-food chains in the cities.

News headlines cut in.

The ocean, slick with oil. Turtles and fish coated in oozing black. Angry men in fishing boats. Suited executives hiding their faces from cameras.

There had been a disaster of epic proportions in the Gulf of Mexico: an explosion at an oil well. I couldn't tell how long the black gold had been gushing into the sea but there were reports of people dying. I remembered that the Vatican's list of modern sins had included environmental pollution. Would they be taking to task the company responsible? The effects of this sin would last lifetimes. The screen showed pelicans flapping sticky black wings and dolphins unable to remove smears of toxicity. I pushed my plate away, all appetite gone.

Leonardo called, his timing always perfect. He and Ricardo had decided I must come to Barcelona after Santiago, so they could care for me. You will be tired. The world will be big and noisy. Our home is quiet, *tranquilo*. You can rest.

They'd given so much, but I didn't know them. I didn't know how it would be to be in their house. We were strangers. Constructions in each other's minds and hearts.

And yet ...

Another voice said, 'You know them. They've always been known.'

I couldn't imagine *camino*'s end. I slipped into my sleeping bag and arranged the pillow under my knees and the blankets above. It was still light outside.

O wind, a-blowing all day long.

I slept.
I woke to blackness and listened.

O wind that sings so loud a song.

I slept again.
I woke at six, before the roosters.
Silence. No wind.
Zamora, a town of nearly seventy thousand people, was only twenty kilometres away.

23

THE WALKING VILLAGE

SUN AND FROST. CROPS and cornflowers. Birdsong.

Spain's mornings are all chirrups and twitters compared to the vehement crow-squawks and magpie-chortles of home.

I breakfasted at a pensioners' club opposite the church in San Marcial, where the barman made me his first coffee of the day, hot and syrupy, with a gingerbread biscuit to dunk. Then I slid over kilometres like oil across water.

Approaching Zamora, I met a shepherd.

Who was I? Was I lost?

I showed him my guidebook, with its abbreviations: KSO, //, veer L, XR.

He scratched his stubbly chin, and shook his head.

'*Flechas amarillas*,' I said. Yellow arrows.

'*Ah! Peregrina!*' He removed a fingerless glove and pumped my hand.

'*Dónde está tu hombre?*' Where is your man?

I'm alone. Yes, I like it. No, not lonely.

He shook his head. '*Vaya con Dios, Rubia*,' he murmured. Go with God, Blondie.

Barely a hundred metres further, a ewe lay on her side, her guts spilled in the dirt. I turned, but the shepherd had moved on. Death was routine. Vultures would take care of her.

The Río Douro raced under Zamora's bridge as I crossed over towards sunwashed stone—now that's blonde! Mediaeval fortified walls, an uphill alley, a shaded square, a library, a *plaza*, a palace, a convent, a bench, a view, a promenade, another *plaza*, another bench. Zamora was made for strolling and sitting, and I'd made it in before midday.

Citizens carried bags from the library, where an exhibition featured advertising posters from the fifties and sixties, in a town that goes back to Roman times. Zamora's heyday was the twelfth century. It has more Romanesque churches than any other city in Europe.

It also had fruit stalls, a post office, and a phone box where I could use a phone card to try, repeatedly, to call my brother. Brett had emailed that he was going through old letters from Sue and 'doing it a bit tough'. A master of emotional understatement, that meant he was struggling, and I wanted to hear his voice even if he did crack hearty. There was no answer.

I rarely experience loneliness, but it claimed me there in Zamora's main square, as I fretted in case my brother needed some crying done.

My feet led me to the cathedral. It had a dome surrounded by smaller domes, towers and flags. It had galleries and a museum space. It had a *Santiago Peregrino* statue, colonnades and buttresses, but it didn't have anything to relieve the ache in my chest. I wandered to the eleventh-century castle, with its ramparts and walkways, crumbling walls and staircases. High in an open turret, as I looked out over the town's gold towers, a breeze took my anxiety and lifted it from my shoulders.

Brett would come through. He was doing what was necessary to heal. My melancholia was for myself, unable to do his crying. The true sorrow was for Brett to navigate. My job was to stay focused and press on for my sinners. To 'get on with living'.

At the *albergue*, a two-year-old splendour built into the old town's walls, lines were inscribed on a column by the door:

The value of camino, and of life, is not in the walking, or the discoveries, or what you are given. The value of camino is in the love you offer by walking.

Point taken!

Inside, I was glad to see Eva and Heike, who were the only other women there. All but one of the thirty-two places had been filled. From where had all these pilgrims appeared?

My *Fräuleins* had caught a bus. The wind and the distances between *refugios* were proving tough for them. We were allocated a room to ourselves, so we could avoid the snores and smells of the bloke brigade. I don't wish to sound unkind about the male of the species—God knows, I'm partial!—but after long days of walking, and without women around, men often reverted to a pack of stinky ferals.

Eva, Heike and I went out on the town. Two local *chicas* had given me a list of their favourite *tapas* bars, so we sampled mussels and *patatas bravas*, eels, whitebait and spices. Eva flirted, with the Spanish and with us. She told me she had lived all over the world, that she loved men, loved bodies, loved flesh, loved food. Eva loved, full stop. And she laughed. Zamora was lit up by her pleasure, and just knowing she was in the bunk below made me smile as my eyes closed.

Next morning, I was the last to leave the *albergue*, but by 11.30 I was twenty kilometres down the road in a café and had overtaken everyone.

It wasn't intentional, but nature was dancing her most seductive moves and the sky was criss-crossed with *caminos* of jet trails. A black-and-white bird came and went with me for at least five kilometres, twittering and wagging his tail, always three metres ahead, landing and lifting off. I was not going to be left behind and before we finished our conversation I was in Montamarta, a run-down *pueblo*, grey from the fumes of the passing trucks on the N-630 and coated with a thick film of resignation.

I had gone too fast. But when the road opens, the skies lift and a bird sings ... well, what's a pilgrim to do?

I removed my boots and made myself known to a *bocadillo* with an oozing omelette centre. I journalled and consulted maps. A Swiss pilgrim stopped at my table and told me I walked 'too fast, too fast'. Others straggled in, greeting each other like prodigals, taking their *café con leche*, planning destinations and catching up.

'Where did you last see ...?'

'They caught a bus with that dark-haired ...'

'He said he was stopping in ...'

Camino gossip or, as a friend would say, details. She always said she didn't like gossip, but loved a detail.

The crowd grew. The word count increased. Time to head out.

Opposite the café was a phone box where I got through to Brett. It was dinnertime in Australia and he was cooking. With the roar of road trains in my ears, I managed to hear him say he was coping, but couldn't deal with things in his normal way.

'This isn't normal,' I shouted over a belching truck.

He said it was good to read those early letters from Sue; they confirmed his memories were accurate, not rose-tinted. That was comfort. He was following me on a map and liked to imagine where I was walking. I wished he could have been with me.

It was a long call, over half an hour before my credit ran out, but I didn't need to do any crying for him. He was strong.

The Swiss pilgrim bowled up, saying he couldn't find a way out of town.

'The *camino* is gone. Which way do you go?'

A *chica* in a floral dress explained that, with the rains, the track was flooded and we had to go over the freeway bridge. Eva and Heike appeared and said they were coming too. No one wanted to spend all afternoon watching Spain's groceries thunder down a highway.

The girls fell behind but my Swiss sidekick accelerated with me. I wanted to be alone, and said as much, but I mustn't have made myself clear. *Herr Stalker* had clearly decided I meant 'alone with only you'.

I walked faster. He increased his pace. I put on my headphones. He kept time beside me. I sang. He smiled.

He was either insane or smitten if my singing pleased him.

We were approaching a sweeping *embalse*, its surface glinting in the sun. I put my pedal to the metal and zoomed, but at the shoreline *Herr Stalker* was still with me, red of face and panting. I had to stop or I'd be responsible for his death. Then I would have a sin to carry!

I said I needed time alone. He said, of course, he too wanted that, and headed off around the lake. I sat, sipped water and wondered at the perversity of humans. *Herr Stalker*'s figure got smaller. I inhaled dry heat.

It was swimming weather, a day to plunge in and laugh at snakes and turtles. A day to picnic or play I Spy. Something beginning with A.

Amigo …

On the opposite bank stood Castrotorafe. More ruin than castle, its crumbling gold walls appeared to hover above the water. Camelot and Rivendell. Sleeping Beauty and Snow White. It had been a stronghold for the Knights of Santiago, an order of warrior monks set up to protect pilgrims and to keep the *camino* paths firmly Christian. Their tapering red cross was the symbol on the first *sello* I'd been given by that nun of few words way back in Granada.

The track took me close to the ruins, which appeared to have pushed themselves up through a mound of turf. Wildflowers lined my path, the sun had the sky to itself, and I had the road. My phone rang.

'*Hola!*' I answered, singing it as the Spanish do when they are glad. Two syllables, two notes that can express delight, surprise, joy, love.

'*Hola, mi peregrina preferida!*'

My *amigo*!

I told him I'd been thinking of him, of swimming, heat and poems. He sounded happy. We talked. Little things. No sadness. *No pasa nada.*

I thanked him for making my day. He asked if he had called before Leonardo and Ricardo. When I said yes, I made his day!

I whizzed along the gravel road, oblivious to the heat. Shaggy goats bleated a welcome to Fontanillas de Castro. A horse neighed farewell. Kilometres disappeared under my swollen feet as mountains began to beckon up ahead and the landscapes morphed into scenic backdrops, less and less plausible.

Too green. Too blue. Too bright. Too clear.

After thirty-five kilometres, I was glad to reach Riego del Camino.

Sad little *pueblo*. Grey. What had happened here? It felt leached of love.

It was late in the day. The next town was another seven kilometres and its *albergue* small. I might not get a bed. Be sensible. Stay and rest.

But who can explain a feeling? I had to go.

Later, down the road, Eva and Heike said they stayed there and had fun, laughed with *Herr Stalker* and scraped together a meal. But I sensed sorrow in the walls of the village, so I booted up and propelled myself on burning feet back out into the heat, to the seven unbending kilometres of gravel leading to Granja de Moreruela.

Oh, the contast between the day's first kilometres, when all is fresh, and a final stint when the day has been long. My legs threatened mutiny and my shoulders went out in solidarity. There was no flying down that road, but we got there, me, my feet and I. And to a welcome, most welcome sight: a one-room, ten-bed *albergue*. The last free bed was mine, a top bunk, beside the bathroom, above an Australian!

I had joined a different village. In the *albergue* were four French gents and a French couple; the surprise Australian and his Dutch walking buddy; and Anton, a Spanish watercolourist whose abstracts captured the land better than any camera ever could. Spanish José, compact and charming, and Italian Giovanni, giant in stature and spirit, were staying up the road at a *casa rural*, where they insisted we all join them for a home-cooked dinner. Forty-two kilometres never ended so happily.

After my evening rituals, I was rushing to the *casa rural* when a woman and girl arrived, both of them petite, red-haired and smiling.

Joan and Lucy, the mythical other Aussies from *albergue* guestbooks. Mother and daughter, they were women of *duende*, no question.

We were full of the joys of Spanish spring as we tried to work out how and where I'd overtaken them. Were they in a bar when I passed? They went to find a room and we agreed to meet in the morning.

Now there were four Aussies in town. An invasion!

Dinner was a multilingual feast of tastes, jokes and bonhomie around a stone well in a garden courtyard. Anton had ligament problems, so I kneaded his calves in Spanish, supported Giovanni's kitchen wizardry in Italian, and reclined in garden chairs with the French collective.

José generated conviviality. He'd spent five years in Australia decades before and had never lost his love for it. He'd worked everywhere from the mining towns of the far north-west to Melbourne's society restaurants. He spoke thickly accented, perfectly constructed English, and was fascinated by our brightly coloured plastic banknotes. He had walked from Valencia, about the same distance as me.

The Australian man wasn't at dinner, but we'd talked earlier as the crimson sun set, his story returning me to Brett's. He said his wife had died the previous year, so he'd moved home after decades of living in Europe. He didn't know where he belonged without her.

'It takes so long to recover,' he said. 'Maybe forever.'

I understood why he didn't want to be part of the group dinner. Walking is salve. Feasting takes energy.

And energy it gave, too. Stories flew around the table. Translations were attempted, and succeeded, and failed, and morphed into new stories. We ate pasta and salad, followed by cheese and *membrillo*, quince paste. We snuck into the *albergue* like naughty children, and I managed to climb up to my bunk with minimal squeaking. It was a *roncar* of a night, but sleep came with earplugs.

Next morning, I made a left turn out of the *pueblo*. I'd travelled north-west for four hundred kilometres from Granada to Mérida. I'd been heading due north for four hundred kilometres from Salamanca.

Now I would veer north-west again, skirting the border with Portugal, climbing into the mountains of Galicia with my new village.

There were dozens of us. Some I knew by name, some by sight. We came and went from each other on the path. They all accepted that I walked alone.

'Very fast,' they would say. '*Muy rápida.*'

But I sat for longer than them, writing or staring, and so paths crossed. I relished the fleeting catch-ups …

Anton, by the side of the road, his easel out, creating a mini-masterpiece before hobbling on, grimacing and swearing.

José, eyes twinkling above his grey moustache, guarding his hips and giving me another piece of my own country's history.

Giovanni, talking of his family in Italy, and lifting his mammoth pack as though it were air.

The French *gentilhomme* with white hair and beak nose, saying he'd tracked me along the Via, wanting to see who walked alone in such small boots.

Eva and Heike, the party girls, two pebbles generating ripples of laughter.

Herr Stalker, wanting to photograph us all, everywhere, in front of everything.

Joan and Lucy, Aussies in a constant state of delighted surprise. They spoke no Spanish but knew how to connect. I watched their hands clasp involuntarily over their chests, or mime sleeping, eating, drinking or joy.

Many of the most compelling pilgrim conversations were these dumb-shows, no matter how idiotic we felt. Just as walking reduces humans to their most basic, so language was reduced to its essence. Mind you, no language could ever express my gratitude for the kindnesses visited on me daily in *pueblos*, by other pilgrims or by the road itself.

I became intrigued by the way we give thanks, needing to say it so often.

Gracias and *grazie*, both words for grace, are my preferred options. I also love the French *merci*, being tied to the idea of compassion.

I like less *obrigado,* as it implies obligation; and *danke,* because I hear no music in it. But even they are preferable to our prosaic English 'thank you', or worse, 'ta'.

On a perilously high outcrop above the Río Esla I wanted to shout thanks in every language. I was looking back to a bridge as a line of pilgrim-ants crossed its arch. I imagined flying out above the gorge, joining the wheeling falcons above the crags of the granite cliffs. I sensed *duende* moving the leaves of the *encinas.* Invisible forces. They were there.

In Tábara, our walking village expanded to fill the *pueblo.* The *albergue* had no beds, so the *hostal* took the overflow. We wandered the town, eyeing new *peregrinos* and greeting intimates we had known for two or even three days.

I retreated and tended my feet with arnica. A hundred and thirty kilometres in four days, they shouted. Hard tracks, they shouted. I'd been going four weeks, and over eight hundred kilometres—further than the Francés.

Il Capitano and his *Soldato* continued to urge me forward. They were a day ahead and texted that the *albergue* in the next town was *ottimo.* As good as it gets!

Barcelona called. 'When are you arriving?'

They had come to seem *normal,* but when I stopped to consider they had never once let me down, I still marvelled at my road-angels.

I left Tábara next morning under grey skies, in a mood to match. An *anciano* stopped me in the square to ask if I had *miedo*—fear. For the first time, I answered that oft-asked question truthfully.

'*Sí,*' I told him. '*Tengo miedo.*' I have fear. '*Pero tengo miedo en Australia, también.*' But I have fear in Australia, too.

Finally I'd been honest. Of course I was afraid. I may be blonde, but I'm not an idiot. I knew very well that I could fall, I could be raped, I could be robbed, I could be mugged, I could be lost. But those things don't stop me from walking into the world at home, so why should they stop me in Spain?

But why had I pretended? Why lie?

It may have been pride, but it was also protection—of myself and of those who love me. We all knew that a woman walking alone in remote areas had risks but we chose not to speak of them. And besides, I carried a whistle!

Regardless of the whys, it was a confession, and I felt stronger for it. Lighter.

Confession as weight loss. Now there's a selling point.

As we talked, we ambled into the Saturday market.

'Peregrina,' stallholders called to me, offering dried fruit and jokes.

So I wandered, the only pilgrim in the *pueblo*. The others had made an early start, racing the rain, but I knew that if I wanted to keep my equilibrium, I should also keep my distance. There were only twenty-two kilometres to walk and when I finally left at midday—midday!—my backpack bulging with tall tales and walnut biscuits, I figured none of it mattered. Go slowly. Get wet. It's only water.

And miracle of miracles, rain held off, so I could see an orange fox dart towards the sheep corralled in a makeshift pen, and shout at him to leave them be, paying my debt for all the sheep's milk cheeses I'd eaten along the way.

It held off so I could inhale *jara* as I climbed, reminding myself that slow is best. I got to see men working their *bodegas*; to sip their wine; and to be taken into the Cultural Association in tiny Bercianos when rain threatened again, and plied with coffee and cake. Slow steps on soft earth. Gentling along.

Finally, I walked into Santa Croya de Tera, the last pilgrim to the *albergue*. As *il Capitano* had promised, it was a highlight. We dried our laundry over a roaring fire. We dined *en masse*, and we were a mass by then—a steamy, grinning gaggle of humanity, clicking photos and tucking into home-cooked meals. We were a mini-United Nations engaged in peace talks, and my *sola* day meant I could participate, too. The *introvertida* had topped herself up and could come out to play.

'There's a message for you,' José said over flan.

My Italians, of course. *Il Capitano*'s familiar scrawl in the visitors' book.

A call from Leonardo. Rain is good, it softens the heart, he said.

From my husband at base camp, words that might have been written for me:

Never did I think so much, exist so vividly, and experience so much, never have I been so much myself—if I may use that expression—as in the journeys I have taken alone and on foot.

That's J.J. Rousseau, patron saint of the lone walker. Amen to him.

There was a wish from my vengeance-seeking sinner that we might meet one day. That particularly moved me. She'd confessed without knowing anything about me.

Another sinner posed a question: *If we can pay you to erase something on the negative side of the ledger, could you be paid to gain a virtue?*

How to admit that virtue still seemed as far off as Santiago? I had no idea how one might gain it, for myself or for an employer.

This from another, with whom I'd hiked demanding trails: *I feel like my face is hot from the smithy where I am watching the uncreated thing being created.*

There were photos of Buddhas, and Irish blessings. There was more Rilke, more love, more encouragement. I went all that way looking for faith when there was already so much faith in me.

We faced four days of rain. Hail too.

The weather is *malo*, the TV said. Clouds will open and stay that way.

It was weather. It wouldn't stop us. Faith can move mountains.

And whole villages.

24

BY HEART

WHEN UNUSUAL DEMANDS ARE placed on muscles, rips occur in the fibres and connective tissue. During periods of rest, the body will repair these rips and build strength so the muscle copes better with stress in the future.

The heart is muscle.

When I set out for the Mozárabe, I thought my heart was pretty resilient but the *camino* kept testing it. The more awake I became to the world around me, the more my heart had to expand.

Camino as personal trainer for the soul.

There was so much to make the muscles twitch: leaves floating to the ground like homing pigeons; the eyes of a cow, black as wet velvet; the precise circle inscribed by the outline of a tree against the horizon; the flick of a lizard's glistening tail; the rainbow that greeted me as I walked out of the *albergue* at Santa Croya de Tera.

And then the rain that followed it!

Rain. Rain. Rain. The first since Act One.

I stopped to put on my plastics, tying my hood tight. My pack's inner lining is waterproof, so I didn't need the cover used by many pilgrims, and while my rain jacket and trousers make things steamy, at least I'm not troubled by the flapping of a poncho. Nonetheless, it was grim walking. Steady grey rain. Not mist. Not drizzle. Rain. Thumping continuous rain.

Cold, too.

A forest was being hacked to pieces on my left, and *Santiago Peregrino* stared at me from a rain-streaked road sign. Puddles became ponds. I had soaked boots, soaked socks, soaked feet.

I saw other pilgrims, but we never spoke. Too difficult. The German *Fräuleins* had left before me, but I caught up to them in a birch plantation, looking like wraiths, their black ponchos fluttering as they weaved between trees. When I overtook them, their eyes never left the mudbath path.

My phone rang. I slid it under my plastic hood and shouted, '*Hola!*' It was my husband, at lunch at a table I know and love. A gathering of jokesters, laughing at the sound of my splashing feet, greeting me from above their plates of chicken wrapped in prosciutto.

What to say? I had chosen to be where I was. I laughed with them. On. On.

After eleven kilometres I staggered into Calzadilla de Tera, a grey *pueblo* outlined against a grey sky. Nothing moved. I followed the arrows, thinking to rest in the portico of a church. The *camino* takes you past one, in every town.

This one tore at my heart.

The roof had caved in and gaping holes were punched in the walls. Icons, crucifixes and statues were scattered at random, in piles and in solitude. The altar was defaced and the choir stalls crumbled. Rain poured into the central aisle and vines grew over the tops of the eaves. Toilet paper curled in corners. Above all that, a steeple rose intact.

In the remains of the entrance, I removed my pack and clicked photos, documenting the end of something. People had asked for help, given thanks, and marked transitions in that place. Had hope died? Or faith? It wasn't so much the loss of religion that troubled me, but the loss of history and of a space to gather in. Of communal *palimpsesto*.

Maybe it was the day, the rain. Maybe there was a vibrant community hall around the corner, hidden from the outsider. And maybe

it was nothing more than that there was another *pueblo* only two kilometres further on and this church had out-lived its purpose. Times
are a-changing ...

But my heart hurt at the sight of that church, rotting in the rain.

It was a reminder. Even things that seem permanent can die.

I kitted up and walked along a canal path, pondering Spain's
Catholicism. During the Franco years, it was the only religion to have
legal status; other forms of worship couldn't even be advertised, and
only the Catholic Church could own property or publish books. Laws
were passed abolishing divorce and civil marriage, and banning abor-
tion, contraceptives and homosexuality. Catholic religious instruction
was mandatory.

In 1978, the Spanish Constitution was amended so that Spain no
longer had an official religion. Now, while most Spanish might still
identify themselves as Catholic, they don't attend church regularly,
and Spain's birth rate, one of the lowest in the world, is testament
to the fact that contraception of some kind is being practised widely.

Change.

In Spain it had been fast and, to my eyes, all to the good in the preceding thirty years. Was the abandoned church related to those post-
Franco developments? The drenched terracotta waymarker didn't
answer my questions:

> *Walker, forgiveness is greatness of the soul. It dignifies those
> who give it, and graces those who receive it. May forgiveness
> inspire your step.*

On bleak days, it was harder to forgive myself or steer my mind
away from sins. That's when I lost sight of my sinners and turned
on myself, unable to differentiate between their cargo and mine.
When it was hot, or I was fording rivers and navigating tricky paths,
I was released. Bitter cold and incessant rain made a fertile environment for recrimination, making me recall my pride, selfishness and

anger. If *camino* is, as some say, taking one's life for a walk, it was on sodden days that I met my least attractive self, and I didn't forgive her readily.

In Olleros de Tera, I stopped for coffee and warmth. It was *fiesta* day for a soaked Virgin, and decorated cakes were being carried under umbrellas to a waiting car. On TV, a presenter tried to make a bulldog jump through a hoop. Outside, the rain kept falling. Commonsense would have dictated staying in the bar, but instinct had taken over and it gave only one command. Walk!

Leaving town, a stooped *anciano* in a cashmere cardigan escorted me to the main road, saying I would never get through on the inundated cross-country *camino* path. He squeezed my hand in farewell and the scent of Imperial Leather soap stayed there for hours, reminding me of my father and all the times I'd snapped at him or failed to pick up the phone and call.

I crossed the swollen Río Tera, and scurried through Vega de Tera after an eagle swooped low, its whooshing wings black and serrated, its talons sharply defined through the rain.

Road-walking in a deluge. Difficult not to fear the worst. Difficult not to recall hurts I shouldn't have given, to punish myself and see myself as a failure. Somewhere on that storm-washed asphalt, anxiety and regret became visceral. At least, I think that was what happened. I didn't have much time to consider. Out of nowhere, I was sobbing. Tears mixed with rain. My chest heaved. What was happening?

Grief erupted out of me like lava from that volcano in Iceland. I couldn't contain it. I veered off the road, oblivious to oncoming trucks, and bent forward to lean on my knees, plastics crinkling and my pack a dead weight.

Several selves operated simultaneously. There was the 'I' who was undergoing something terrifying and the 'I' who judged it, deeming it unattractive and unseemly. There was another 'I' who was fascinated, like a scientist—'So this is what meltdown looks like.' And there was the Head Girl 'I' telling the first 'I' this was nonsense and to pull the selves together.

Except she couldn't. None of them could.

My thinking was confused by rain and panic, my field of vision was limited to the spot below me as I tried not to vomit and my body spasmed as though trying to eject something poisonous.

I've no idea how long the onslaught lasted. It had its way.

Finally I heaved myself out of the mud and reached for my dropped walking poles so I could inch to a standing position. My pack pulled me off balance. I steadied myself and tried to breathe, looking around for an answer.

Nothing. Just the rain.

I made my way back to the road, focused on placing one foot, then another. To get somewhere, anywhere, would be enough.

I got to Bar Jesus.

In Junquera de Tera, a town of diminishing population, that was the first sign I saw. I walked in to smiles and hot tea. The barman, my saviour, insisted I sit at a table under a heater, beside a painted tile showing a man bowing before a priest. It read: *It's better to sin little than to confess much.*

I took out my journal and wrote, trying to comprehend what had made my heart crack open. It wasn't food poisoning. I'd had only coffee after a breakfast of bread, cheese and fruit. Was it the church? A response to the desecration of a sacred place?

More often than not, the sacred places I'd encountered were full of images that only spoke to me of suffering. I could see the power of those symbols and the history of the places, but I was beginning to think that *my* sacredness would never be found in them. When I finished the Camino Francés, I'd watched other pilgrims arrive in Santiago, some dazed and overawed, some dancing and partying, some shouting, some praying, some silent. All footsore.

I was glad for those who stood in front of the cathedral and experienced completion. I was also glad for those who found meaning inside the cathedral. But nothing happened for me. Mostly I was confused and numbed by the 'showbiz' aspect of the rituals. I left thinking I had failed. Clearly there was something wrong with me. Something missing. I was doomed to be an onlooker in the world of the spirit.

I realised in Bar Jesus on a dripping Sunday, with football blaring from the TV and my pot of tea fogging the window, why the Santiago cathedral bell never resonated for me. It said, 'In here. Come in here. This is the place to be forgiven.'

I prefer bells that say 'Maybe ... maybe ... maybe you'll sit and reflect awhile ...'

I believe in personal accountability, and betterment via example, I wrote. *And I believe in possibility over certainty.*

Even using the word 'believe' felt too certain.

Not that I wasn't grateful to 'sacred places', or respectful of those who found meaning in churches, temples and mosques. The Catholic Church had given me rich and potent stories, and rules against which I could measure my life. It had given me the *camino*.

I questioned myself about my roadside meltdown. I had left something behind out there near the Río Tera. Was it faith?

No. No it wasn't. I still believed.

In the possibility of union and peace. In kindness and in our longing to express that kindness. In goodness. Pure and simple.

What I decided I had left behind was the hunger for a particular kind of faith.

My faith may not fit in cathedrals, or dwell in temples, or nest in mosques, I wrote. *But it is no less meaningful for that.*

I could learn from the teachings of the enlightened, from people who believed and from those who believed only in the here and now——just as I had always learned from poets. All had something to offer me. But for now, the road was my instructor. It was both benevolent and ruthless, but it sure could teach.

I sipped tea and looked at the tile by my side.

Sin little rather than confess much.

It wasn't that I needed more churches or chanting, but rather a stronger heart; one that could withstand self-scrutiny and help my mind to make better choices.

My heart seemed to function optimally in ordinary places, and if my lived experience was any guide, clarity could mostly be found where silence prevailed: dung-laden paddocks, barren plains, forests, mountains and places where the hush of humility had fallen.

They are my churches, I wrote, *where I see the possibility of who I can be. As Will Shakespeare said, sermons in stones, and good in everything.*

Perhaps I had found a way. It was dirt and often rocky. Sometimes it was wet and treacherous. But I didn't need talismans or bishops. I just had to turn up and be ready to meet myself.

Who knew I would find answers in Bar Jesus! I wrote.

I began another sentence, documenting what had happened in the lead-up to the meltdown.

I walked, I wrote.

I looked at the words. Looked again. I placed a full stop after them.

I walked.

That was enough.

I closed the journal and got ready to go back out into the rain.

It wasn't easier. The rain still fell and the asphalt still bit, but my heart chugged along. My wet feet were in wet socks in wet shoes, with wet plastics over wet trousers and wet jumper. *De nada.* It's nothing. Walk on.

I was nigh drowned when I arrived in Rionegro del Puente, five saturated kilometres later. At the new *albergue*, the walking village was settling in for a *fiesta* out of the weather. I stopped, de-booted, considered, re-booted and left. The roadside meltdown had left me raw. I didn't want to be a party pooper, so rain triumphed over company.

The N-631 was a puddled ribbon of bitumen with a headwind rippling its surface. This was my church! Six slogging kilometres later, a four-wheel drive pulled over to ask why I was not on the *camino*.

I had missed an arrow in the rain.

Carlos, a cigar-smoking Andalucían, told me I was a kilometre or two short of the *albergue*-town of Mombuey; that he would take me there, to his bar of choice, and I could buy him a coffee. I got in. En route, he said how difficult it was for a southerner in the north, where people are more serious. He missed the south's *no pasa nada* attitude. It had been days since I'd heard my *amigo*'s phrase. Things had begun to matter.

In Mombuey, there was hot coffee and an *empanada*, but no bed. Not at the *albergue* or the *hostal* or the closed hotel. The next room was in Palacios de Sanabria, twelve kilometres down the road.

Joan and Lucy arrived, bedraggled but smiling, a welcome taste of Australia. They were followed by a Spaniard with a limp and a tanned Austrian. We were all bedless. There was nothing for it but to make for Palacios.

Carlos told me to ring Hostal Teresa. The owner told me she had five beds left.

Meant to be.

A taxi arrived, driven by a man named Santiago. Meant to be.

We arrived at a two-storey whitewashed building. My phone beeped. *Il Capitano*, saying he and his *Soldato* would be in Puebla de Sanabria the next night. I texted back, saying I would see them, as I was in Palacios. He texted back to say he was too. I opened the door to discover they were sleeping across the hall. Meant to be!

Mirth, hugs, a torrent of Italian. Both had added beards to their moustaches since I last saw them. They would shave in Santiago, they said.

To the bar we went for televised bullfights, porcini mushrooms, weather and stories.

Back to the *hostal* for stracciatella, goat ragù, roast pork, potatoes, salad, bread, wine, bananas. Three hours earlier, Teresa had only two Italians to feed. Had she intended to give them all that food?

I bedded down with Joan and Lucy. A hush never feels deeper than when a wind rages outside. My heart was a reliable metronome as my eyes closed.

Next morning at the bar, Ana Balen Rey told us there would be snow!

Il Soldato handed me his gloves, which I took to be my orders to walk with them. I gulped down my coffee and toast, and followed.

More rain. More puddles. And mountains dressed in muted grey with pink heather highlights. From the primary colours of the *meseta* to the pastels of the peaks, Castilla y Léon had it all. And we were preparing to leave it.

My Italians walked like locomotives. We sang, we marched, we laughed. Much of the time I was unable to understand them, so rapid was the chat, but the instructions were clear. Up and on. Forward and fast. Take no prisoners, only an Aussie pilgrim.

We trooped into Puebla de Sanabria and up a million stairs to the castle. Leaning against 500-year-old walls and looking out over the swathe of countryside we'd walked, my heart and legs pumped fire. In front of me was a quilt of grey. Granite houses. Slate sky. Charcoal road. Dove mist.

To my left stood the grey-haired *Soldato*, surveying the vista like an Easter Island statue. To my right, *il Capitano*, bubbling like a child on a sugar high, pointing out landmarks and congratulating us on moving fast. We could press on, he said, and get ahead of schedule.

Puebla de Sanabria has a storybook heart. The castle is a Cinderella fantasy, and the historic centre is cobbled with flagstones. Balconies tumble with flowers and cats doze under stone lintels. We managed to convince *il Capitano* to lunch in a restaurant where candles gleamed against copper. We shopped for gloves and a warm top for me, made from some mystery synthetic that acted as a wearable heater, but there was a movement order for our garrison and we were off.

We were three. A difficult number, but somehow, with them, easy.

Through industrial estates, past milking cows and abandoned houses, I walked with the old soldier as *il Capitano* made phone calls and consulted his GPS. *Il Soldato* spoke of his regrets about having been a stern parent. Severe. Expectations are cruel, he said, and they were his sin.

His word, not mine.

He was as economical a talker as he was a walker, travelling lightly across the earth, a legacy of his years living in mountains. He liked silence, he said. And people with whom he could achieve it.

Il Capitano appeared, at full throttle. He'd bought a Coke at a vending machine and said he'd beat us to the *albergue*. Refuelled, he zoomed ahead, his white hair standing out from his head like a cartoon cat.

Kids alighted from a school bus as we arrived in Requejo. They led us to a private *albergue*, where *il Capitano* waited, tapping his feet. We paid twelve euros for a bed, sheets, towels, a stylised shell *sello* in our passports, and a place to be warm and dry.

Leonardo called. It was sunny and warm in Barcelona. I told him I was in company with Italians and he said that I would eat well!

The town was closed. We washed clothes and hung them on heaters as the rain persisted. We flicked between TV stations, searching for news of better weather. There was none. Only images of oil belching into the Gulf of Mexico, the purity of blue water inked black by corporate error. We played with Italian playing cards. I won two of five hands, though I had no idea how. The old soldier napped. *Il Capitano* and I looked at each other's photos, comparing our days. We had seen different things in the same places at the same time. A reminder, if I needed it, that there is no one way, no definitive truth.

We dined late, taking our time, savouring green beans, casserole and flan. Savouring each other. We worked to have conversation.

They held chairs for me, poured wine for me, tucked my scarf around me. *Il Capitano* had his whisky and warm milk, and we returned to the *albergue* where they had chosen the best bunk for me.

Angels and saviours, finding good in everything.

Sacred hearts.

25

RETURN TO GALICIA

INTO MOUNTAINS AND THE *dénouement* of the third act.

The act of the spirit.

A pale sky greeted us. A snow sky, my Italians said. *Il Soldato* checked I had warm layers and gloves, checked I had coffee, checked I had eaten. He was like my father, a gentleman from another era, and made me rue the times pride made me tell Dad I didn't need his help. Accepting assistance is not weakness, as I kept on learning.

Our exhalations made miniature clouds as we climbed past skeletal birches to where vegetation thinned and gorse bushes ruled, then higher to the tundra, where pylons rose from the earth into the sky and an *autovía* roared above us. The land folded and unfolded. Clouds lay in its deep pockets, stopping the sun's rays from reaching whole valleys.

We were at thirteen hundred metres: rarefied air and bone-chillingly cold.

I'd travelled from winter into spring in Andalucía, through flooded creeks to poppies and mustard flowers. Summer arrived in Extremadura, so I swam with tadpoles and dipped in Grimaldo's blossom-strewn stream. Autumnal blasts and falling leaves greeted me north of Salamanca. And finally, as though Proserpina had returned to the Underworld, I was entering a wintry kingdom.

All this in under five weeks.

Il Capitano announced that so much rain had fallen in the night that the *camino*'s valley path would be flooded and we must take the high road all the way to Lubián. Twenty kilometres of *carretera*. His foot soldiers' faces must have told quite a story but he wouldn't be swayed. Up we went, air cutting like knives into exposed skin. It was easy to see why.

Snow.

There it was. Barely a kilometre to our left. Almost touchable.

Water gushed on all sides. Creeks where there had been trickles. Rivers where there had been creeks. I thought of *Herr Theologie* and of our plodding days. I hoped he was not out in the rain. My Italians were years older than him, yet they were like teenagers, sustained by an appetite for laughter and life.

Il Capitano told me of the walks he planned for the years ahead. Would I join him? He would like to have his *libellula* with him. His dragonfly. He said it was the right name for me because I flitted from side to side as I walked, stopping, looking, speeding up, turning and dancing. He imitated me and was so accurate I groaned in recognition.

We sang '*A Modo Mio*'—'My Way'—into Lubián as the rain stopped. The town was silent, the granite buildings forlorn. At La Casa de Irene, a private *albergue*, we gulped homemade *empañada* and hot coffee at Angelus time.

To walk or to stay?

Not fancying another long, locked afternoon, we voted to push on. I had become part of a regiment, just like that. We marched out of Castilla y Léon, crossing the border without fanfare.

Into Galicia.

Land of witches and little people, where the Celts left traces of themselves in the haunting music of bagpipes and the stone architecture. It's called 'the bathtub of Spain' with reason. It rains. All year. Moss coats walls and grows like cushions on stone; the air is heavy.

Right on cue, rain returned.

We ploughed up inclines and skittered down fast-moving watercourses where sharp rocks lurked, waiting to trip us up. The old soldier was like a rabbit. His feet barely touched the ground. *Il Capitano* and I brought up the rear, my walking poles keeping me from slithering into mud. Eventually, though, I began to flail.

My period started, out on the road in the rain. It was the final straw. I had walked over thirty kilometres of up, down, up, down, and I had to stop. I insisted they leave me at Vilavella, ten kilometres past Lubián, at a *hostal* on the N-525, beside a service station. I said I'd catch them up, but I had nothing left. They took women's business in their stride, making sure I didn't need a *farmacia*, waiting until I had a room, taking tea with me, and then heading back into the rain to make for the big *albergue* at A Gudiña. In spite of the lowering skies, they were going to do a forty-plus day. They said they felt at home in the mountains. 'Just as our dragonfly loves the *meseta*, so we love altitude.'

In my room, I crumpled. Let's just call it hormones.

After my roadside meltdown, I'd thought all collapses were behind me, but mountain-walking in torrential rain with mud underfoot and oestrogen cavorting though the body, undertaken while searching for words in another language, after eight consecutive days without a break, will probably produce a result!

My journal entry was a litany of misery.

I was sick of handwashing and smelling rancid, of throbbing feet and aching back, of guarding physical steps and mental state, of roadside rubbish, and of waste, like the multiple layers of packaging on the tampons.

I was sick of sins. So sick of them. And maybe sick from them. What idiocy was this, to fill the mind and spirit with pain, and hold hands with it across an entire country?

I wanted to drop my bundle but was afraid I'd never pick it up again, so I went to the bar and sat looking out over petrol pumps to the mountains where windmills twirled, slicing into the passing grey clouds. I texted my husband to tell him not to worry, that I was okay. A text came back asking if he should have been worried. I had forgotten that my world was not his! I really was losing it.

I watched television, but couldn't focus on bullfighters, no matter how dazzling their looks and moves. The government had changed in England. The Spanish king had been operated on in Madrid. Emerging from a public hospital, he declared Spain's health system the pride of the nation. I tried to imagine a king of England checking into the Royal London on the NHS, but didn't think it likely. Spain's movie-star president was in close-up announcing rescue measures for the economy. Still the volcano belched, houses were washed away like toys, and oil spilled into the Gulf of Mexico. Insurance companies baulked at payouts. These were Acts of God, they said.

What did they mean? Did insurance companies know something I didn't?

I wanted the companies to disclose the god who was their excuse: the one who sent floods to wrench babies from the arms of mothers; the one who rained down locusts to eat crops; the one who shook whole cities until people were pulp under buildings; the one who washed away continents of topsoil where food had grown.

A wanton god, this god of insurance.

Outside, the grey stayed. Fog closed in. *Niebla.*

I hadn't had a rest day since Salamanca, nine days earlier. Since then, I'd travelled far under threatening skies and in *mucho* company. I was numb, aside from a dread that, as I approached Santiago, I was no wiser. I hoped my sinners were faring better. My great fear was always that the walk would prove pointless: that I would make no discoveries, learn nothing, and waste the time and faith of my supporters. Worse, that I might have asked them to own up to painful self-truths, only to return with no offering. The fear that the whole exercise might be empty was too terrible.

What if there was no point to all this plodding?

To search for meaning assumes that there is a meaning and that it is findable. But how will we know it? What will it look like?

I opened my journal and began to make notes. *Meaning has begun to sound like the crunch of boots on gravel, but what use is that to anyone else?*

I took a deep breath and tried to slow down. Snail-writing.
Paso a paso. Step by step.
That's my mantra, I wrote. *That's my rosary. That's the prayer for me.*
I kept on writing as the sky turned from dove to lead outside.

For me, prayer is walking. Every step is a prayer. And if there are sacred places, then the ones I have seen are roads that stretch to the horizon, empty of all save perhaps a fellow traveller, dotted in the distance, walking a separate but connected way.

A saint is a tree beside a road, the branches wide enough to give comfort and solace in equal measure.

A sermon is a story told at sunset, two spirits meeting to pay attention, to listen, and to learn.

Divinity is the moment when heartbeats and footsteps align, find each other, and mark miles together.

Miracles ask little and give much. Like a woman tucking homemade food into a stranger's pockets, miracles quicken the step, light the way in the early morning dark, and are the first star of the evening cool. Miracles are journeys from emptiness to fullness, from heartbreak to heartache to heartburn to heart's ease. And back again.

And heaven?

Heaven is a place where good people do bad things and bad people do good things and somewhere out on the miraculous road, good and bad people look into each other's eyes and realise there is no separation. They are the same.

And 'buen camino' is a blessing.

Good road. Good path. Good way.

Perhaps it is the only blessing.

The woman proprietor of the *hostal* sat down opposite me. Her dark hair was tinged with grey and she moved as though each action gave her pain. She took my hand, saying the pilgrim road was not easy. That I should eat and sleep. There was soup, special soup from

Galicia. *Caldo gallego*. And fish, too. Fish would be good for me. And maybe I should have some cake.

Galicia is soft, she said, but hard too. People are not rich. They have little. They know what it is to work and to be tired. You must rest, she said.

And one more thing. Very important, pilgrim. *Muy muy importante.*

Remember that you don't walk the *camino*. The *camino* walks you.

I made her repeat it. I wrote it down. I wanted to tell her that that day the *camino* had walked all over me. I think she knew.

I remembered my shepherd. Life: hard but beautiful.

Was everyone in Spain a philosopher?

We stood, but before I could move into the dining room, she hugged me, squeezing me tight. It was a shock to feel the warmth of her. A relief.

The body is a work of wonder, but it needs care. Basic food and drink, sufficient sleep, and connection. Bodies need it. Feet certainly do.

'Hold the sole and you hold the soul,' a lanky Canadian with fierce blisters said to me when I rubbed his feet. I think he was right.

'You're the yeast to my dough. You make me rise!' said an Irish lass with purple bruising at her waist and shoulders from her backpack, as she cried at being touched.

I didn't want to cry there in Vilavella with those arms around me, so I clamped my jaw and told myself to harness a bit of *duende*.

When she brought me my soup, steaming and aromatic, the owner said I had only two hundred kilometres to go to Santiago. *Más o menos*. More or less.

Really? Two hundred? Then I had covered a thousand kilometres!

Some trudging, some flying, some singing, some weeping, some sheer sinful delight. I'd carried sins for a thousand kilometres, and I was in Galicia, a land of mists and mellow fruitfulness, if ever there was one.

Land of *tormentas* too, if the scene outside the window was anything to go by. Lightning illuminated the bowsers. *Gaitas*— bagpipes—played on the sound system. I was in Macbeth territory.

A group of men filed past to the next table, all with that scrubbed, just-showered glow. They raised glasses and laughed. Their energy bounced off the walls and off my back, battering me with bonhomie. I finished my celebratory *vino tinto* and stood to go. I had no energy to party.

My hugger appeared and thrust a plate into my hand.

'Something sweet. It's important.'

A slice of the Santiago almond cake, with its cross of Saint James outlined in icing sugar on the top. It's the traditional cake of the pilgrim, made throughout Galicia. Two friends cooked it for my birthday, before I had even contemplated a *camino*. None of us viewed it as anything more than a display of their culinary prowess. Hindsight makes me see it as a sign!

As the sky flashed outside, I stood staring at the cake. The men fell silent. I opened my mouth but nothing came out. A man with salt-and-pepper hair raised his glass.

'*Buen camino*,' he said.

I sat back down and polished off every crumb. As I ate, I had a *palimpsesto* moment, going back in time to the final day of the Francés, when I'd walked—or rather, flown—for fifty-three ecstatic Galician kilometres. I'd bounded down country lanes between dry-stone walls set with rickety wooden gates and benches; along narrow paths lined with chestnuts, sunflowers, pumpkins and pears; through cobbled streets past the inevitable bakery filled with Santiago *torta*; by bronze cornfields swaying in late afternoon sun and haystacks glowing gold under a rising moon.

Galicia's granite villages are built to last. They are plain, undecorated. Maybe that's because the landscape is so dramatic that the inhabitants don't feel the need to dress them up. Also, landhold-ings are small and making a living is *difícil*.

The people, too, are different. They have the pale skin and dark eyes of the Irish. They are elvish and weathered, living with fog all year round. It makes dreamscapes of their land. Stone walls wind across it and spiders' webs are barriers of filigree across entire fields.

The Galician food is hearty and stew-based, their most famous dish being *pulpo gallego*, a kind of octopus hotpot, pungent and rich red. They have their own language, a re-worked Spanish with a bit of Portuguese flung in for good measure. They say *Bom dia* instead of *Buenos días.*

I remembered all that, from a piece of cake.

Palimpsesto.

I was fortified.

I was a pilgrim and I would keep on walking, to the end of the third act.

26

REGALOS

GIFTS.

Next morning I received my first at breakfast.

Sleep and Santiago cake had worked wonders, and in spite of hormone heaviness and grey skies, I wanted to walk. A Gudiña was fourteen kilometres up the road. Even if I only made it that far, I could check into an *albergue* and explore a Galician town.

As I was finishing my *café*, *tostada* and sin-reading, a familiar face greeted me—the man who had wished me *buen camino* the previous evening. He wore red and yellow Lycra, and asked where I was going and how far I had come. When he heard my story, he called the others over. They were cycling the *camino* in a group, their support van loaded with puncture equipment, spare tyres and luggage. They took it in turns to drive, going ahead to find coffee, forage for lunches and track down necessities from pharmacies or lottery agents!

The designated driver invited me to ride for an hour or two in the van with him, saying it would be a pleasure to have some 'kangaroo company'.

Would I have gone sightseeing with a group of stranger cyclists at home? Undoubtedly no.

But here I was, surrounded by smiling faces insisting I should see more of Galicia than simply the path of the yellow arrows; that they would return me to my road; that it would be a chance to see the *camino* through cyclist's eyes.

And so I rode high in the white Transit van, gasping at panoramas that must surely have reached to world's end at Finisterre. The rain stopped. The sky cleared. The van turned corner after miraculous corner, and the day expanded with the vistas.

Travelling at car pace was an adrenaline rush after walking. Colours blurred and speed made fields merge into one another. Mountains were vast, then nothing, then gone. On foot, there is only the next step. Up high, in the van, I could see the separations, the folds of land, the *pueblo* hidden behind that hill like a child behind a mother's skirt. And fast. So fast.

Fifty kilometres per hour was Formula One frenzy.

We stopped in Verín, off the walking path, and met the riders for coffee. They ate mammoth *bocadillos* of cheese and *jamón*, and skulled coffee like water. I bought them a box of strawberries and they washed them down with *grappa*. They bought me a lottery ticket so I might come and live in Spain.

I didn't win, but I kept the ticket—a reminder of their gifts.

The cyclist's *camino* is a *fiesta*, a bonding exercise played out on big roads and in larger towns. I saw why they were always calling to each other on the road. Speed is an intoxicant.

Nonetheless, I was back in my natural habitat when my feet hit the earth. I was way past A Gudiña and so let myself drift, a karma-collecting breeze at my back and cows at my side, snail-walking downhill to Laza, where I checked into my first Galician *albergue*, its modern steel structure incongruous above the stone buildings of the *pueblo*.

The Galician government must have spent a fortune upgrading *albergues* for the Holy Year. This one was built around a central grassed courtyard, its glass walls allowing floods of light to enter. The communal sitting and cooking areas were clean, practical and inviting. It was inhabited by a new village, mostly German.

I collected a key from the office of the *Protección Civil*. When the officer saw me limping, she led me through to the on-duty doctor, who checked my knee (no problem) and my sore toe (perhaps a small break) and my other vital signs (*normal*). All free for the pilgrims.

The wiry-haired matriarch at the supermarket told me about her family, saying the young don't value anything but money now. It's all that matters. So marriages fall apart and children ignore their history.

Then we talked about mothers. Hers had died only a year before, at the age of eighty. I said that I often walked with mine; that I still felt her loss, after fifteen years. I told her about the death of my sister-in-law. Suddenly, we were both crying, hugging like intimates.

Her sternness and disappointment vanished. She said life is *sol y sombra*—sun and shadow. Like the *camino*. And you can't value one without the other. Then she said the young were not so bad and history was not everything, and we laughed. I walked out into the late afternoon, completely oblivious to the possibly broken bone in my right toe.

Sol y sombra.

I think she was right. We value the sun more when we have known shadow. Why is that? I don't want to believe that suffering is necessary for happiness but it certainly puts it into sharper relief.

I strolled past a donkey of palest grey. He pottered with me part way to the church. Finding it closed, I investigated the cemetery. Behind a wall, a row of open graves lay ready and waiting, their marble headstones already inscribed with family names. Pedro Perez Serra. Mauricio Jurado Rodriguez. Luisa Barbero Martín.

Long names, each telling a story. The Spanish take two surnames: the first surname of their father and the first surname of their mother. It's possible to comprehend something of a family's history through the surnames, which may hail from different corners of the country or even the world. Like Pablo Richter Miramontes!

The impressive names were prepared for death. It was coming. It was part of their lives and must be given its due. Looking into those gaping rectangles, I thought what a curious exercise it is to claim we are immortal.

We are born. We die.

That is it, Brett and Sue would have said. They had no faith in anything other than life, and no expectations beyond the pleasure of the day they were in and the connections they made along the way.

I'd often questioned their certainty about that, just as I'd questioned certainty about an all-knowing god. At Sue's funeral, overflowing with friends and family, I saw how unnecessary religion is as comfort when there's an abundance of love. Faith was present, in the eyes of friends as they reassured my brother and his childen. Faith in each other. In the here and now and the goodness that can be done.

There are kinds of immortality.

It may sound morbid, but looking into those open graves, I imagined myself, like Mum, long gone. Particles of me had been eaten by a fish, perhaps, that swam to a distant sea, only to be plucked by a hungry seabird winging to a beach in the north of Spain, where it landed and watched feet trudging along a path to a lighthouse, where people burned things in flames on rocks, and other birds wheeled overhead. I was there, in that bird.

I imagined myself as dust. Clay.

A potter scooped up a handful of me and made me into a bowl, turning it on a wheel, his hands shaping it into something useful, then fired it, fired me, then placed it on a table to hold fruit to feed a hungry child.

Earlier in the day I had stopped under an oak tree. I'd closed my eyes and imagined my feet still walking, crunching seeds from acorns that had been crunched under other feet that had already walked that path before me. I'd imagined those seeds being pushed into the soil, sprouting tendrils and growing down into the earth.

I'd opened my eyes, and by my side a grasshopper sat rubbing its feet together.

Somewhere, a crow called.

As I looked into those graves in Laza, I wondered whether, in hundreds of years, another oak would spread its shade over another pilgrim wandering that same path. By then, I might be in Australian earth, feeding another tree.

Or a crow.

Or even a grasshopper.

These imaginings are types of immortality. They have mystery and beauty aplenty. And if there is more, I will surely discover it in time. But for now, this world, these mysteries, are ample. And accepting mystery, celebrating it, is a kind of faith.

'*Gracias,*' I whispered to the wind as it whipped through the graves, blowing ice off the mountains. '*Gracias.*'

I turned to find *il Capitano* watching me from a distance.

He was waiting for me to finish my prayers, he said.

They'd arrived earlier in the day. *Il Soldato* had mild food poisoning, so they checked into a *hostal*. Also, *il Capitano* whispered, there had been many snorers in the refuge at A Gudiña, and they hadn't slept.

We went to dinner. Of course!

I was glad to have a chance to shout him, as he'd insisted on giving me a memory card for my camera the day before. We wolfed down soup, a mixed grill and half of Spain's potato crop, ice cream, bread and wine. *Il Capitano* downed his whisky with hot milk and declared that we would meet in the bar at 7.30 next morning, because of course I would be walking with them.

I grinned all the way home.

At the *albergue*, I met another woman—a German in her early fifties. Elfin and fair, she walked with her tall lean husband. She gathered wildflowers as she walked, pressing them between the pages of a book of poems by Rilke. I told her he was leading me to Santiago, that friends sent me his words. She said Rilke helped her to survive when she stopped menstruating at forty and was told she would never have children. Poetry had lifted her from darkness.

She translated a poem called 'God Speaks'. I went to bed with her gift of Rilke's words:

Flare up like flame
and make big shadows I can move in.
Let everything happen to you: beauty and terror.
Just keep going. No feeling is final.
Don't let yourself lose me ...

I didn't feel I had lost any connection to the divine in the revelations of the previous days. In fact, I had found a new peace. Certainty belonged to childhood, and the acceptance of mystery worked best for me now.

No feeling is final.

The mystery of how some flowers open at night to release their perfume, while others won't reveal their hearts without sun. The mystery of knowing one's clan. The mystery of love.

More than enough.

My bunkroom was peopled entirely by men; the snorers who'd wrecked the Italians' sleep the previous night. It was as though I was inside the grumbling timpani of a full orchestra. I gave up on the idea of sleep and tried to hold the words of the poem as booming waves of sound crashed around me, making me nervous for a couple of the men when they paused too long before a thundering inhale.

At around three the room began to quiet, save for rhythmic breathing and a few rattles. A rumble. An isolated snort. As though someone was conducting.

Then peace. Minutes passed. Silence.

I was too nervous to move, afraid of disturbing the sleepers.

Then a new sound. A whimper. Small, tender, high-pitched. A cry of pain.

The conductor at work again, making other music.

It rose to a crescendo of loss and sorrow. Cries, mumbles, gasps; the sounds of children, trapped and afraid, like a boarding-school dormitory on the first night of term.

I wondered about the masks worn by men. All that bravado and machismo, is it only a façade? How painful to be inside those minds. I hoped Mr Rilke was right and that no feeling was final. I would have hated the sleepers to remember their night-time grief.

Next morning I navigated downhill through a whiteout to Bar Picota. The tall girl who ran the place had a long thin face and straight dark hair. When I told her I liked her sweet-smelling bar, she produced a pocket notebook for me.

'*Un regalo para usted,*' she said. A gift for you.

I tucked it into the back of my journal, and when I see the smiley faces on the cover, I picture her bar, with the president of Spain warning of cuts to funding for *funcionarios* and *pensionistas*. I see two *ancianos* in the back corner shaking their heads. And I see my Italians bursting through the door, ready for coffee and *camino*.

We walked in wispy fog, climbing on soft Galician earth. Together, apart, by a river, along a valley, past dogs and chickens, up, up, up. The shuffles, squeaks and growls of the waking landscape evoked the sounds of my Australian bush and the mantra I often repeated to myself when I walked alone through it—the words of Caliban in Shakespeare's *The Tempest*:

> *Be not afeard. The isle is full of noises,*
> *Sounds and sweet airs that give delight and hurt not.*
> *Sometimes a thousand twangling instruments*
> *Will hum about mine ears, and sometime voices*
> *That, if I then had waked after long sleep,*
> *Will make me sleep again; and then, in dreaming,*

The clouds methought would open, and show riches
Ready to drop upon me, that when I waked,
I cried to dream again.

Was that what they were doing in the *albergue*, all those big men/
little boys? Crying to return to their dreams? On the road they looked
so certain and fearless.

High on a peak, windswept and fog-free, I took out my camera. I
turned in all directions but could not fit even a corner of the landscape into a frame.

I descended to the veiled human-scale world of fog. An arthritic
farmer with a flock of Jersey Caramel cows whispered, '*Hola,*' as
though mindful of what might lurk in the whiteness. I asked him if
the *niebla* would lift.

He shrugged. '*Galicia!*' he whispered.

Further along the path I heard wailing, a sound from the gut of
something. I felt my way off the track, along a low stone wall, peering
into the white. At a gate, I stopped. The sounds were coming from a
sheep, barely six feet from me.

It groaned and a bloody bundle dropped from it.

The sheep stepped back and the bundle bleated.

The sheep stepped towards it, licking blood and something viscous
from it.

The bundle tried to move, to raise itself on spindle legs.

The sheep and I were motionless as it got up, fell, and got up
again.

The sheep stepped forward. Her lamb began to suckle.

I've no idea how long I stood there, but I had nowhere better to
be than watching that lamb fall and finally rise, in the silent white
stillness.

The Bar Rincón del Peregrino is a kind of Wild West outpost covered in scallop shells. In pride of place on the bar was a shell signed
by an Australian called Tony Kevin, whose book about walking the

Mozárabe was being read by my husband as I walked. He was following me on the map, through Mr Kevin's eyes, another *palimpsesto* as our experiences converged and diverged.

Tony Kevin had walked in the height of summer, at a different pace, staying in different places. When I read his book, I was struck by our opposing impressions. Weather, company or mood can alter an experience profoundly, but we agreed on Bar Rincón. It was a place of charm and eccentricity, and Luis, the patron, gave grinning welcome.

Sipping coffee at the wooden table on his verandah, I watched pilgrims arrive, sign a shell and leave, escorted by local dogs. The moving village kept shaping and forming itself, over and over. I pinned my shell near the entrance and tucked in beside my Italians, who had caught up with me.

We sang and were silent together through heather and gorse. I photographed them standing on either side of a rudimentary wooden cross. It towers above them, the sky a blue and grey backdrop. At their feet, white stones are piled in front of pink-flowering Erica. They lean in against the trunk of the cross, their bright rain jackets a contrast to the muted Galician tones.

Down we came, into Albergueria for lunch—always, with them, a proper stop, seated at a table, with boots off and rest shoes on. Always time and conversation. Tasting the food. Smelling it. Noticing each other. Energy levels, moods, preferences.

Then on, apart, along a stretch of flat gravel lined with flowering gorse. The daily call from Barcelona, my daily gift. Open land. Open heart. Then up, into pocket-handkerchief *pueblos* and an overdose of green and stone. Then up again into more heath, and then … then …

The top of the world.

Wind at my back. At my feet, a stone marker, carved with a shell and arrow. Sun on the far hills. Brown chocolate earth in blocks. Enough vegetables for a village in every plot. No stone unturned. Outrageous gifts from a landscape simultaneously rich and poor.

Down I went along muddy byways, light peeping though lacy tree cover and moss creeping up stone walls. My Italians caught me. *Il Soldato* streaked ahead. I side-stepped puddles with *il Capitano*, and when eventually we found our soldier, he was snoozing on a stone bench by a fountain, just outside a *pueblo* with an unpronounceable name: Xunqueira de Ambía.

Galician twists the tongue!

After thirty-four kilometres, another modern *albergue* greeted us. The government was spending on pilgrims, as pilgrims put money back into the economy. More than fair exchange, I thought, as I paid five euros for bed, shower and tissue sheets.

My Italians would have none of it. To a *casa rural* for them and some three-star silence, without *roncadoras*, as they called the snorers.

I ate with them down in the village. After the laundry, the ecstasy!

Chicken and pimentos. Jokes and stories. They talked of the Germans they had met who were doing a 'Mercedes *camino*', town to town in air-con luxury. *Il Capitano* described us walking into Santiago together: the captain, the soldier and the dragonfly. He gave me 'our' plan, and I thanked him for it. My acquiescence was the gift I could give. I smiled with *il Soldato* as another list of phone numbers was produced, another GPS co-ordinate cited.

Walking back to the *albergue*, the sky was full-blown rose. I'd had a text from home to tell me all was well. The Italians were tucked in, digesting my story. I'd told them about my cargo over flan and *il Capitano*'s hot milk with whisky. They said I was crazy to walk with sin because I was an angel!

I was a mud-smirched blonde harridan who got grumpy with unshow-ered Frenchmen in *albergues*, but I would be an angel if they bestowed it on me. It was their gift and a reminder to me to try to be better.

In my hand was the plan. In five days we'd arrive in Santiago.

Looking into the sky, I saw the first star's glimmer. I wondered if there might be particles out there of my mother, and of Sue, and of others I've loved and farewelled. Science tells us the stars we see disappeared long ago. I was looking back in time. I squinted to see further. Were they out there?

The word for 'starry' in Spanish is *estrellado*.

The phrase for 'to give birth' is *dar a luz*. It means 'to give light'.

I whispered those words to the Spanish skies.

Only five days until we reached the field of stars. Could that be possible?

I waited at a pedestrian crossing as a car passed.

'*Buen camino*,' the driver called.

I waved back. So far, so *buen*.

27

RISING

NEXT DAY, AFTER ONLY twenty kilometres, we let ourselves take stock in the city of Ourense. Or at least, *il Capitano* allowed it. We booked into a *hostal* above a *chocolatería*, amid cobblestones, arcades and courtyards.

I'd been walking for five weeks and was in advance of my schedule. The sins had felt lighter in the mountains of Galicia. I was becoming clearer about where my own faith lived, something I had not expected to be a side effect of the journey. Maybe the three-act structure was right, and I was reaping spiritual rewards in the third act. Whatever the cause, I felt confident that the worst was behind me, so I made a decision. I would carry the sins on, beyond Santiago, to Finisterre.

World's end.

There's a pilgrim tradition of burning boots, clothes or anything you want to release, there on the cliffs. I would write up the sins and let flames carry them to the ether. I imagined an orange sun dropping into the Atlantic, my pilgrim toes digging into white sand and achievement radiating from me like a halo as I looked up into the field of stars. After all, it had been the stars, the road and the elements instructing me along the way. I'd have to walk an extra hundred kilometres or so, and hoped I wasn't tempting fate, but it felt right.

Of course, *il Capitano* was thrilled at a chance to update my itinerary.

In a *ciber* in Ourense's bustling main street, I opened my inbox to find poems, news and encouragement from home:

From my Buddhist friend: *The way is not in the sky. The way is in your heart.*

The story of a sixteen-year-old Aussie girl who had sailed solo around the world ...

A traveller in Bangkok, watching as the people's uprising was quashed ...

A picture of Reepicheep, the mouse from the Narnia stories I loved as a child. There he was, high in the ship's rigging, with his sword and coracle, off on an adventure.

And sinners.

One wrote of a new sin. The sin of not pausing. A sin that seemed very modern.

Mostly, though, it was as though all the sinners had formed into a cheer squad and the string of emails contained only encouragement. And love.

At the end of email after email: *love.*

From husband, family, friends, peers, saints, sinners and strangers.

There was a call from Barcelona as I sat at the computer.

Come, they insisted again. Come and let us care for you. You are family.

To complete my trinity of affection—Australia, Spain and Italy—*il Capitano* and his *Soldato* sat beside me in the *ciber*, waiting to go to lunch.

'No' was unthinkable. I said I would come to Barcelona.

In a restaurant called *La Fuerza* we talked of my decision. *Il Soldato* nodded and said it was good. Proper. Such loyalty must be acknowledged.

They ate *pulpo gallego* and smacked their lips over the juices. I ate spinach pasta, which they pronounced acceptable. We all chose lemon mousse. When I paid, *il Soldato* was horrified. I had breached a rule. The woman does not pay.

He accepted my being independent and paying my way, but to pay for him? For the man? No, no, no. It was good when I gave them each a shell from Australia, but this … this was impossible.

I tried to explain it was gratitude for their kindness. They had been with me since the first day of the Via. They'd let me make my own road, but always welcomed me back to theirs without question. They had shown me how to walk.

I couldn't say all that and *il Soldato* wouldn't have listened anyway.

Il Capitano said it was *niente*, that *il Soldato* was too proud, too proud, that pride was the sin of the ego. I tried to explain to him that I knew it well, that his soldier and I were fellow travellers in the land of pride. *Il Capitano* just laughed and said it would all be good.

And it was. Eventually.

Il Capitano and I went shopping for phone cards and found a sub-urban mall with all the worldwide same-name brands. After completing the *camino* of capitalism, we went to the museum to marvel at bronze wings and weeping granite women from the first century BC, and to the cathedral to see Santiago slaying Moors above the entrance. The mediaeval streets closed in around us as evening fell.

When we rejoined *il Soldato* he presented me with a rucksack of ironed laundry and would take no money. At dinner, after a dessert of cheese drizzled with honey, we all paid our share, down to the last cent.

The morning brought another twenty-kilometre saunter to the next *albergue* at Cea, so it was agreed over dinner that I'd make a late start and walk *sola*. You will be happier, they said, with time to write.

That's what they called my preference for solitude. Writing time.

I heard whispers in the hallway but resisted popping my head out, instead sitting up like a queen in my single bed. And I did write.

My room had no window, but images flooded in from the previous days: the grey-haired, black-eared mule nibbling grass from my hand; frail balconies overhanging crumbling stone walls; the road sign to

Granada reading 888; chandeliers of corn cobs drying on low veran-
dahs; the doll's clothing pegged above a brown donkey who sniffed it
for taste; the *hórreos*, granaries, like miniature temples, raised off the
earth to protect the produce; the land, furrowed and burrowed and
harrowed and barrowed; the row upon row of saints in the gloomy
cathedral; the jubilant *niño*, kicking his goal against a stone crucifix;
and rain, mist, haze, fog … shrouds …

When I went to pay the bill, there was confusion about my Italian
friends. No, the owner said, they had paid for me already. I handed
over my breakfast money with my key and waved farewell, vowing to
tackle *il Soldato* about his double-dealing.

Passing the Church of Santa Eufemia del Centro, I was compelled
to go inside. It was starker than other churches I'd seen and elegantly
proportioned, but I still wasn't sure why I was there. I offered a prayer
to Eufemia, wherever she was, asking her to help my sinners, then
stood, not knowing what else to ask. As Mark Twain said, 'You can't
pray a lie.'

In a pew by the exit, a woman sat weeping. She was plump, with
lustrous long dark hair, and she wore an inky-blue cashmere wrap.
Her grief halted me. I put a hand to her cheek and wiped away tears.

'*Sufro*,' she whispered. I suffer.

'*Sí*,' I said. '*Lo siento.*' Yes. I'm sorry.

'*Por amor.*' For love.

Tears spilled again. I leaned down and hugged her, my pack almost
tipping me into her lap. She clung to me, her sobbing echoing to the
ceiling, but eventually she calmed. We held hands a moment, then
she said '*Gracias*' in that same whisper, and we separated.

In the weak sun on the worn entrance steps I said the prayer I've
made all my life when someone is in trouble: 'Please let everything
be all right.'

Distant sounds of cannon fire marking the feast day of the Virgin
of Fatima farewelled me as I clattered across the Roman bridge,
hoping the prayer was heard above the din.

I exited Ourense via lanes and alleys, *frutas* and *pastelerías*, past granite and marble sellers and industrial estates, past the bus station, uphill. I strode along, confident my eyes would locate the next yellow arrow, my feet would fall into place and my heart would keep pumping in time with my lungs. The body doing its thing. Remarkable, wonderful machine. And somewhere above it, like a kite at the end of a tether, I flew, watching the snail crawling up, ever up ... To meet a weathered face that widened into a grin when I called out, 'Hola, Señora, buenos días.' She laughed and laughed, amazed at my courage, at my force, at my strength, at my *anima*. She showed me her knees, scars bisecting both, and her knobbled hands. She spoke of her pain.

'But you smile,' I said.

'Like you,' she said, going on to talk of the heart and the spirit, of the soul, and of the little people who live on the mountain I was about to climb, insisting they are real, true. She had seen. Dragging me into her garage, a jumble of chairs, boxes, preserves and pickles, she grabbed two beers, filled a bag with fresh walnuts, and stuffed them all into the pack.

I don't even like beer and it weighs a ton, but how to say no? A sin!

'Dame un beso.' Give me a kiss.

I did, on that cheek of wrinkles. Once, twice, three times. Four. Walk with God. Say a prayer for me. Remember me in Santiago. Think of me.

I did. I do.

I climbed. My pack was heavier, but I was lighter.

I wondered how I would recall them all. So many *promesas* for Santiago. The Angels, Lucia, *Herr T*, the cyclists, the men with *duende*, my Australian saviour and my Spanish *amigo*.

An Italian text. They were only seven kilometres ahead of me. The road must be steep.

And so it was. I climbed. And climbed. And climbed.

For two kilometres, I went straight up until all was green and the air sparkled. The mountain lifted me with it as the valley dropped away. A breeze played on my back and around me hung a sky so vast I could have fallen up into it.

The *meseta* and the mountains are two sides of the same coin. They both ask you to expand. The *meseta* says, 'Be big enough to fill my emptiness' while the mountain says, 'Rise to meet me.' I kept thinking my heart couldn't expand any more, then I would turn and look back or up, and it had to, in order to meet the wide world I was being shown.

All I want to do, I thought, is write a love letter to this ridiculous country, because I'm infatuated. I see only good and am met with nonsensical beauty and kindness. All the way.

First love. It was like that.

I walked, that morning, for all the loves of my life, including Spain, the newest. And as the lady said, maybe Santiago was walking with me. In love, anything is possible.

I danced, too. Left alone, I turned cheerleader.

Those walking poles!

They strode out in mantis mode, praying a prayer all their own. They stretched my shoulders when I placed them horizontally in cross-carrying style. They remade me into a swordsman or gunslinger. Or Reepicheep! I braked with them, hung clothes to dry on them, and forded rivers with them. I was yet to poke another pilgrim with them, but I had pulled down the branches of fruit trees, tested water depths, and even walked with them. Just as my *mochila* had become part of me, so the poles were mood barometers.

While I was prancing, Galicia behaved like a showgirl, flashing all her best bits. Granite of all shapes and sizes, covered in lichen and moss, glinting in sunshine. Bowers, dells and glades. Yellow arrows on vineyard walls, beside wooden gates, on wayside rocks and the arch of bridges. The land rolling up and down, opening and closing, stretching and bending.

Carved marker stones showed abstract swords, crosses, pilgrims and stars to point me to Santiago. I grinned my way past them, waving to farmers, calling to crones. Twice I stopped on the path to click a photo of myself and inspect it, thinking, 'No. You look normal. No one would know.'

Sin-free and *sola*, I sang to the *cielo*.

At Mandrás, a hamlet where I stopped for a lemon drink, three sisters worked the bar. We talked of the approach of summer. They told me they had bushfires, just like in Australia. They spoke of the pain when a blaze is deliberately lit. Someone always knows someone. Communities, tiny communities, are cleft in two.

It was hard to imagine the rural peace of Galicia being shattered. Entering one *pueblo* almost as soon as I left another, I was struck by the way generations came out to play. Cars disgorged adult children returning for the weekend, unloading treats. Grandparents played with toddlers beside stone fountains and siblings sang to each other as they hoed vineyards.

I was flying again. Galicia took me out to the sky, where I met up with my sinners. This time, we flew together.

Finally, I understood something the mediaeval pilgrims may have learned, too.

It is easier to walk for others than for yourself.

When I considered what had been entrusted to me, the pain that had been disclosed, what it had cost to tell me, and what was hoped for and from my walk, my personal woes lifted. The thing people had worried about most was actually the thing that made pavement softer. Remembering my sinners stopped my feet from throbbing or my knees from aching, and demanded I do better. Walking for another is a gift and teaches us how to walk with our own failings. It is grace, if there is such a thing.

High in the hills above mediaeval Ourense, I realised I'd been blessed by my sinner-teachers, and I hoped to depict their grace in a flame at Finisterre.

Act Three. The spirit stage.

Leonardo called. Happy, happy. The pilgrim is coming.

Il Capitano texted. Hurry, hurry. You have the best bed. By the wall. Up high.

I wept my way into Cea, tears staining my stretched, grinning cheeks.

The *albergue* was chock-full. Overnight the numbers of walkers had doubled.

In order to get a *compostela*, the certificate issued by the cathedral stating you've completed the pilgrimage to Santiago, it's necessary to walk a minimum of one hundred kilometres. For this reason, the town of Sarria on the Camino Francés has ten or more *albergues*—it's exactly the right distance for the hundred-kilometre pilgrim. Ourense is at approximately the same distance on the Via de la Plata.

Beginner pilgrims nursed blisters and talked of aching backs. I felt so sorry for them. These newbies would have barely broken in their packs before they reached the cathedral, and would never know the euphoria of the well-oiled body. The focus of their pilgrimage would remain their feet, their calves and their anguished spines. They deserved their *compostelas*. Those of us who had walked for weeks got our reward from the road and the weightless freedom of the third act.

I strolled the streets of Cea with the Italians, photographing each other in the *plaza* under the clock, sampling bread at family bakeries, sniffing overblown roses, waving to other pilgrims and greeting locals. We sat at Bar Vaticano, sipping white wine and nibbling the walnuts I'd been given. *Il Soldato* opened them by squeezing two together in his palm. I won a bet that the photos on the wall were really of Rome. My Italians couldn't see the Holy See!

It seemed a lifetime since I had been there. The photos reminded me of words given to me by a scholar at the British School. Richard Pollard, a mediaevalist, had been intrigued by my undertaking and had slipped a piece of paper under Susan's door the morning I left. It was his translation of a quotation from Pope Gregory I's *Dialogues*, describing his feelings after becoming Pope. Richard felt it might have relevance for me. After all the weeks of walking, the words of a Pope from 590AD resonated:

> *And so I weigh what I now bear, I weigh what I have lost; and when I look upon what I have surrendered, what I bear is made heavier. For look: now I am struck by the waves of a great sea, and in the ship of my mind I am hammered by the winds of a fierce storm, and when I recall my previous life, as if I have sighted the shore with a backward glance, I sigh. And what is still harder to bear, as I am savaged and roiled by immense waves: I now can scarcely see the harbour I left behind.*

How differently we felt about our burdens. Not that I imagined sin-walking was anything like being Pope—compare the shoes! But looking over Gregory's words, I recognised that although I could scarcely see the harbours of Rome or home, what I carried was lightening. My storms were behind me. I was being lifted by kind breezes.

And kind Italians.

We agreed we could feel the end. I wanted to slow, to savour everything, but some other force pulled me forward. *Duende?*

No. But mysterious, certainly.

I tried to thank them for that day of solitude. All day, I said, I walked as though on air. I told them how I'd seen an elderly couple emerge from a grey stone cottage into the sunlight. How they blinked then kissed each other. A few paces on, I watched two yellow butterflies fly around and around each other in a tight circle, oblivious to me.

I said I walked inside a dream of flying.

There's still no other way to describe it. In my body but also outside it. Watching myself, feeling my feet but not the ground, feeling air moving above and below me, lifting, soaring, rising. Rising with the sun ...

They raised their glasses to flying and we talked on.

But I will forever rejoice in and be mystified by my flight. I never found an answer for why it happened or how. I never knew when it would kick in, but suddenly there I'd be, looking down on my self.

Grateful. So grateful for another mystery.

I came to love that body walking below me, getting me where I had to go and waiting for me to return to it. I loved its resilience, its steady forward motion. I came to love my body 'in spite of'. I'd always loved it when we flew but I'd finally learned to love it when it was earthbound.

I celebrated and mourned the end of that day's walking. A kind of sane delirium. Ecstasy, I guess.

Sky-dancing.

It was my last full day *sola* before reaching Santiago.

28

THREE'S COMPANY

IL CAPITANO AND *IL SOLDATO* were natural carers, like Leonardo and Ricardo, determined to ensure my safety and happiness. In some ways, *Herr Theologie* and my *amigo* had softened me for them. Had I met *Herr T* in a Galician lane, he might not have recognised the cheery pilgrim in convoy. My *amigo* might have wondered too. Back in Salamanca, he said the Italians would protect me. I bridled at the suggestion. I had forded torrents and stared down turtles. I needed no one.

Pride. My boon companion.

The Italians taught me that the opposite of giving is not taking, but receiving.

A big lesson.

I watched the two of them, friends for decades, play out their relationship. I never really knew who was boss: the texting, flirting *Capitano* or the watchful, dignified *Soldato*, who would say, 'When the Captain decides …' just before walking out and choosing a direction. Sometimes they bickered, but I couldn't tell how much of that was for my benefit. They were both actors. *Il Capitano* was perennial clown to his soldier's king.

And they claimed me for their own.

Finally I gave in to the road, my teacher, and embraced being part of a team. I even stopped keeping tabs. Mostly.

I did get a shock when I interrogated them about paying my *hostal* account at Ourense. They flatly denied it, and after insisting they promise, I realised the man on the counter must have made a mistake. I tracked down a phone directory, called the *hostal* and said it was the Australian pilgrim. He laughed, said it was *nada*, that his wife had mis-marked the ledger, it happened often. He was happy I had called but very surprised.

I didn't want to tempt fate. I wrapped cash in tissues, found an envelope and despatched it. To do otherwise would have been thieving and not a good look for a sin-carrier two days short of Santiago.

The next day, I strode up, and occasionally down, hills, ascending three hundred metres over twenty kilometres in a little over three hours. Along the way I encountered Yuji, a Japanese pilgrim who laboured under a twenty-kilo pack and a gargantuan camera; laid-back Chris, who was twice Yuji's height, and said he wanted to be 'less German' in his ways; a quizzical Canadian, who was intrigued by our sin conversation, as it was his first talk of things spiritual on the *camino*; the bony Dutch pilgrim with the perpetual limp and gritted teeth; the French gentleman with the love of Spanish *vino*; the Spanish heartthrob with the love of Italian beer; the Austrian singer with a love of Australia; and the Belgian loner who kept his eyes on the road and marched.

The sky was open. The plateau was wide. The air was thin and heating up. Layers were removed. Arms bared. The day sprawled.

Team Italy convened in a lush green pocket, where a wooden slab doubled as a table. Boots came off and toes wriggled in long grass. We picnicked on Cea bread, sheep's milk cheese, anchovies and wine. The beers I'd carried up the mountains were polished off and we cracked open the last walnuts to eat with an apple. We talked about endings then avoided talking about endings.

We walked on, past vegetable gardens, across multi-lane freeways, above sky-blue wildflowers necking with humble bees and bumble-bees, and into the laneways, the mystical little-people-laden laneways of Galicia. We came together and separated. A foal tottered towards me and a cow shied away.

Cows.

Black-and-white. Deep brown. Caramel. They looked straight into me, their eyes black pools of acceptance.

An ancient *señora* talked to her herd as she'd done for centuries, her profile so craggy I wondered if she was hobbit, gremlin or goblin. Another called to her flock of ten sheep, shooing them, entreating them, scolding them and shoving them like wayward children.

Grasshoppers raced me along the track, startling me with their blue underwings, reminding me over and over of Mary Oliver's hopper in the poem that had first made me walk in Spain. Reminding me again and again to relish every heartbeat, because after all, it is this life, this one right now, that is the one to cherish, to relish, to live well and with integrity.

'This life,' I called to the racing grasshoppers. 'It's enough.'

And if there should happen to be a life beyond this, I told them, then I will meet it with wide-eyed surprise. But this life is enough. I have heaven, here and now.

I walked on, full and thankful, praying all through that long summery Galician day.

Praying with my feet.

Moss thickened. Slugs slid. Heat rose, and so did the Italian battalion, and after thirtyish kilometres we handed over our *credenciales*, received our *sellos*, and checked in at the *albergue* at A Laxe. We sprawled on the grass with our expanded pilgrim village, to watch washing dry, to journal and to drift. The sun made everyone dozy, like sleepwalkers.

At dinner, we requisitioned the local bar to watch a tennis match between Rafael Nadal and Roger Federer. One new pilgrim sat alone, spruce in clean khaki cotton, his shirt and trousers sporting sharp creases. There was something of the star about him. He was German and ascertained that I spoke English but my friends spoke only

Italian. He told me he had walked *caminos* before and learned many lessons. He gave his opinion on wines of the world, and Australia fared well; on architecture, and Spain fared badly; and on the changing face of the *camino*. This was his eighth time, having travelled the Francés first back in the '70s. He was disappointed by the changes there, including the attitude shifts as locals learned what pilgrim money could buy. He feared the same for the Via.

It's difficult, I said. No one would want people to stay 'poor and simple'. As in any country, an influx of money is an influx of choice, and people don't always choose as others would wish.

He agreed, saying he was enjoying the conversation. He liked to speak English, he said. It was, like German, a civilised language. He asked why a woman like me was allowed by her husband to walk alone across a country. When I said our marriage was built on trust, he shook his head and said I did not know real freedom. He laughed as *il Capitano* made repeated attempts to contact a *hostal* in Santiago, trying to book a room for me. *Il Soldato* noted phone numbers and addresses.

'Why do you walk with these old ones?' the German asked.

'They're my friends,' I said.

'But they are old. You could find other companions. More congenial to you.'

'No,' I said. 'They make me happy.'

'So do they pay for you?'

'I don't understand. What do you mean?'

'Your meal? Your lodgings? Do they pay?'

'No. Of course not. They're my friends. Why would they pay?'

'You should let them pay for your company. A woman like you. You should take what you can get.'

I pushed my chair away but said nothing. *Il Soldato* was watching. He raised his eyebrows and I laughed, hoping he would be fooled. I had no words to explain.

Take what you can get.

Back in my bunk in the still-light dormitory where snoring had already begun, I replayed the conversation. No matter how I interpreted it, the hurt didn't diminish. Was he inferring I was some kind of escort service for elderly pilgrims? That I was the kind of person who could be bought? Was the implication that my friends were gullible fools? The kind of men who would trade in women? Why say such a thing?

He had either tried to enlist me or he had offended me and my friends. I couldn't be sure which, but either way, something had been violated.

I lay awake planning methods of retribution.

Next morning, we set off as the sun rose. I clicked a photo of our shadows, elongated on the road in front of us. *Il Capitano* is obvious from the shape of his muscled legs in shorts. I'm identifiable by my hat brim and walking poles. *Il Soldato* curves under his enormous pack.

Tre amici. Three friends, side by side down the narrow way.

It was our last full day's walking before Santiago. We passed fields of patterned mown grass, the smell of it a herbal nectar. Oak trunks sprouted boles, suspiciously like homes for gnomes. Jets left vapour trails above ancient belltowers in sleeping hamlets. Vines trailed into the path, and sprigs of white, blue and yellow flowers accumulated on my hat.

In Silleda, we stopped for coffee. *Il Soldato* asked if I was okay. He said that something was not right. 'No,' I said, 'it's just the last day. I am fine.'

'No,' he said, 'tomorrow is the last day. This is just another.'

I had been talking, laughing and picking flowers, but I guess when you walk, eat, sleep, and share intimacies about hormones and history, you get to know someone. Why should they not see through me when I knew the moment there was a shift in their moods?

I walked ahead, letting them talk as I resorted to the iPod to take my mind off the German. I'd thought I was done with sin, but the day before arriving at the cathedral steps, I was a seething mess, wanting only vengeance. I imagined holding an *albergue* pillow over his face as he slept, stopping his flow of spite. I wished him thistles and thorns to rip his pristine smugness. I summoned words like brigand, outlaw and bandit, hoping they could be enlisted to take shape and attack him.

If thoughts were sins, I was toast.

I did also consider the German's sin.

'Take what you can get,' he had said. That seemed a very modern sin: grab it all, because what matters is who has the most, or the biggest.

I liked him less with every step; wished him pain with every breath.

We stopped to picnic in cool woods. The day had worked its temperature up, along with mine. We were boiling together. *Il Capitano* pinned a rose to my hat as *il Soldato* opened a bottle of wine. I spread out cheese, bread and tomatoes. Our bare toes lined up in the shade. We raised water and wine glasses to each other and toasted our last road lunch.

I tried to give them money for the wine. I didn't realise they were going to buy it and hadn't contributed enough. They were adamant. It was a gift. I was equally adamant that I pay my share. *Il Capitano* argued with me that it was only a couple of euros, they might be old, but they could buy me a wine. *Il Soldato* watched, saying nothing.

And then I cried.

Il Soldato said it was good. That he knew I was unhappy. He asked what had upset me. Was it the phone call from my husband?

No, no, that was a gift.

Then what?

I told them, as best I could. Slowly, searching for words.

Il Soldato's face turned to stone. The Easter Island statue had returned. *Il Capitano* stepped onto the path as if to face down the German.

Il Soldato pronounced the German *maleducato* and *brutto*—ill mannered and ugly—as *il Capitano* wiped my tears with his napkin-sized handkerchief. *Il Soldato* said he knew I was unhappy at dinner; my face was pink, and so he knew the man had said something. I laughed. My face was always pink. We all laughed. That was true.

Time to move on. I said I'd sit for a while and write. They would see me down the road. No problem.

I did write.

When my husband called, he'd asked if this *camino* had been like the first. Had I loved it as much? I told him that it had been harder and deeper. The Francés had been in no small part a life-lesson about letting go. Having found my acupuncturist *compañero*, my long-lost-lifetime-friend, I then learned how to release him. Each time we said goodbye, it was simple.

That had never been possible for me before the *camino*. I always experienced parting as pain, as though each 'see you soon' was a final farewell, like the ones I'd made after the deaths of those I loved. The Francés, and my *compañero*, changed that. Just knowing he was on the planet meant I could finally relax about everyone I loved and let them walk their ways. I still don't understand why finding him was a home-coming, but mystery sits easier now.

This road was tougher.

Yes, it had asked more of me physically, because it was harder and longer, but it had asked more of every part of me. The unbending, uncompromising part of my nature had been broken down on the Mozárabe. Carrying the sins made me watch myself every minute of the day. I'd been my own critical observer, an active conscience monitoring my actions as fully as I could, fronting my failings.

Also, language had played a part. In spite of the conversations I'd managed, in *Herr T*'s formal English, in Spanish with my *amigo*, and in Italian with my garrison, I never had the release into commonality that had been possible with my *compañero*. I'd had no choice but to go deep into self. And mostly, I found a companion who was prepared to stay the course. Mostly, I was peaceful company, seeking little except to understand the path. As a result, it was a pleasure to travel with that self, and equally pleasurable to learn, finally, to travel gracefully in company. It had been hard, I answered my husband, but full of quiet joys.

Sitting there, remembering what I'd said on the phone, I decided it would be a sin to allow the German to take my joy. It would be my sin. *I can't fix anyone else*, I wrote, *but I'll fix myself right now. If joy has been the gift of this camino, then joy it will be.*

And an hour later I was sitting on the verandah of a white farmhouse, enjoying Italian coffee and homemade *biscotti* with my garrison and a young couple who had moved from Umbria to Spain after walking the *camino*. It was easier to have a good life in Spain than in Italy, they said. Cheaper. And the people are more real. *Il Capitano* was suitably appalled.

Il Soldato toured the house, looking at the joinery and making suggestions as *il Capitano* flirted with the slender, curly-haired maker of biscuits. Behind her, in long black letters on the whitewashed wall, was the phrase *Per Aspera Ad Astra*.

By hope you will get to the stars.

Rome again! I had last thought of that phrase back in the eternal city after seeing the Pope. I had first seen it in Ventosa on the Camino Francés. Full circles.

Palimpsesto.

I'd got to the stars. Thanks to my Italians, I found myself in a home, telling stories and sharing food, forming family.

We walked on in scorching heat, together and apart, past ripening figs and blooming roses, and beside freeway constructions that straddled mountaintop and valley floor.

I stopped to talk to a woman in a field. Wearing trousers and gumboots, she explained that Galician women had to be farmers. They worked like men. No, harder than men. 'But we would not walk alone across Spain,' she said. 'That is work for no good reason. *Loca, loca.*'

I pressed on, the sun my accelerator through chapels of beech forests and across manicured fields cultivated with sweat and devotion. Those fields made me think of my friend Ida, an irreverent sage, whose favourite phrase of the Catholic Mass is 'by the grace of God and the work of human hands'.

Grace. The grace to be on this planet at this time, free to walk the earth. And work. Turning up each day, even when dispirited or afraid.

Snakes crossed my path, reminding me to shed what was left of my angry skin. I'd met my devil, and he could take his pressed khaki and try it on with someone else.

Rounding a corner I caught *il Soldato* sitting on a wall. He leapt up and walked, as though he hadn't seen me. He was carrying a staff of rough wood and I asked where he had found it. By the path, he answered. He showed me how he had whittled the end of it into a grip. If he saw the German, he would use the rod to teach him manners.

I hoped we wouldn't see him now. The last thing I wanted was for my soldier to get hurt—or hurt anyone else, which was, I suspect, quite possible.

Up we went, catching a young Spaniard who said he could barely keep pace with *il Capitano*. I photographed them out in front and it's impossible to say who is younger, the backs equally straight, legs equally muscled and strides equally sure. I strolled with *il Soldato*, watching him accustom himself to his new friend. He'd had staffs in the past, he said, and liked the feel of this one. Maybe the German had given him a gift. He thought he might take it with him when they left Santiago to walk the Francés in reverse direction, going home. Having walked a thousand kilometres from Seville, they were going to do the eight hundred back to the Pyrenees before flying home. Magnificent.

We got lost. The *Guardia Civil* stopped traffic for ten minutes in order to find our way. Fingers pointed, foreheads glistened, two-way radios buzzed. Ultimately, it transpired we were on the right road!

Just because you're wandering, it doesn't mean you're lost.

Up further, with the world at our feet, windmills dotted along distant hills, and the land below us like an aerial photo, we saw a sign: SANTIAGO 20.

Up higher still, we were met by a group of thirty horseriders out for a trail ride. We climbed with them along dappled bridle paths.

Suddenly there were eucalypts, the smell potent in the afternoon heat.

Home. I was coming home.

I picked leaves, squeezed them, inhaled them and pocketed them, like a koala let loose with her drug of choice. I tucked them inside my bra, close to my heart, and breathed them in.

The eucalyptus, the heat and the light conspired to make me fly.

'You are so fast,' the horseriders called. 'You will get to Santiago before us. You will get there tonight.'

It was tempting. But no.

We would have one final *albergue* night. One final road dinner. And besides, the gossip on the pilgrim hotline was that this was the Parador of *albergues*. Perched above the world, the glass and blonde-wood building was immaculately clean and spacious. We laundered and nested, but just as I'd finished unpacking, *il Capitano* appeared, miming conspiracy, and collected up my belongings. I followed him to the end of the hall, where, behind the arrival desk, he'd discovered a single dormitory. He arranged my belongings, announcing it was my apartment. The dragonfly suite!

Dinner followed. Downhill to a café, in company with German Chris, Japanese Yuji and our Spanish companion. Salad, roast chicken, potatoes and Santiago tart. Most others had walked on or planned their stages so they didn't overnight there in Ponte Ulla at the Albergue de Vedra.

I'm glad we did. To have rushed into the city at day's end would have been *maleducato*! We celebrated each other's achievements and listened to stories. Chris had married an Australian girl and was preparing himself for big changes by walking to Santiago. Down under, he wanted to work outdoors, to make himself over from a computer-oriented German to a labouring Aussie, exploring alternative medicine and southern sun.

Before we left the bar, the Italian army decided to have a special drink.

Sol y sombra. Sun and shadow.

It's brandy and anise. Powerful stuff. It celebrates duality.

Life is, as the lady said in Laza, sun and shadow, and we'd certainly had both that day, but we'd ended in the blazing sun of friendship. We drank to the *camino*. I was, and am, so grateful that it exists and knows what to do with all of us. That it's endlessly generous and forgiving.

Like Spain. Like love.

'*Buen camino!*' we said, as we raised our glasses. That wish never felt more like a blessing.

The burning spirits slid down, and I tucked into the silence of the dragonfly suite for my final night before greeting the saint. I took out my journal, and wrote by torchlight:

What have I learned in twelve hundred kilometres?

Well, I do have faith: in the simplicity of walking, the power of forgiveness, the kindness of Spaniards, the goodness that wants to prevail, the ache to be better and the impulse to serve.

I believe in the restful set of evening and the pale wispy promise of morning. In the hope of rain on parched soil.

I believe in confession with all my heart, telling the true story of ourselves, eye to eye with another human being, owning up to all that we are.

I believe that stories shape our lives, and that the more honest we are in our stories, the more freedom we will gain.

I know there's nothing more sacred to me than the act of putting one foot down on a dusty road, and then putting down the other. Again and again. For as long as it takes. Turning up and doing the work.

And I know that the work never ends.

I know there is beauty in effort.

I know slow is sublime. Slow food. Slow dance. Slow talk.

I know snails are gurus.

I know we are all connected, whether we like it or not, and we owe it to this astonishing planet, and those we hope might come after, to acknowledge that fact in our actions as well as our words.

I don't know any more than I ever did about what comes after, or if there even is an after, but one thing I do know. I absolutely know.

I will die.

And I'm perfectly happy to die wondering.

There are so many wonders ...

I closed my journal, flicked off the torch, zipped up my sleeping bag and shut my eyes. What would I dream?

Perhaps of a pilgrim walking along a dirt road, leaving a trail of footprints etched into the dust. Of others walking north over muddy ground. Of the thousands walking out their doors, across hills and valleys, treading trails into the earth.

Their trails are tales. Their trails are prayers. Their trails are hopes, wishes and intentions, stories being inscribed into the Spanish soil.

Perhaps I'd dream of the man I'd seen leading his donkey down the road.

Both wore coats, but the donkey's was best: bright blue with a red Santiago cross on his flank. They plodded, inscribing the path with their own hard but beautiful story.

Mediaeval, they looked.

Out of time.

Like a dream.

29

SUNNY SANTIAGO SUNDAY

IT BEGAN WITH WORDS on a page and it ended the same way. This is the final email I sent home to my village from Spain.

Well, it is done ...

For those who like a statistic, thirteen hundred kilometres completed in forty-three days. Approximately thirty kilometres per day, if you are interested in such things.

But how do you measure love? Or experience? Or learning? Or gratitude?

Maybe by steps ...

I walked into Santiago with my Italian pensioner angels on Tuesday morning in bright hot sunshine.

Galicia, the bathtub of Spain, had turned it on for us. There has been a week now of temperatures in the thirties, and they are melting here in the land of lush green.

I, of course, have been in my element—wide blue skies, eucalyptus all around, good strong heat to warm my blood, and a task nearing completion.

We arrived in pilgrim central, were awarded our *compostelas* (the certificate from the Church that says we have made it here in this Holy Year), and in true Italian fashion, went out to lunch!

Those seventy-something boys taught me a thing or two about life.

Don't eat on the run. Make a meal of a meal. Laugh. At every turn. Laugh.

I think it is the laughter that gives them the energy to walk and live as they do. Everything is funny. Even when they bicker. Which they do, like little boys, partly to show off to me, I suspect.

I miss them.

We went to Mass together in the cathedral on Wednesday at noon, along with the Galician government!

I heard the statistic read out: 'One pilgrim from Australia from Granada.'

So quick, to summarise such wonders.

The *botafumeiro* (enormous incense burner that takes six men to swing it through the air, cleansing the cathedral of the waft of pilgrim sweat!) flew over our heads.

We had A Reserve seats because we arrived an hour early, at *il Capitano*'s insistence, so I had time to write a long list of thankyous to all my sinners and benefactors and beloveds. You were all with me in the cathedral.

But I also knew it was not the end. My instinct was right. I reckon the pre-Christian pilgrims knew a thing or two.

The end of the world called.

I went out into the vast square in front of the cathedral with my Italians beside me and began to walk. Out through the narrow, baking lunchtime streets of the city, as it snoozed through the *siesta*.

Out towards the green woods that surround it, which were blessed cool on that hot afternoon. Out towards the first bridge, where we parted.

They were going east along the Camino Francés, back towards their homes in Italy. I was walking west to the sun, another hundred kilometres with my sins and my village.

We clicked photos. Said farewells. I cried. Leaving them was hard. The only parting that has felt difficult. I could always manage being in their company, and I came to love them so. Like fathers, friends, angels ... *amici* ...

They text me every day. They miss me, and my laugh that they call 'allegra e contagiosa'.

They made me laugh like that. That was their gift.

I am in danger of weeping as I write about them, so that is enough now.

The walk to Finisterre was like a dream.

Hot, clear, greener than green—like being under the sea and in the air simultaneously.

Yet always on the ground. Feet on the ground. The blessed earth of Spain: furrowed, gravel, hard, squelching, muddy, dusty, stony. Spain. Under my feet, in my pores, in the fibres of my clothes, in my lungs.

The first sighting of the sea on Friday, the third morning, was a shock. Suddenly there it was.

Really? In all the shimmering heat, maybe it's a mirage?

But no. It's the Atlantic.

And then, oh then, from the top of a high hill, there is a headland and a lighthouse at the end of it.

Finisterre. Land's end.

I cry, I laugh, I tell myself, 'At the top of that hill, I have made it.' For the first time, with the end in sight, and only fifteen kilometres to go, I have made it.

And with that, I fall!

My first, my only fall in thirteen hundred kilometres, and it was right at the moment that I had prematurely congratulated myself! Yes, I can now vouch for it: pride goeth before a fall, indeed.

Pride.

My sin.

I have wrestled with that from the moment this journey began and I had to ask for help.

I have wrestled with it daily when Leonardo and Ricardo and *il Capitano* and *il Soldato* and my *amigo* have tried to care for me.

Pride. Just as I let myself wallow in it, it tripped me up!

Fantastic, this road. This teacher.

And so I walked very very carefully in blinding heat into Finisterre.

The last two kilometres were barefoot, along the beach, collecting shells for all of you. They are wrapped in plastic, and you will have one on my return, in pilgrim tradition.

Pilgrims walk with a shell on their pack now, but originally they only walked with the shell on their return journey, as proof they had made it all the way.

You will have your proof!

The sun sets here at 10 p.m., so that night (Friday) I hobbled out the last three kilometres to the Cape, and sat on the rocks high high up, and waited.

It's easy to see why they believed the world ends there. The Atlantic swirls away and disappears into mist. There is nothing but blue. No horizon.

SINNING ACROSS SPAIN

It was sublime. A perfect red sun dropping into an *azul* sea.

I had my list with all your sins, all my sins, all your gifts, all your names, all my thanks. And at 10 p.m., I placed it under a small rock to hold it firm, I borrowed a lighter from a Dutch pilgrim, and I set it alight.

It burned.

Really beautifully.

All but one tiny piece, with one word on it: 'for'.

For what?

For love, for gratitude, for pain, for sorrow, for anguish, for scrapes, for bruises, for joy, for release, for compassion, for lessons.

For privilege, for Spain, for friends, for colleagues, for life, for death, for sun, for shadow.

For newborn lambs and pensioners, for silence and for laughter, for Australia, for the world, for peace.

Within and without.

For love. Always for love.

I burned that last scrap. The sun dropped away. And a man on the rock above me said in Spanish, 'And now the sun is rising on the other side of the world. Maybe Australia.'

I said, 'I'm from Australia.'

He said, 'Then it is rising on your home.'

And he was right. It would have been 6 a.m.

I did cry then. Just a little. I thought of you all, and of how much I care for and about you, and how lucky I am to have had such faith placed in me.

Faith.

I have wondered about it all down the road. Asked questions. Sought answers. In the end I come back to something simple.

We were taught as little things that God is Love.

Well, I think that love is god.

That's all.

And that loving well is the test and the gift.

I walked back downhill like an invalid, my body suddenly aware of every step I had taken. But the happiest invalid on the planet.

My job done. My task accomplished.

I had served.

On Saturday I slept until 8 a.m.

I threw my naked body into the Atlantic (it's okay, I had the beach to myself, so didn't terrorise any locals!).

And I caught the bus back here to Santiago, where every dreadlocked new-age wannabe and cross-carrying devotee and obsessive hiker is partying up a storm, while the Spaniards watch yet another football final. I tucked into clean sheets and an actual room with bathroom in Hostal Fornos. Silence and cleanliness and a towel.

Bliss.

And today I walked out the first ten kilometres towards Finisterre at dawn, because I wanted to. Without my pack. Fast. Flying.

And I realised that I missed the pack.

Why?

Well, it keeps me upright and straightens my shoulders, and it slows me down. So I see the world and stand tall when I have weight on my back.

Another lesson. Maybe we do need our weights, if we carry them with care and consciousness.

I don't know.

I forgot! I lost a good friend, and it was a terrible, difficult farewell.

When I fell, one of my hiking poles took my weight and it bent in the middle. My beloved pole, which has made two *caminos* with me, as well as many walks through central Victoria—well over two and a half thousand kilometres. I have danced with it, twirled it, been supported by it, argued with it, climbed with it, tapped rhythms with it, carried it across my shoulders and in my holsters. It saved me from having anything worse than bruising and scratching, but it had to stay at Finisterre because I couldn't straighten it out to bring it home.

A loss.

A twenty-dollar Ray's Outdoors loss.

How to quantify an experience? How to put a value on anything? How to define loyalty?

It is out at Finisterre, and maybe someone will rescue it and it will be a sculpture. I have one left to bring home. I'll have to be lopsided for a while.

On Tuesday I fly to Barcelona to complete my pilgrimage.

Yours is done, but I must see Leonardo and Ricardo. They have walked every day with me, called me, asked if I needed money or assistance. They have loved a stranger as though I were their own. And so they have become mine, and I will go and complete that stage with them.

After that ....

Well, I'm not entirely sure yet, but I'll keep you posted.

I have about ten days and want to try to sift through the six thick notebooks and the two thousand photos before I get home. I don't know what, if anything, I have made out here on the road. Hopefully a bit of stillness will answer that question.

For now, there is gratitude and there is the present.

This moment.

The sun is shining brilliantly. It will be thirty-four or thirty-five degrees today. Among the cool stone colonnades of Santiago, I won't be bothered. I've had my walk, so the body is happy. I can watch and ask a few questions.

And be still.

Thank you, my village, for your care and your support. There are not words. That is the truth of it. There are not words enough for you.

I send love and gratitude from Santiago. From world's end. And from my full, full heart.

Ailsa x

CURTAIN CALLS

AFTER WORDS

This email was waiting for me in Santiago, from my sinner who confessed to adultery, and who thought she would never find a relationship.

> *And while you have been journeying, I've been having a quiet*
> *pilgrimage of the soul in a room in Australia.*
>
> *I have met my fella.*
>
> *I have just spent the day with him and we spoke our true*
> *feelings for each other, and we are so happy to have finally*
> *met. Or, as he says, met again.*
>
> *It's a lovely story, which I won't go into here. But we both*
> *feel the same, and we want to share our time, our minds and*
> *our hearts together.*
>
> *I am so happy.*
>
> *The sin you carried for me is now well and truly put to bed.*
> *I don't have to carry the weight of it anymore. It is now ash. In*
> *Finisterre. On the Cape. Done. Dusted. Clean cleared away.*

Less than a year later, I read a poem at their wedding.

Other sinners made changes, too. Big and small, lasting and temporary. The more honest they were with themselves and me, the greater the change. Or at least, that is what they have told me. I remain in awe of their courage.

My brother is well. Brett did some crying for me when I called from Finisterre! He mourns, talks, goes silent and laughs. He remembers. He's getting on with living.

Leonardo and Ricardo gave me ten days of pride-testing love in Barcelona. They call me *hermana*—sister. They are my new, and yet not new, brothers.

German Chris is now a happy Aussie. When last I spoke to him he was on top of a crane on a building site. He said he could see for-ever—all the way back to Spain.

Paul has left the white apartment in Salamanca, but he emails about books he has read and journeys he is making. His mind and his door remain open.

My *compañero* continues his work. Not a day goes by without me making my simple prayer for him: 'Please let him be all right.'

Il Capitano and *il Soldato* enter downhill ski competitions, rescue hikers in the mountains and send messages about future walks. They keep walking.

My *amigo* didn't return to the world of high finance. He is volunteering for an aid organisation. He says he is still deciding about his life. But he did complete his *camino*. He kept his *promesa*.

I don't hear from *Herr Theologie*. I hope he is happy. And strong.

THE STUFF IN THE SWAG

On top of the sins, this is what I carried. All weights are in grams.

The beloved *mochila*   1500
I carried an Aarn backpack. It hails from New Zealand.
Kiwis know all there is to know about walking, hiking and feet.

Inside the *mochila* or on my body
Sleeping bag   500
Merrell Siren Ventilator boots. Loves of my life   920
    (now discontinued)
Crocs. Ugly but good!   280
2 × New Zealand thick wool socks (100g each)   200
3 × quick dry Nanna undies. Uglier, but good! (40g each)   120
2 × crop top/bras   120
2 × hiking pants (Target and Kathmandu—well worn in!)   800
2 × black fast-dry Silk Body T-shirts   200
Rain pants with a split!   180
Rain jacket/godsend   370
Pashmina. An essential   140
Sarong. Modesty-protector, tablecloth,
    bedsheet, sunshade and more   140
Icebreaker thermal top and leggings. New Zealand again   280
Mini quick-dry towel   150

Mini Maglite torch	20
Camera. A borrowed baby Canon	400
Notebooks. They got heavier, but I got stronger	500
Purse with comb/credit card/cash/passport/drivers lic, etc	300
Mini Swiss Army knife	20
Electrical adaptor	30
Buff. For keeping neck and ears warm or hair off face	30
Mobile phone. A chum's old Nokia	100
Mobile charger	60
Sunglasses	20
Hat	80
iPod	80
Medical bag—elastic bandage, essential oils, Panadol, hair ties	250
Pens	20
Needle and thread, safety pins, whistle and cleats	40
Soap, deodorant, toothpaste, toothbrush, sewing kit, razor	300
Moisturiser and sunblock	200
Plastic bags for food carrying and rubbish collection	20
Toilet paper and tampons	100

Olive oil is the best nurturer for the body. I bought it along the way and mixed it with ti-tree, peppermint, rosemary or lavender essential oils to make my rubbing oil.

I didn't carry water holders. I bought 1.5-litre plastic bottles and refilled as I went. On long days I had to carry three of them—an extra 4.5 kilos!

SINNERS, SAINTS, GUARDIAN ANGELS ...

Heartfelt thanks to my friend-colleague-sponsor-benefactors. They had faith at the beginning, when it sounded like I had lost a large bag of my marbles. Their faith sustained me every day ...

Anthony Adair, Janet Andrewartha, Jeni Bethell, Donna Blake, Paul Brasher, Hugh Colman and Anthony Fong, Beverley Dunn, Liz Egan, Paul English, Alan Fletcher, Carrillo and Ziyin Gantner, Susan Greaves, Diana Greentree, Sonia Gurbiel, James Hagi, Elizabeth Horne, Robert Kirby, Nina Landis, Tamblyn Lord, Tracy Mann, David Pledger, Angela Punch-McGregor, Hannie Rayson, David Ross, Graeme Samuel, Pierre Sauzier, Michael and Helen Sedgley, Kat Stewart, Adele Swain, Leith Taylor, Louise and Theo Van Embden, Nicki Wendt, Janet Whiting, Necia Wilden, Jackie Woodburne.

Particular acknowledgement goes to the Australian Business Arts Foundation, and my project officer, Sharon Nathani, who grasped the concept immediately.

My gratitude to all at MUP, and most particularly, heartfelt thanks to Colette Vella for seeing the book that could be and editing with *amor* and *atención*. Also to Anouska Jones for her eye for style and ear for tone.

James Laurie. Friend, agent, good counsel and touchstone.

Alanna for computer wizardry, reading, re-reading, and saving me when a hacker hacked. And for being a most excellent *hermana*.

Sue in Manly, for reading the first manuscript, which led me back to Spain.

Hannie, for the courage to give tough feedback.

George, writing and life teacher extraordinaire.

Louise, for going so many extra miles.

Tart, for the big lesson and the big faith.

Susan May, for shelter and commonsense in Rome.

Carl and all my walking buddies, who warmed me up for Spain as only walkers can!

My poetry hounds, who kept feeding me the good stuff.

My extended *camino* family, who 'get it' without explanation.

My home village, so many of whom are not named specifically here, but who wrote and wished and cared. And amazingly, still do.

My family—sisters, brothers, in-laws—who are without peer. The best.

My father, for making me a book of my walk before I had begun to make my own.

Brett. For saying yes. To me and to life.

Mum and Sue. For walking with me.

All the people I met on that hard but beautiful journey.

And Peter at base camp …

For letting me go and welcoming me home, all the days of our lives together.

Gracias. Grazie. Merci. Obrigado. Danke.

Thank you.

I walk with you in my heart.